# Sacred Landscapes in Anatolia and Neighboring Regions

Edited by

Charles Gates
Jacques Morin
Thomas Zimmermann

BAR International Series 2034
2009

Published in 2016 by
BAR Publishing, Oxford

BAR International Series 2034

*Sacred Landscapes in Anatolia and Neighboring Regions*

ISBN 978 1 4073 0611 7

BAR Publishing is the trading name of British Archaeological Reports (Oxford) Ltd.
British Archaeological Reports was first incorporated in 1974 to publish the BAR
Series, International and British. In 1992 Hadrian Books Ltd became part of the BAR
group. This volume was originally published by Archaeopress in conjunction with
British Archaeological Reports (Oxford) Ltd / Hadrian Books Ltd, the Series principal
publisher, in 2009. This present volume is published by BAR Publishing, 2016.

Printed in England

# BAR
PUBLISHING

BAR titles are available from:

BAR Publishing
122 Banbury Rd, Oxford, OX2 7BP, UK
EMAIL    info@barpublishing.com
PHONE    +44 (0)1865 310431
FAX    +44 (0)1865 316916
www.barpublishing.com

# TABLE OF CONTENTS

# CONTRIBUTORS

Birgül Açıkyıldız is a research associate at the Khalili Research Centre of the University of Oxford. At present, she teaches as a visiting lecturer in the Islamic Art and Archaeology Department of the University of Paris I (Panthéon — Sorbonne). Her research areas are Yezidi material culture, Kurdish history and art, and late Ottoman art and architecture. Her current research project explores the administrative construction of a provincial monument, the Ishak Pasha Palace at Doğubayezıt during the late Ottoman period of the eighteenth century.

Soi Agelidis is an Assistant Curator in the Antiquities Collection of the Staatliche Museen, Berlin. Her research interests center on ancient cult practice and festivals, particularly in Asia Minor; Greek sculpture; and German collections during the Nazi period.

Susanne Berndt-Ersöz, the author of *Phrygian rock-cut shrines. Structure, function and cult practice* (2006), has concentrated her research on the history and religion of Iron Age Anatolia with a special interest in the interaction between cult and power. Affiliated with Stockholm University, she is currently working on a project entitled "Cult and cult formation in Asia Minor 600-300 BC" that examines the Persian influence on local cults in Asia Minor during the Achaemenian period.

Jacques des Courtils is a Professor of Archaeology at the University of Bordeaux, and director of the Xanthos and Letoon excavations.

Owen Doonan is an Associate Professor of Art History, California State University at Northridge. A classical archaeologist, he has directed the Sinop Regional Archaeological Project since 1996.

Ivonne Kaiser, head librarian at the German Archaeological Institute, Athens, is a member of the excavation team in Bronze Age Miletus. Her research interests include household archaeology, statistical methods in archaeology, and the transitional period between the Late Bronze and Early Iron Age in the Mediterranean.

Veronica Kalas, a specialist in Byzantine Cappadocia, is based in Detroit, Michigan. She has taught art and architectural history at Middle East Technical University, Ankara; Wayne State University, Detroit; and the University of Michigan.

Christina Maranci is the Dadian Oztemel Chair of Armenian art at Tufts University. Her 2001 book, *Medieval Armenian architecture: constructions of race and nation,* explores the role of Josef Strzygowski in the field of medieval Armenian architecture. She is currently at work on a study of four seventh-century Armenian churches.

Anneliese Peschlow-Bindokat, a classical archaeologist now retired from the German Archaeological Institute, has devoted over thirty years to the exploration of Heracleia-under-Latmos and its hinterland.

Lynn Roller is a Professor of Art History at the University of California, Davis. A member of the Gordion Excavation Project since 1979, she has published two volumes in the Gordion Publication Series as well as several papers on Phrygian art, culture, and religious practices. She has also completed a major study of the cult of the Phrygian goddess, Matar, and its impact on the Greek and Roman worlds. Future projects include studies on the influence of Greek culture on the pre-Greek peoples of Anatolia and on connections between Thracians and Phrygians.

John Senseney is an Assistant Professor in the School of Architecture at the University of Illinois at Urbana-Champaign. His research focuses on ancient Greek and Roman design process and the Greek invention of linear perspective and scale ground plans. Currently, he is completing a book on the importance of Greek technical drawing, theories of vision, and astronomy for the Roman invention of "architecture" as an entity distinct from the craft of building.

Anja Slawisch, a classical archaeologist, is a research associate at the German Archaeological Institute, Istanbul. She previously worked as a research assistant at the University of Halle and as a Humboldt/ Feodor-Lynen research associate at Bilkent University. A member of the Didyma excavation team, she is currently working on the analysis and publication of metal finds from Didyma, and the publication of Roman tombstones from the Isparta museum collection.

# PREFACE

The ritual dimension of land use in both prehistoric and historic societies is a flourishing research issue examined by a growing number of archaeologists, historians, philologists, and anthropologists today. Anatolia, because of the time depth of its human settlement and its geographical as well as cultural diversity, offers a great potential for such studies. Many local cults are well known, and the ever-increasing endeavors to reveal Turkey's past through surveying, excavations, and the (re)examination of written sources continue to enrich our database for pre- and early historic monuments, features, and findings in their sacred as well as profane contexts. Such studies, however, tend to focus on a particular culture, period, or region. Neglected in recent Anatolian research, it seemed to us, have been wider comparative and contextual themes. To remedy this lack, "Sacred Landscapes in Anatolia and its Neighboring Regions," a symposium organized by the Department of Archaeology and History of Art at Bilkent University, October 18-21, 2007, aimed to bring together a wide array of international scholars interested in both the local and comparative aspects of this extensive subject. Almost two dozen prospective disciples then embarked on a pilgrimage to autumnal Ankara, and many of them received indulgence with timely contributions to this volume.

Although the project as originally conceived embraced a wider range of cultures (including Hittite, Seljuk, and Ottoman, e.g.), we believe that the present collection of articles, by reflecting many dimensions of approaching such a complex subject, offers a stimulating examination of how the "Sacred" has manifested itself in landscapes of Anatolia from pre-Classical to Greek, Roman, medieval, and modern times. The thematic variation among the papers is large. Certain contributors explore the "big picture." In her keynote address, Lynn Roller investigates how religious practices changed over a millennium in a single region, Phrygia. Change in practice, even in cult, is a theme addressed also by Susanne Berndt-Ersöz (Iron Age Phrygia), Soi Agelidis (Pergamon and nearby mountains), and, on a vast chronological scale from Chalcolithic to Byzantine, Anneliese Peschlow-Bindokat (the peaks of Latmos). Related to these diachronic studies are the difficulties of identifying, classifying, and interpreting sacred sites during archaeological surface survey, as Owen Doonan makes clear. A broad regional survey of sacred architecture and ritual within the larger cultural context of Yezidism is presented by Birgül Açıkyıldız.

In contrast, other contributors take a "micro" view, examining aspects of the sacred at a single site in a specific period. Ivonne Kaiser discusses cultic artifacts and their spatial context in a Minoan sanctuary at Miletus. Anja Slawisch, at nearby Didyma but some 1000 years later, evaluates the archaeological and epigraphical evidence for a still puzzling problem: collapse or continuity of religious practice at the Sanctuary of Apollo after the Persian sack of Miletus in 494 BC? The relationship between landscape and sacred architecture is a theme of several papers. John Senseney explores the geometric underpinnings, visible and invisible, of Hellenistic planning at Pergamon and their connections with landscape features. The defining role of water at the Letoon, suggested by Ovid but only fully understood after modern excavation, is the theme of Jacques des Courtils's essay. Christina Maranci demonstrates how at Mren, at the opposite end of Anatolia from the Letoon, the setting of the seventh century church helps us understand its role as an expression of the volatile network of local Armenian dignitaries and imperial Byzantine rulers, in the shadow of conflict with nearby Persia. Mren was an aristocratic construction; in contrast, Veronica Kalas explores the religious architecture of the anonymous inhabitants of the settlement of Selime-Yaprakhisar in Byzantine Cappadocia. By examining the interplay of chapels, settlement, and landscape, she distinguishes different functions among the religious buildings.

The chronological span of these papers stretches from the enigmatic world of Chalcolithic cave paintings at Latmos to the contemporary yet no less mesmerizing reality of sacred spaces in the Yezidi religion. Space in terms of its geographical aspect is equally well covered, reaching from the western and southwestern shores of Asia Minor to the Anatolian highlands, Cappadocia, and the Black Sea littoral, finally touching and crossing the easternmost borders of modern Turkey.

Concerning the papers, choice of spelling where variations exist (Miletus vs. Miletos, American vs. British spellings, e.g.) has been left to the individual author. References to ancient writers follow the abbreviations of the Oxford Classical Dictionary, third edition revised.

Good faith alone would not have sufficed to guarantee a successful assembly, so our sincerest thanks go to the many individuals and institutions who contributed substantially to the success of this symposium. Colleague Oya Pancaroğlu, now at Boğaziçi University, was instrumental in the development of the program. The support and encouragement of Bilkent University and, notably, Prof. Talât S. Halman, Dean of the Faculty of Humanities and Letters, and Prof. Bülent Özgüç, Dean of the Faculty of Art, Design and Architecture, were invaluable. Substantial funding was further provided by the Turkish Research Association TÜBITAK and by ALABANDA Tourism. Thanks are also due to Lynn Roller and John Devreker for enlightening commentary at Gordion and Pessinus during the post-conference excursion, to Ertan Turgut for organizing in exemplary fashion the excursion and a dinner in the Ankara citadel, to Tuğba Şardan, the secretary of the Department of Archaeology and History of Art, for assistance throughout the preparations and the symposium, and to our departmental colleagues for their interest and participation.

We believe that the three days of dialogue thus generated have contributed to a deeper awareness of how the sacred landscapes of Anatolia developed from early times to the present. The printed proceedings may be taken as proof of this and as encouragement to continue the discussion, and as a companion to set directions for future research.

Charles Gates, Jacques Morin, and Thomas Zimmermann

Ankara

July, 2009

# THE SACRED LANDSCAPES OF MATAR:
## CONTINUITY AND CHANGE FROM THE IRON AGE THROUGH THE ROMAN PERIOD

### Lynn E. Roller

Landscape has long played a major role in determining human relations with the divine. Landscape, however, is a fluid concept that meant more to the peoples of the ancient Mediterranean world than merely their geographical surroundings. Ancient peoples experienced their environment as co-existing landscapes of the natural, the human, and the imagined worlds.[1] The natural landscape, clearly, comprises the physical features of the land, the mountains, the plains, the rivers, springs, and other water sources, in which a particular community was situated and to which the community needed to adapt in order to survive. The human landscape may be defined as the human imprint on the natural environment: the settlements of village, town, and city, the tilled land, the routes of transportation and communication, and the political units that demarcated and controlled these, all of which reflect the human community's efforts to alter the natural landscape and make it more responsive to human needs. The third landscape, the imagined landscape, is the most difficult to define, although it seems certain that this landscape weighed very heavily on human experience in the ancient world. The imagined landscape was joined to the known world, but extended beyond it to include unseen beings and powers that affected both the natural and human environment; it also included those parts of the human experience that transcended the known physical world, such as the dead and those still living who could communicate with the divine.

The ways in which human cultures interact with all three landscapes and integrate the experiences of these landscapes into their lives form one of the chief markers of ethnic identity. In this the Phrygians were no different from other peoples of the ancient world: their responses to the landscapes in which their society developed clearly conditioned their cultural and political character. In this paper I would like to use the cult of the Phrygian Mother

goddess, or Matar, to explore the Phrygian response to the imagined landscape and its relationship to the natural and human world. The Phrygian Mother has received special attention in the study of Phrygian cult because she is the only deity in the Phrygian pantheon that is represented in anthropomorphic form and because of her prominence in Greek and Roman cult. She was surely not the only deity in the Phrygian pantheon, and not all Phrygian cult monuments should be ascribed to her.[2] Yet images of the natural landscape figure prominently in the goddess's cult, primarily through the use of predators for her principal attributes and the rural settings of many of her sacred places, and so the concept of landscape offers a good focal point to examine the dynamics of a cult experience in which the forces of the natural environment seem to have played a significant role. Several scholars, including myself, have suggested that the goddess's relationship with the landscape, particularly the natural landscape outside the human environment, was a key element in her character (Haspels 1971: 110-111; Roller 1999a: 113-115). A more nuanced assessment of the role played by landscape in different phases of the goddess's cult may enable us to refine this hypothesis, determining how the cult's relationship to the Phrygian landscape changed with the changing status of Phrygia.

The origins of the Mother Goddess and the character of her cult in the Early Iron Age are still unclear. The Phrygians became established in central Anatolia in the early first millennium BC,[3] but their response to the imagined landscape of their new homeland is hard to gauge. Gordion, practically the only known Early Phrygian site,

---

[1] The concept of three landscapes is drawn from the work of Cole 2004, 7-9.

[2] Berndt-Ersöz 2004, and Berndt-Ersöz 2006, 170-172, on the evidence for a dominant male deity whom Berndt-Ersöz calls the Male Superior God.

[3] Phrygian migration into Anatolia from southeastern Europe, Herodotos 7.73; Strabo 7.3.2. The ancient literary testimonia are corroborated by the material culture of the Early Iron Age levels at Gordion, which show marked affinities with Balkan material, Sams 1988; Sams 1994a: 19-22. One should recall that the term "Phrygian" is a Greek name; we do not know what these people called themselves.

has yielded definite evidence for the formation of a complex state during the ninth century BC (Voigt and Henrickson 2000; Voigt 2005: 28-31), but virtually no artifacts that can be clearly connected with cult. There is no unequivocal evidence for cult installations, nor any objects that indicate the identity or character of the deity or deities venerated by the community.[4] Several of the symbols that were later connected with the cult of the Phrygian Mother, such as birds of prey and lions, figure in the imagery found in the Early Phrygian city, but it is uncertain whether they alluded to cult practice at this time.[5] The most definite evidence for early Phrygian cult activities comes from the site of Dümrek, about 40 km northwest of Gordion, on a high cliff overlooking the Sangarios River. The presence of numerous altars and stepped monuments in this remote spot indicates that the site was a sanctuary, perhaps a place of pilgrimage, and ceramic finds indicate extensive usage that began during the Early Phrygian period and continued into the Middle Phrygian period, the ninth through sixth centuries BC (Grave, Kealhofer, and Marsh 2005; Berndt-Ersöz 2006: nos. 101-107). The deity (or deities) venerated at Dümrek are unknown, but the site's continued use as a cult center for several centuries clearly indicates that the confluence of the natural and the human landscape was of high importance to the early Phrygians.

Evidence for Phrygian cult practice increases markedly during the Middle Phrygian period, the eighth through sixth centuries BC. It is during this period when many of the extensive series of monuments that form the core of our knowledge of Phrygian cult, including step monuments, idols, cult images, and architectural façades, were created.[6] This is also the time when the Phrygian Mother becomes a visible and vivid presence in Phrygian cult. The locations of the shrines of the Phrygian Mother help define the Phrygian sense of critical spaces that were sacred to this deity. Most are not found within an urban center, as is regularly the case in Hittite and Greek settlements where a temple or shrine formed the central nexus of a community, but on the boundaries of the human and the natural landscape. Some have been found near city gates; these include the anthropomorphic images of the deity from Boğazköy (Bittel 1963; Roller 1999a: fig. 10) and Gordion (Mellink 1983: 349-50, pl. 70; Roller 1999a: fig. 7), and the step

monument at Midas City (Berndt-Ersöz 2006: no. 68).[7] The recently discovered stepped monument and idol near the so-called Cappadocia Gate at Kerkenes Dağ reinforces this pattern. The idol, a typical Phrygian aniconic form consisting of a rectangular stele with a round disk on top, has no clear markers connecting it with a specific deity; thus it is uncertain whether the idol belonged to the cult of Matar, although the surrounding niche is incised in several places with the letter M, which makes this likely (Summers 2006b). Another regular setting for monuments to the goddess is a location along a road or other transportation route; the Arslankaya monument, situated near the road that gives access to a valley with rich tilled land, furnishes a well-known example (Berndt-Ersöz 2006: no. 16), as does the Büyük Kapıkaya monument (Berndt-Ersöz 2006: no. 17), and some of the architectural façades that lack images, such as the Bahşeyiş Monument (Berndt-Ersöz 2006: no. 28). Sanctuaries of Matar could be placed on a high point that offers a commanding view of the surrounding area, signifying the extension of human activity beyond settled territory into the natural landscape; the peak sanctuary of Karahisar provides an excellent example of this (Berndt-Ersöz 2006: no. 108). Cult monuments to the Mother could also be found on the boundaries between the human and the imagined landscape of the dead. We see this in the two well known reliefs from Ankara that were set up near burial tumuli (Roller 1999a: fig. 8, 9), and in the use of cult iconography for funerary monuments such as Arslantaş (Roller 1999a: fig. 34). That she was not the only deity associated with such ritual settings is certain: an image of a male figure, probably a deity or heroized ruler, was set up near the Monumental Entrance to the Palatial Complex at Kerkenes Dağ (Summers 2006a: 11; Draycott and Summers 2008: 8-21), and there are several indications of a pair of deities who were worshipped together, in the Phrygian Highlands and in central Phrygia, near Ankara (Berndt-Ersöz 2006: 161-66). Moreover, there is a rich series of discs, aniconic idols, and step monuments that have no obvious association with one particular deity and could be connected with the cult of other deities, male and female (Berndt-Ersöz 2006: 158-172). Nevertheless, the monuments dedicated to the Phrygian Mother dominate the physical artifacts of cult during this era in their size, detail, magnificence, and geographical breadth.

It has become commonplace to speak of the Phrygian Mother as a deity with age-old roots in the Anatolian sacred landscape, extending as far back as the Neolithic period, and to cite figurines from Çatal Höyük and other Neolithic centers as evidence for continuity of her cult (Haspels 1971: 110-111; Vermaseren 1977). What we know of Phrygian cult practice, however, suggests the opposite, namely that the growing prominence of the Mother goddess cult represents a break with past practice. The sanctuaries of the Mother build on characteristic elements of Phrygian cult, such as the importance of shrines in high places

---

[4]   While several of the buildings from the Early Phrygian Destruction Level were impressive structures that contained rich finds, each contained a variety of material that points to a mixed domestic use, DeVries 1980: 36-37.

[5]   Numerous drawings of the lion and the bird of prey appear on the walls of Megaron 2, one of the Gordion Destruction Level buildings; see Young 1969; Roller 1999b: fig. 2, 6, 8; Roller 2005: fig. 1, 2. Because of this Mellink 1983, 357-9; Sams 1995, 1156-1157; and Prayon 2004, 612, have suggested that Megaron 2 was a temple; however this interpretation is not supported by any objects or cult installations found in Megaron 2 and is unlikely to be correct.

[6]   For a thorough and comprehensive study of Phrygian rock-cut monuments used as cult centers, see Berndt-Ersöz 2006, which examines all known Phrygian rock-cut shrines. Sivas 1999 provides an excellent survey of cult monuments from the Phrygian highlands. These should be used together with the still valuable work of Haspels 1971, especially 73-111.

[7]   On the relationship of the Matar cult to city gates, see Berndt-Ersöz 2006: 148-52.

and along transitional boundaries such as a city gate, but at the same time introduce several new elements into Phrygian cult tradition. The most significant of these are the appearance of the anthropomorphic image of the deity and the creation of the architectural façade with a central doorway; in several cases the image of the deity standing in the doorway of the architectural façade combines these two elements. The placement of several of the most striking of these monuments in dramatic settings in the Anatolian landscape almost suggests that the cult of the deity was being used to stake a claim to territory beyond the settled community, in effect extending the dominance of the human community into the natural landscape. The Phrygian affinity for the natural landscape of the open countryside and high places was being redirected specifically to the cult of this one deity.

How would this have happened, and why? The monuments of the goddess from the Middle Phrygian period, the eighth through sixth centuries BC, are diverse in location and degree of elaborateness, but have a key feature in common: they show an increasingly close connection with the symbolism of Phrygian royalty, as if the rulers of Phrygia were using the cult of this deity to enhance their own position of power. We can see this in the images of the goddess herself, in her costume and her attributes, and in the cult façades decorated with architectural elements and elaborate geometric designs.

The emergence of the anthropomorphic image of the goddess in itself signals a new direction in Phrygian cult. The visual source of this image can be determined with some certainty. As has often been noted, the image of Matar found in Phrygian cult reliefs, especially the well preserved images from Ankara and Gordion, reveal strong formal similarities with the cult images of Kubaba, a prominent deity in the Neo-Hittite pantheon who was the protector of Karkamiš in the Early Iron Age (Mellink 1983: 354-55; Roller 1994: 190; Roller 1999a: 71-72). This is not unexpected, since extensive contact between Neo-Hittite and Phrygian visual images had been attested since the Early Phrygian period (Sams 1974: 181-94; Sams 1989: 449-53). If, as seems likely, early Phrygian cult images were aniconic, the Neo-Hittite visual material offered a readily available model if and when the Phrygians wanted to create an anthropomorphic image of a deity. These circumstances, however, do not explain why Matar alone in the Phrygian pantheon was depicted in anthropomorphic form, nor why the deity Kubaba was chosen as the model.[8] The answer seems to lie in the special relationship between Phrygian Matar and the ruling elite of Phrygia. The Phrygians were surely aware that Kubaba's title as the Queen of Karkamiš

and the close relationship between Kubaba and the rulers of Karkamiš, emphasized in the program of visual relief in the city, offered the rulers of Karkamiš a powerful ideological tool to consolidate their position (Denel 2007: 193-95). A Phrygian ruler could well have capitalized on a similar ideological concept by claiming a close relationship with Matar and emphasizing that relationship by depicting the Phrygian goddess in human form, and in a costume that presented her as both goddess and queen.

The Phrygian Mother's attributes, particularly the images of predatory birds and lions, also served to reinforce the deity's status as a protector of the ruler. Both of these predators were symbols of long-standing in Anatolian cult, valued for their imagery of fierceness and power (Collins 2004). The image of a predator communicated power and dominance over the natural landscape. The predator also carried a strong connotation of elite status: the use of the lion to symbolize kingship was widespread (Collins 2004: 90), and the raptor, or bird of prey, also implied elite status, through its symbolism of power and its connection with hunting and falconry, both privileges of the aristocracy (Mellink 1983: 351-354; Canby 2002). When coupled with allusions to a ruler, particularly a ruler protected by an important female deity, the predator conveyed a powerful message, namely that the ruler had extended his dominance beyond the human landscape into the natural environment. The combination of visual form and attributes found in the anthropomorphic images of Phrygian Matar emphasize her high status and her control over human and natural landscapes, to the benefit of the ruler who served her.

The cult façades imitating architectural frames convey a similar picture. The basic elements of the façades' decorative scheme from both central Anatolia and the Phrygian highlands in western Anatolia are consistent: they comprise a relief representing the architectural frame of the short end of a building with a central niche that is frequently surrounded by geometric patterns; the niche, often depicted as a doorway, usually contains an image of a standing female figure, the goddess Matar (Roller 1999a: 72, 84-5). In some examples, e.g. the Midas City relief (Berndt-Ersöz 2006: no. 30), the figure of Matar is not present, but cuttings within the niche demonstrate the provisions made for attaching a portable statue of the deity (Berndt-Ersöz 2006: 200). Thus the goddess's association with these architectural façades is uncontestable.

The evidence for the façades' association with Phrygian rulers is more subtle, and lies in part in the geometric ornament of the façades. While the Phrygian preference for geometric patterns in the visual arts is well known, the decoration on the architectural cult façade is consistent and complex enough to imply that it communicates something more profound than mere aesthetic appeal. The decorative scheme found on wooden serving stands from burial tumuli at Gordion offers a suggestion of what this meaning is. On three serving stands from two Gordion tumuli of the

---

[8]    Some scholars have explained the visual similarity between Kubaba and Phrygian Matar by assuming that the two deities were the same figure, e.g. Laroche 1960; F. Naumann 1983: 17-38; Munn 2008. I find more persuasive the arguments of Graf 1984; Roller 1994; Collins 2004: 91; and Berndt-Ersöz 2006: 200-202, who have shown that the two deities were in fact separate entities with little in common apart from the visual representation.

mid-eighth century BC, one from Tumulus P and two from Tumulus MM (Young et al. 1981: TumP 151, MM 378-379), the geometric patterns used in the serving stand decoration are consistent: on each of these three objects the wooden screen face was divided by a horizontal bar into two sections, each of which was inlaid with geometric ornament built around a series of interlocking cross and square patterns. The same decorative scheme can be found in the geometric ornament on several of the architectural façades from the Phrygian Highlands (Berndt-Ersöz 2006: 35-38, fig. 96-104). There are five extant façades with extensive geometric ornament, and here too the decorated face is divided by a horizontal bar and covered with geometric decoration consisting of a series of cross and square patterns.

The chief difference between the decorative schema on the tumuli serving stands and that on the cult façades lies in the lower half of the decorated face. In the lower section of the three screens from Tumuli P and MM, the main element is a central rosette that is surmounted by a pattern of semi-circles that suggest horns, and it is likely that the rosette with its superimposed horns was a symbol of a divinity (Simpson 1998; Roller 2006, 127-128). On the cult façades, however, the position of the rosette is occupied by a doorway, in which an anthropomorphic image of the Phrygian goddess Matar stands (or once stood). Thus the carved façades repeat the overall imagery of the decorated serving stands from the Gordion tumuli, but substitute the figured image of the goddess for the rosette. This visual shift served to direct the viewer's attention to the deity, who is surrounded by symbols taken from objects used in the burial rituals of the ruling elite.[9] The effect is to stress the connection between the ruling elite and the deity, and to place that visual connection on a public cult monument where it would have been visible to all.

The architectural features depicted on the façade reliefs convey a similar concept. As has long been recognized, the façade reliefs of several prominent monuments, such as Midas City, Büyük Kapıkaya Monument, Arslankaya, and others, include several architectural features that imitate actual Phrygian buildings. The view of the building depicted on the façades, namely the short end of a rectangular structure with a central doorway, is consistent with the foundations of actual buildings in Phrygian centers such as Gordion and Kerkenes Dağ (Sams 1994a: Plan A; Summers 2006a: 5). The façades also depict construction details such as a wooden framework, windows in the pediment, and horn akroteria on the roof; these are similar to actual construction features attested on structures from the Early and Middle Phrygian levels at Gordion.[10] These features tell us that the façades reproduced the form of an actual

Phrygian building, although they do not tell us the identity or function of the building. The architectural elements on the façades have been interpreted as representations of a temple of the Mother (Haspels 1971: 105; Mellink 1983: 356-59), but it seems more likely that the façades depict the house, or palace, of a Phrygian ruler.[11] On the façades, the architectural elements that signify a ruler's palace have been combined with the geometric ornament used in a ruler's funerary apparatus to create a monument dedicated to the cult of the Phrygian Mother. The function of the façades may be not to celebrate the Mother's relationship with the natural landscape, but to take the iconography of the Phrygian royal elite and impose it on cult spaces in landscape settings that were already venerated as sacred. In the architectural façades, the iconography of goddess and ruler has been transferred to a conspicuous public setting, where it would have been visible to all.

From this I would like to propose that the goddess *Matar*, far from being an ancestral symbol of a fertility cult, was originally one of a male-female pair of deities, the male being the dominant male divinity who remained aniconic until the Hellenistic period. The Mother may even have functioned primarily as a household deity, and the adoption of her cult as the principal deity of the household of the ruler led to the prominence of the cult in a public setting, one which functioned both to advertise the goddess within the traditional sacred spaces of Phrygian cult and concurrently to advertise the authority of the Phrygian ruling elite. The human landscape dominated the natural landscape with a forceful statement of power and authority. We do not know exactly when this practice started, but the similarity between the ornament on the Gordion wooden serving stands, dated to the latter half of the eighth century BC, and that on several of the large cult façades, suggests that the goddess gained special prominence during the eighth century BC. Her cult probably retained its dominant position as long as an independent Phrygian state (or states) survived.

The close association between the cult of the Phrygian Mother and the Phrygian ruling elite helps explain the conspicuous examples of the Mother's cult from sites east of the Halys River during the later seventh and early sixth centuries BC. These include the striking image of the goddess from Boğazköy, placed in a niche near the city gate, and the evidence for Phrygian cult practice near the Cappadocia Gate at Kerkenes Dağ. At both sites the placement of prominent cult objects near the city gate point to a continuing association of the deity with Phrygian rulers

---

[9] Note the comments of Vassileva 2001: 59-61, on grave goods, especially bronze belts, found in tumuli P and MM and their symbolism of the bond between ruler and female deity.
[10] Evidence for wooden timber construction, Young 1963, 352-3; horn akroteria of stone from the Early Phrygian level, Young 1956, pl. 93, fig. 41, Sams 1994b, fig. 20.2, pl. 20.3.2, 20.3.4; horn akroteria and window

in the pediment illustrated on a drawing from Early Phrygian Gordion, Young 1969, 272, Roller 2005, 127, fig. 3.
[11] Roller 1988, 49; Berndt-Ersöz 2006: 205. This interpretation is based in part on the similarity of the architecture depicted on the façades to structures from Early Phrygian Gordion that were almost certainly elite residences, e.g. Megaron 3, see Sams 1994a, Plan A, and in part on the complete lack of evidence for a cult structure such as a temple from Phrygian centers in the early first millennium BC.

and Phrygian power.[12] Such pointed and public monuments of Phrygian cult practice in these eastern extensions of Phrygian presence may have been intentional statements of Phrygian policy in the face of growing Lydian control of the Phrygian centers such as Gordion west of the Halys River.

The vivid picture created by imposing monuments such as Midas City and Arslankaya imbues the cult settings of the Phrygian Mother with a certain timeless quality, as if the cult of the Mother and her predators was an eternal part of the Anatolian landscape. In practice, sacred landscapes, especially those that mediate between human and numinous powers, are cultural constructs that are subject to the whims of historical events.[13] Therefore it is no surprise that decline of Phrygian power following the Achaemenid Persian conquest of Anatolia in the mid-sixth century BC had an impact on Phrygian cult monuments. The close relationship between the Phrygian Mother and the ruling elite of Phrygia meant the cult of the Mother would have lost important patronage as the Phrygian elite lost power.[14] As a result, the sacred spaces of Phrygian cult that had figured prominently in earlier cult practice underwent significant changes. Several shrines located near a city gate disappeared, as Phrygian settlements such as Boğazköy and Kerkenes were destroyed and not rebuilt (Bittel 1963: 7; Summers 2006b: 648). The striking cult façades that marked the territory of the Phrygian Highlands for the Phrygian Mother ceased to be made after the mid-sixth century BC, in part because the Phrygian elite no longer had the resources to support such efforts and also because the political ideology that the façades advertised was no longer acceptable in the face of Achaemenid dominance. Several of the façades in the Phrygian Highlands, including the Areyastis Monument (Berndt-Ersöz 2006: no. 37) and the Unfinished Monument at Midas City (Berndt-Ersöz 2006: no. 34), were left incomplete in the mid-sixth century, a circumstance that is likely to be a result of this changed political situation.[15] The main cult center at Midas City continued to be used, but its economic circumstances were significantly reduced (Haspels 1971: 140-1). Extra-mural sanctuaries in high places also declined, as is illustrated by Dümrek, near Gordion. This open high place along the Sangarios River had been a major center of cult activity in the Early and Middle Phrygian periods, but its usage decreased significantly during the Late Phrygian and Hellenistic eras (Grave, Kealhofer, and Marsh 2005: 155, fig. 12-4).

During the Hellenistic and Roman periods, the deities in Phrygia most regularly acknowledged in cult dedications were male figures, primarily an older male who was regularly identified with the Greek Zeus, and a younger male, who was variously identified with Apollo or Hermes (Drew-Bear and Naour 1990; Mitchell 1993: II, 22-24). It is likely that these deities had been part of Phrygian cult practice before, but had been represented only in aniconic form. The Mother was still a forceful presence in Phrygian cult, however, and it will be valuable to inquire how the changed political situation of Phrygia affected the deity's relationship with her sacred landscapes. I will focus on two time periods, the Hellenistic era, and the second century AD, during which evidence for Phrygian cult suggests that affinity with the past played a significant role in Phrygian religious practice as an identifier of Phrygian ethnicity. I will focus on evidence from central Anatolia to explore the staying power of the goddess in the Phrygian heartland, and thus will not discuss the highly Hellenized cult sanctuaries of Meter in western Anatolian Greek cities such as Pergamon and Ephesos.

Material from late Classical Gordion demonstrates that the Mother continued to be venerated there. Visual images are rare: a crude alabaster statuette from the fifth or early fourth century depicting the standing deity (Roller 1991: 131, pl. IIIb) is one of the very few, and there is still no evidence for a temple or cult building dedicated to the goddess in the urban area of Gordion. However, material from the Hellenistic period is considerably richer, and includes a number of representations of the deity, in terracotta, stone, and on jewelry,[16] as well as several objects that suggest that the goddess was the object of household cult practice and personal devotion. A striking group of objects from a private house of the second century BC offers a good case in point. These include a marble statuette of the seated goddess, a marble statuette of a draped woman holding a torch, and two stands, one a lathe-turned alabaster with the name of the dedicator ΜΙΣΤΡΑΒΟΥΤΑΣ, and the other a small alabaster stand with an image of a tree carved on three sides and a paneled door on the fourth, presumably front side; on both stands the top surface is concave, as if to support a bowl.[17]

The material is an intriguing mix of traditional Phrygian features found in the earlier Matar cult with other cult aspects that reflect the increasing impact of Hellenism.

[12] The identity of the Iron Age population at Boğazköy is not known (Seeher 1999: 331-2), and it is not certain that there was a Phrygian presence at the site much before the seventh century BC. The conspicuous shrine of Matar near the gate at Büyükkale could well be a Phrygian imposition on an earlier, and different ethnic group. On the evidence for a Phrygian palatial complex and shrine near the Cappadocian Gate at Kerkenes, Summers 2006a: 11; Summers 2007. The population of the Kerkenes settlement is likely to have been mixed, with the Phrygian element in a position of dominance.

[13] Note the comments of Alcock 1993, 172.

[14] See Voigt and Young 1999: 236, on the transition of the elite quarter in Gordion from massive stone structures to small houses and industrial areas during the Achaemenid period.

[15] See Berndt-Ersöz 2006, 208-209, for a discussion of unfinished façades. I disagree with Berndt-Ersöz's proposal that some of the façades were built after the mid-sixth century BC; it seems very unlikely that Phrygian elite would have had either the financial or the political resources to make such a major investment in cult installations after the loss of Phrygian independence.

[16] Marble image: Roller 1991: pl. IIIc; terracotta images, Romano 1995: 22-28; a gold ring, Dusinberre 2005: no. 74, fig. 84, 198 (Berndt-Ersöz 2006: 107 n. 159, incorrectly identifies this as a work of the fourth century BC, but it was found in a private house of the second century BC and uses the Hellenistic Greek iconography of the goddess).

[17] These are discussed in detail in Roller 1991: 132-4; for the inscription, see Roller 1987: 128 no. 52.

Greek influence is clearly recognizable in the two marble statuettes, both of Greek style and workmanship. The alabaster stand with the tree and the paneled door, on the other hand, signals the survival of Phrygian cult features. The imagery of the tree may allude to the natural landscape, and the paneled door recalls the goddess's association with funerary monuments, since the paneled door was a regular decoration on a large number of Phrygian funerary monuments of the Hellenistic and Roman periods.[18] The objects are likely to be artifacts of a private household cult, and their presence in this context may signal a broadening of the deity's appeal to the local Phrygian population. Features such as the association with funerary monuments, which in earlier times had been addressed primarily to the Phrygian elite, now appear in ordinary household settings, where they form the cult offerings of a wider cross-section of Phrygian society. Even the terracotta representations of the deity found at Gordion that are thoroughly Hellenized in style and iconography may allude to Phrygian concerns, since several of the Gordion Meter figures show close affinities with cult images of the Mother from Pergamon (Roller 1991: 137-8). These may be the offerings of Gordion residents who identified their traditional deity with the goddess worshipped in Pergamon and her role as the guardian of the city gate there. Thus the urban material reveals the continuation of traditional Phrygian areas of cult emphasis amid the growing influence of Greek style and form.

The tension between Anatolian and Greek aspects of the Mother deity was not limited to central Phrygia. An indirect testimony to the role of the Mother as a symbol of Phrygian identity is found in an inscription of the fourth century BC from Sardis (Robert 1975; Gschnitzer 1986). In this text adherents of a cult to Zeus sponsored by an official of the Achaemenian satrapy are specifically forbidden to have any contact with the cults of native Anatolian deities; these include Angdistis, Sabazios, and Ma. The Angdistis mentioned in the Sardis decree is another name for the Phrygian Mother, one that emphasized her connection with the mountains of Phrygia (Strabo 10.3.12, 12.5.3; Haspels 1971: 200; Roller 1999a: 196-8). This suggests that Angdistis was closely identified with the Anatolian, specifically Phrygian and Lydian populations. The text records the evident desire to separate Phrygian cult practice from the cults sponsored by prominent public officials who were not of Anatolian origin.

Evidence for the Phrygian Mother's cult during the Roman Imperial era, particularly the later first and second centuries AD, offers a different perspective on the goddess's continuing impact on the sacred landscape of central Anatolia. At this time Phrygia was a rural district, far from the major centers of power and culture of the Hellenized elite of Roman Asia Minor, and lacking in notable urban centers that might have drawn the economy or the

intellectual life of the region more towards the center of the Roman world (Mitchell 1993: I, 165-197 and passim). In this setting the Phrygian Mother seems to have played a dual role in the structure of Phrygian society. On the one hand, the Hellenized goddess had long since been adopted into the mainstream of Greek, and even more prominently Roman cult practice. In this capacity Meter had entered the dominant Graeco-Roman culture of Asia Minor and gained an official, public character supported by the cult apparatus characteristic of Graeco-Roman centers. Within Phrygia a conspicuous indication of this trend can be found at the site of Aizanoi. There the cult of the Mother had earlier been a local phenomenon centered on a cave, where her image was displayed along with a throne, reminiscent of the stepped monuments from the Iron Age, and two circular stone foundations above (Roller 1999a: 337-40). The enclosed cave-home of the goddess was transferred, probably during the Flavian period, to a vaulted underground shrine that was situated below an impressive pseudodipteral Ionic temple of Zeus (R. Naumann 1979; Levick et al. 1988: xxxiii-xxxv). The temple was built on an artificial platform that raised it above the surrounding countryside, and was evidently a source of pride to the local people, with funding coming from the income of the temple estates. The whole architectural complex and undertaking seems an unusually conspicuous installation in a small community and a rather isolated region, but Aizanoi's position as a center of the Mother goddess cult helped keep it from being too isolated, for we know that Aizanoi sent delegates to the Panhellenion in Athens, a prestigious mark of the community's status in the wider Empire (R. Naumann 1979: 8-11). The cult offered the community a means of capitalizing on the traditional position of honor held by Meter in Greek cult practice, especially in Athens. The Phrygians must have been keenly aware that their major flourishing period lay in the long distant past, and that they were viewed as inferior by contemporary Greeks. Yet the cult of the Phrygian Mother, a deity recognized as distinctively Phrygian by Greeks and Romans as well as by the indigenous people of Asia Minor, offered the potential for a statement of ancestral pride in one distinctive feature of the region's past. The sanctuary of Aizanoi also offered a recognizably Phrygian version of cult practice, as we can see from the choice of cult spaces at the sanctuary: the most prominent space in the temple was given to the Male Superior deity, here identified as Zeus, while the underground enclosed space of the structure was given to Meter. This reinforces the cult duality seen in the Iron Age monuments, where the presence of dual step monuments and thrones acknowledges the importance of two figures worshipped jointly.

At the other end of the scale, the Mother goddess was still an important figure in the sacred landscape of the Phrygian countryside. There is no evidence for the cult of the goddess in the older Phrygian center of Gordion, and the high sanctuary of Dümrek had long been abandoned,[19]

---

[18] The Gordion stand most closely parallels Waelkens' Type A, Waelkens 1986, 4, nos. 9, 363, 806.

[19] On Gordion during the Roman period, Goldman 2005. Gordion seems to have been primarily a military station during the first and second

but evidence from the region of the Phrygian Highlands demonstrates the goddess's continuing impact on this rural area, where the concerns of the agricultural population were far removed from the need for a public statement of prestige and power. Several inscriptions and votive dedications to the Phrygian Mother attest to her presence in the remote rural villages of this region (Haspels 1971: 163-204). In addition, at least one formal cult center was active, a small sanctuary of the Mother Goddess Angdistis on the citadel of Midas City, at the foot of a large stepped altar from the older Phrygian period (Gabriel 1965: 46, fig. 27; Berndt 2002: 26, fig. 38). The site had been used as a sanctuary during the Hellenistic period, probably in the second century BC (Haspels 1971: 154-55), but this had long been abandoned by the second century AD. One wonders what would have brought worshippers back to this area after a hiatus of several centuries, when the important cult centers of the early first millennium BC, including Midas City, were no longer in use as residential sites. This is not a case of continuous cult, but rather a deliberate revival of a sacred landscape that recalled the earlier and more glorious days of Phrygia. The Roman period offerings at Midas City took the form of dedications to Angdistis, the Phrygian name of the Mother attested in the inscription from Sardis noted above. This material is very far from the earlier Phrygian cult of the deity: the intimidating images of predators, the lions and birds of prey that characterized the Phrygian Mother's cult in the early first millennium BC, are no longer present, nor are the inscriptions and geometric ornament that advertised the close association of deity with the royal household. Household concerns still predominate, but they are the concerns of the people of the rural countryside for whom agriculture was the primary way of life. The dedications to the deity are simple altars, often crudely carved. The most frequent decorations on them are an ox head, a symbol of the rural agricultural economy, and a star or sun, radiating the all-seeing rays of the deity (Haspels 1971: 199-202).

The votives from the sanctuary of Angdistis at Midas City, although unprepossessing, point to another reason for the revived consciousness of ethnic distinctiveness among the Phrygians. The altars decorated with the star or radiant sun allude to Phrygian concern with upright moral behavior and the desire to invoke divine justice in the cults of their local deities. This distinctive regional phenomenon of rural Phrygia and Lydia is confirmed by contemporary observers, on whom the desire of the local people to hold themselves apart from Greek customs seems to have made a significant impact. Writing in the first century BC, Nicholaus of Damascus comments on the Phrygians' unwillingness to swear oaths or to participate in oaths sworn by others, presumably because they did not want to risk being put in the position of having to break their word. He also comments on the harshness with which they treated lawbreakers (*FGrH* 90 B 130i). His observations were reinforced with reference to the Phrygians' Christian

character by Socrates of Constantinople in his *History of the Church*, written in the mid-fifth century: "The race of the Phrygians seems to be more temperate than that of other peoples; and indeed the Phrygians seldom swear oaths. [Other races, i.e. the Skythians and the Thracians] are slaves to their passions, but the peoples of Phrygia and Paphlagonia have no inclination towards any of these things. Among them there is little enthusiasm for horse racing or theater entertainments. And among them prostitution is thought to be monstrous and an abomination" (Socrates, *Hist. eccl.* 4.28). Inscriptions of the Roman Imperial period reinforce these observations. One text from a mountain top in the Phrygian highlands records a vow on behalf of the donor's children to the Mother of the Gods and Hosios, the Holy; the accompanying relief shows a male figure wearing a crown with radiating rays of the all-seeing sun (Haspels 1971: 342-343, no. 116 and fig. 633; Ricl 1991: no. 42). A text recording a dedication by Zosas the Gallos, a priest of the Phrygian Mother, also bears a relief with a male figure crowned by the sun's rays; the inscription was found in Smyrna but in style and workmanship is very close to comparable reliefs from rural Phrygia and Lydia.[20] Another example, from the region of Dorylaion, is a dedication to the Mother of the Gods, who is invoked along with Phoibos the Holy, Men the Just, and Justice (Dikē) (Frei 1988: 25-8; Ricl 1991: no. 25; Mitchell 1993: I, 191).

The most vivid testimony to this quality lies in the so-called confession inscriptions, a series of religious dedications from the second and third centuries AD found in several rural villages in Phrygia and eastern Lydia. While the Mother is not the only deity who was petitioned in these texts, the Mother goddess of a local community is invoked frequently enough to indicate that to the rural people of this region of Anatolia, the Mother was one of the key deities especially concerned with justice.[21] The Mother goddess whom we meet in this rural setting seems far removed from the urban, Hellenized deity of the coastal cities of Greek Asia Minor. Instead, this Mother, addressed with a variety of local and regional epithets, is primarily concerned with maintaining order among the people of the local villages. The inscriptions record punishment inflicted by the goddess for wrongs committed by the petitioners until the guilty party confessed. Some confess to unspecified errors, while in other cases the Mother is called on to right very explicit ills, such as the return of livestock, disputes over money, theft of the goddess's property, or failure to observe proper ritual behavior in cleanliness of body, clothing, or speech. The texts, often laden with vivid details of village life that are sometimes amusing, sometimes sinister, provide

---

centuries AD, see Bennett and Goldman 2007. On the lack of activity at Dümrek during the Roman era, Grave, Kealhofer, and Marsh 2005: 160.

[20]  Petzl 1987: II, no. 745; the attribution to Phrygia or Lydia is suggested by Petzl.
[21]  The confession inscriptions of central Anatolia have been studied as a group by Petzl 1994. The goddess could be addressed as *Thea*, Petzl 1994: nos. 70, [84], 85, 87, [88]. The goddess Meter appears in Petzl 1994: nos. 39, 40, 41, 42, 49 (theft of a sacred slave), 50 (theft of pigeons from the goddess's sanctuary), 54 (dispute over repayment of a loan), 55 (wearing dirty clothes in the goddess's sanctuary), 57 (failure to serve the deity when called), 68 (missing livestock), 72 (failure to observe proper lustration rituals), 83, 86, 89, 90, 94, 95, 97, 122.

ongoing testimony of the power of the Anatolian Mother to punish wrongdoing. As examples, we may cite Aphias, who gives thanks for release from pain in the buttocks, inflicted as punishment for an undisclosed offense; she (Meter) "makes the possible out of the impossible," says the grateful penitent (Petzl 1994: no. 122). On a more disturbing note, Hermogenes and Demainetos disputed the ownership of three pigs that had wandered away; the power of Meter Anaita was invoked with the resulting death of Hermogenes (Petzl 1994, no. 68). Tatias honored Meter and Men in expiation of theft and perjury committed by her father; he too had been punished by death (Petzl 1994, no. 54).

These "confession inscriptions" have attracted a great deal of attention because of the information they convey on rural attitudes towards morality and the rural justice system in Asia Minor during the Roman Empire (Mitchell 1993: I, 187-195; Petzl 1994; Petzl 1995; Chaniotis 2004). They also, however, tell us a good deal about the desire of the rural Phrygians and Lydians to maintain their own identity in face of the pressures to adapt to the dominant Greek culture of Asia Minor and their use of traditional Anatolian deities to express values that they felt kept them apart from Greek attitudes. It was the Mother, along with the Lydian deity Men and the dominant male god, the local Zeus, all divinities of the rural landscape, who were responsible for maintaining these standards, standards that helped define the concept of ethnic distinctiveness for the people of Phrygia.

The Mother goddess of Roman Phrygia seems a highly localized figure, far removed from the impressive figure who advertised political power and cultural dominance by means of predators and architectural façades during the first millennium BC. Yet in one key way her function was the same, to represent the concept of Phrygian identity. The patronage of the goddess by Phrygian rulers in the first half of the first millennium BC gave the Mother unusual prominence as a symbol of Phrygian culture, and the evidence for the revival of her cult during the early Imperial period highlights the determination of the local Phrygian people to maintain their independence from the now dominant Hellenic culture. The very lack of political power among the people in this region made the power of their local divinities that much more important. To return to the metaphor expressed at the beginning of this paper, the Mother goddess provided the means to express the values of the human community through shared experiences with the imagined landscape. In this regard, the impact of the deity never lost its force.

## References

ALCOCK, S. 1993. *Graecia capta. The landscapes of Roman Greece.* Cambridge: Cambridge University Press.

BENNETT, J. & A.L. GOLDMAN. 2007. Roman military occupation at Yassıhöyük (Gordion), Ankara Province, Turkey. http://antiquity.ac.uk/ProjGall/bennett/.

BERNDT, D. 2002. *Midasstadt in Phrygien. Eine sagenumwobene Stätte im anatolischen Hochland.* Mainz: Philipp von Zabern.

BERNDT-ERSÖZ, S. 2004. In search of a Phrygian male superior god, in M. Hutter & S. Hutter-Braunsar (ed.) *Offizielle Religion, lokale Kulte und individuelle Religiosität. Akten des religionsgeschichtlichen Symposiums "Kleinasien und angrenzende Gebiete vom Beginn des 2. bis zur Mitte des 1. Jahrtausends v. Chr." (Bonn, 20-22. Februar 2003). Alter Orient und Altes Testament* 318: 47-56.

——2006. *Phrygian rock-cut shrines. Structure, function, and cult practice.* Leiden: Brill.

BITTEL, K. 1963. Phrygisches Kultbild aus Boğazköy, *Antike Plastik* 2: 7-21.

CANBY, J.V. 2002. Falconry (hawking) in Hittite lands, *Journal of Near Eastern Studies* 61: 161-201.

CHANIOTIS, A. 2004. Under the watchful eyes of the gods: divine justice in Hellenistic and Roman Asia Minor, in S. Colvin (ed.) *The Greco-Roman east: politics, culture, society*: 1-43. Cambridge: Cambridge University Press.

COLE, S.G. 2004. *Landscapes, gender, and ritual space.* Berkeley and Los Angeles: University of California Press.

COLLINS, B.J. 2004. The politics of Hittite religious iconography, in M. Hutter & S. Hutter-Braunsar (ed.) *Offizielle Religion, lokale Kulte und individuelle Religiosität. Akten des religionsgeschichtlichen Symposiums "Kleinasien und angrenzende Gebiete vom Beginn des 2. bis zur Mitte des 1. Jahrtausends v. Chr." (Bonn, 20.22. Februar 2003). Alter Orient und Altes Testament* 318: 83-115.

DENEL, E. 2007. Ceremony and kingship at Carchemish, in J. Cheng & M. H. Feldman (ed.) *Ancient Near Eastern art in context. Studies in honor of Irene J. Winter by her students*: 179-204. Leiden: Brill.

DEVRIES, K. 1980. Greeks and Phrygians in the Early Iron Age, in K. DeVries (ed.) *From Athens to Gordion. The papers of a memorial symposium for Rodney S. Young. University Museum Papers* 1: 33-49. Philadelphia: University of Pennsylvania Museum of Archaeology and Anthropology.

DRAYCOTT, C. M. & G. D. SUMMERS. 2008. *Sculpture and Inscriptions from the Monumental Entrance to the Palatial Complex at Kerkenes Dağ, Turkey. Kerkenes Special Studies 1.* Oriental Institute Publications 135. Chicago: Oriental Institute of the University of Chicago.

DREW-BEAR, T. & C. NAOUR. 1990. Divinités de Phrygie, *Aufstieg und Niedergang der römischen Welt* II.18.3: 1907-2044.

DUSINBERRE, E.R.M. 2005. *Gordion seals and sealings: individuals and society. Gordion Special Studies 3. University Museum Monograph* 124. Philadelphia: University of Pennsylvania Museum of Archaeology and Anthropology.

FREI, P. 1988. Phrygische Toponyme, *Epigraphica Anatolica* 11: 25-28.

GABRIEL, A. 1965. *Phrygie, exploration archéologique* IV. *La Cité de Midas, Architecture*. Paris: E. de Boccard.

GOLDMAN, A.L. 2005. Reconstructing the Roman-period town at Gordion, in L. Kealhofer (ed.) *The Archaeology of Midas and the Phrygians: recent work at Gordion*: 56-68. Philadelphia: University of Pennsylvania Museum of Archaeology and Anthropology.

GRAF, F. 1984. The Arrival of Cybele in the Greek East, in J. Harmatta (ed.) *The Proceedings of the VIIth Congress of the International Federation of the Societies of Classical Studies* I: 117-20. Budapest: Akadémiai Kiadó.

GRAVE, P., L. KEALHOFER & B. MARSH. 2005. Ceramic compositional analysis and the Phrygian sanctuary at Dümrek, in L. Kealhofer (ed.) *The Archaeology of Midas and the Phrygians: recent work at Gordion*: 149-160. Philadephia: University of Pennsylvania Museum of Archaeology and Anthropology.

GSCHNITZER, F. 1986. Eine persische Kultstiftung in Sardeis und die 'Sippengötter' Vorderasiens, in W. Meid & H. Trenkwalder (ed.) *Im Bannkreis des Alten Orients. Studien zur Sprach- und Kulturgeschichte des Alten Orients und seines Ausstrahlungsraumes. Karl Oberhuber zum 70. Geburtstag gewidmet*: 43-54. Innsbruck: Institut für Sprachwissenschaft der Universität Innsbruck.

HASPELS, C.H.E. 1971. *The highlands of Phrygia*. Princeton: Princeton University Press.

LAROCHE, E. 1960. Koubaba, déesse anatolienne, et le problème des origines de Cybèle, in O. Eissfeldt et al., *Éléments orientaux dans la religion grecque ancienne*: 113-128. Strasbourg: Université de Strasbourg, Centre de recherches d'histoire des religions.

LEVICK, B., S. MITCHELL, J. POTTER & M. WAELKENS. 1988. *Monumenta Asiae Minoris Antiqua* IX. *Monuments from the Aezanitis. Journal of Roman Studies Monograph* 4. London: Society for the Promotion of Roman Studies.

MELLINK, M.J. 1983. Comments on a cult relief of Kybele from Gordion, in R. M. Boehmer & H. Hauptmann (ed.) *Beiträge zur Altertumskunde Kleinasiens: Festschrift für Kurt Bittel*: 349-360. Mainz am Rhein: Philipp von Zabern.

MITCHELL, S. 1993. *Anatolia: land, men, and gods in Asia Minor*. I, *The Celts in Anatolia and the impact of Roman rule*; II, *The rise of the church*. Oxford: Clarendon Press.

MUNN, M. 2008. Kybele as Kubaba in a Lydo-Phrygian context, B.J. Collins, M.R. Bachvarova, and I.C. Rutherford (ed.) *Anatolian Interfaces. Hittites, Greeks and their neighbours. Proceedings of an International Conference on Cross-Cultural Interaction, September 17-19, 2004, Emory University, Atlanta, GA:* 159-164. Oxford: Oxbow Books.

NAUMANN, F. 1983. *Die Ikonographie der Kybele in der phrygischen und der griechischen Kunst. Istanbuler Mitteilungen Beiheft* 28. Tübingen: E. Wasmuth.

NAUMANN, R. 1979. *Der Zeustempel zu Aizanoi*. Berlin: Walter de Gruyter.

PETZL, G. 1987. *Die Inschriften von Smyrna*. Bonn: Rudolf Habelt.

——1994. *Die Beichtinschriften Westkleinasiens. Epigraphica Anatolica* 22. Bonn: Rudolf Habelt.

——1995. Ländliche Religiosität in Lydien, in E. Schwertheim (ed.) *Forschungen in Lydien*: 37-48. Bonn: Rudolf Habelt.

PRAYON, F. 2004. Zum Problem von Kultstätten und Kultbildern der anatolischen Muttergöttin im 8. Jh. v. Chr., in T. Korkut (ed.) *60. Yaşında Fahri Işık'a Armağan: Anadolu'da Doğdu. Festschrift für Fahri Işık zum 60. Geburtstag*: 611-622. Istanbul: Ege Yayınları.

RICL, M. 1991. Hosios kai Dikaios, Première partie: catalogue des inscriptions, *Epigraphica Anatolica* 18: 1-69.

ROBERT, L. 1975. Une nouvelle inscription grecque de Sardes, *Comptes rendus de l'Académie des Inscriptions et Belles-Lettres*: 306-330.

ROLLER, L.E. 1987. Hellenistic epigraphic texts from Gordion, *Anatolian Studies* 37: 103-133.

——1988. Phrygian myth and cult, *Source* 7: 43-50.

——1991. The Great Mother at Gordion: the Hellenization of an Anatolian cult, *Journal of Hellenic Studies* 111: 128-143.

——1994. The Phrygian character of Kybele: the formation of an iconography and cult ethos in the Iron Age, in A. Çilingiroğlu & D.H. French (ed.) *Proceedings of the Third Anatolian Iron Ages Symposium*: 189-198. Ankara: British Institute of Archaeology, Monograph 16.

——1999a. *In search of God the Mother: the cult of Anatolian Cybele*. Berkeley, Los Angeles, London: University of California Press.

——1999b. Early Phrygian drawings from Gordion and the elements of Phrygian artistic style, *Anatolian Studies* 49: 143-151.

——2005. A Phrygian sculptural identity? Evidence from Early Phrygian drawings in Iron Age Gordion, in A. Çilingiroğlu & G. Darbyshire (ed.) *Proceedings of the Fifth Anatolian Iron Ages Symposium*: 125-130. Ankara: British Institute of Archaeology, Monograph 31.

——2006. Midas and Phrygian cult practice, in M. Hutter & S. Hutter-Braunsar (ed.) *Pluralismus und Wandel in den Religionen im vorhellenistischen Anatolien. Akten des religionsgeschichtlichen Symposiums in Bonn (19.- 20. Mai 2005)*: 123-135. Münster: Ugarit-Verlag.

ROMANO, I.B. 1995. *The terracotta figurines and related vessels. Gordion Special Studies* 2. *University Museum Monograph* 86. Philadelphia: University of Pennsylvania Museum of Archaeology and Anthropology.

SAMS, G.K. 1974. Phrygian painted animals: Anatolian orientalizing art, *Anatolian Studies* 24: 169-176.

——1988. The Early Phrygian period at Gordion: toward a cultural identity, *Source* 7: 9-15.

——1989. Sculpted orthostates at Gordion, in K. Emre, B. Hrouda, M. Mellink & N. Özgüç (ed.) *Anatolia and the ancient Near East. Studies in honor of Tahsin Özgüç*: 447-454. Ankara: Türk Tarih Kurumu.

——1994a. *The Gordion excavations 1950-1973: final*

reports IV. The Early Phrygian painted pottery. University Museum Monograph 79. Philadelphia: University of Pennsylvania Museum of Archaeology and Anthropology.

——1994b. Aspects of Early Phrygian architecture at Gordion, in A. Çilingiroğlu & D.H. French (ed.) *Proceedings of the Third Anatolian Iron Ages Symposium*: 211-220. Ankara: British Institute of Archaeology, Monograph 16.

——1995. Midas of Gordion and the Anatolian kingdom of Phrygia, in J. Sasson (ed.) *Civilizations of the ancient Near East* II: 1147-1159. New York: Scribner.

SEEHER, J. 1999. Die Ausgrabungen in Boğazköy-Hattuša 1998 und ein neuer topographischer Plan des Stadtgeländes, *Archäologischer Anzeiger*: 317-344.

SIMPSON, E. 1998. Symbols on the Gordion screens, *XXXIV<sup>ème</sup> Rencontre Assyriologique International: 6-10 VII 1987 Istanbul: kongreye sunulan bildiriler*: 630-639. Ankara: Türk Tarih Kurumu.

SIVAS, T.T. 1999. *Eskişehir – Afyonkarahisar – Kütahya İl Sınırları İçindeki Phryg Kaya Anıtları*. Eskişehir: Anadolu Üniversitesi Yayınları no. 1156.

SPAWFORTH, A. 2001. Shades of Greekness: a Lydian case study, in I. Malkin (ed.) *Ancient Perceptions of Greek Ethnicity*: 375-400. Washington, DC & Cambridge, MA: Center for Hellenic Studies, Harvard University Press.

SUMMERS, G.D. 2006a. *Kerkenes News* 9: 1-16.

——2006b. Phrygian expansion to the east. Evidence of cult from Kerkenes Dağ, *Baghdader Mitteilungen* 37: 647-656.

——2007. The Kerkenes Project, http://www.kerkenes. metu.edu.tr/kerk2/temp/new/07kreportdj.pdf.

VASSILEVA, M. 2001. Further considerations on the cult of Kybele, *Anatolian Studies* 51: 51-63.

VERMASEREN, M.J. 1977. *Cybele and Attis: the myth and the cult*. London: Thames and Hudson.

VOIGT, M.M. 2005. Old problems and new solutions. Recent excavations at Gordion, in L. Kealhofer (ed.), *The archaeology of Midas and the Phrygians. Recent work at Gordion*: 22-35. Philadephia: University of Pennsylvania Museum of Archaeology and Anthropology.

VOIGT, M.M. & R.C. HENRICKSON. 2000. Formation of the Phrygian state: the Early Iron Age at Gordion, *Anatolian Studies* 50: 37-54.

VOIGT, M.M. & T.C. YOUNG. 1999. From Phrygian capital to Achaemenid entrepot: Middle and Late Phrygian Gordion, *Iranica Antiqua* 34: 191-241.

WAELKENS, M. 1986. *Die kleinasiatischen Türsteine. Typologische und epigraphische Untersuchungen der kleinasiatischen Grabreliefs mit Scheintür*. Mainz: Philipp von Zabern.

YOUNG, R.S. 1956. The campaign of 1955 at Gordion: preliminary report, *American Journal of Archaeology* 60: 249-266.

——1963. Gordion on the Royal Road, *Proceedings of the American Philosophical Society* 107: 348-364.

——1969. Doodling at Gordion, *Archaeology* 22: 270-275.

YOUNG, R.S., K. DEVRIES, E.L. KOHLER, J.F. MCCLELLAN, M.J. MELLINK & G.K. SAMS. 1981. *The Gordion excavations: final reports* I. *Three great early tumuli*. University Museum Monograph 43. Philadelphia: University of Pennsylvania Museum of Archaeology and Anthropology.

# SACRED SPACE IN IRON AGE PHRYGIA

## Susanne Berndt-Ersöz

This paper aims to examine and analyse the changes of sacred space that occurred in Phrygia during the Iron Age.

### Characteristics of Phrygian Sacred Space

We may begin with a characterization of Phrygian sacred space. Contrary to many other cultures, we lack evidence for normal built Phrygian temples apart from one or two built shrines at Boğazköy, situated in the eastern Phrygian periphery (Beran 1963; Seeher 1999: 325-327, figs. 6, 9-11).[1] Instead of built temples we have a large number of rock-cut shrines and monuments.

The rock-cut monuments can be divided into two main groups, one group consisting of so-called step monuments and idols, and the other group of façades and niches (Berndt-Ersöz 2006a).

A step monument has a number of steps with a kind of seat or throne situated above the steps (figs. 1-2). The step monuments themselves may be divided into two groups depending on how the upper part of the seat was made. The majority of the step monuments have a seat where the back consists of a thick semicircular disc, representing a deity in the shape of an idol (fig. 1). This kind of step monument is usually situated on top of a rock and some of them are even so high up that they are more or less inaccessible. They all look out onto a good view. I have earlier suggested that this type of step monument might be connected with a Superior Male god rather than the Mother Goddess (Berndt-Ersöz 2007; 2006a: 170-172).

The other type of step monument also has a kind of seat on the top but it lacks the idol image. Usually both the steps

and the seats of these monuments are larger. In addition, in contrast to the other group of step monuments, they are not situated on top of rocks but are instead located at ground level and they all have an easy access (fig. 2; Berndt-Ersöz 2006a: 47-48).

The second group of rock-cut monuments consists of façades and niches. This type of monument may consist only of a tiny niche without the surrounding façade or may be a huge imitation of a building façade measuring several meters in height and width, in which the niche itself represents the door entrance of the building (figs. 3-4). Usually there is an image of the Mother Goddess standing inside the niche (Berndt-Ersöz 2006a: 21-40).

### Distribution of the Two Groups of Monuments

The distribution of the various types of monuments differs between sites. It is my intention to demonstrate that this difference is to a certain extent a chronological difference: the group with façades and niches is a type of monument that cannot be found in the Early Phrygian period,[2] in contrast to the type of step monument with a semicircular disc at the back.

There are three large clusters of step monuments; the first group is at Dümrek, just north of Gordion, where there are ca. fifteen step monuments (table 1 below; Berndt-Ersöz 2006a: 264-266). The second group is at Fındık, in the northern part of the Phrygian Highlands, i.e. in the area between Afyon and Eskişehir, where there are ca. thirty-four step monuments (table 1 below; Berndt-Ersöz 2006a: xx, n. 4, nos. 42-48). The third group is at Midas City in the Highlands, where there are also about thirty-four step monuments (table 1 below; Berndt-Ersöz 2006a: 247-263)

---

[1] Megaron 2 at Gordion is a possible candidate for a built temple but the sparse inventories from the building itself do not confirm that the building was used for cultic activities (Young 1957: 322-323; Young 1958: 142-143). It has been suggested as a possible temple by Mellink (1981:101) and Sams (1997:241). Cf. Roller 1999, 79 n. 84, 112.

[2] The following periods are used throughout the paper: Early Phrygian ca. 950-800 BC, Middle Phrygian ca. 800-550 BC and Late Phrygian ca. 550-330 BC.

*Figure 1. Step monument with semicircular back at Dümrek (photo: S. Berndt-Ersöz)*

Besides these areas there are several places with only a single step monument and also some with a few. The Köhnüş Valley, for example, has eight step monuments (Berndt-Ersöz 2006a: nos. 54, 56-61; Tamsü 2004, 64-65, no. 43), whereas Menekşe Kayaları, close to Demirli Köy, has four step monuments (Berndt-Ersöz 2006a: 52-53, 111-112). We will now compare these sacred spaces with each other.

**Chronological Comparison of the Sacred Areas**

*From Step Monuments to Façades*

The step monuments at Dümrek have indirectly been dated through surveys, since 70% of the collected pottery for which a date could be provided belonged to the Early or Middle Phrygian periods, with an emphasis on the Early Phrygian period, while hardly any Late Phrygian pottery was found (Grave, Kealhofer, and Marsh 2005: 155, 160, figs. 12-3, 12-4). Since a large amount of the Early Phrygian pottery was found below the kale in the area around the step monuments, we may suggest that at least some of the step monuments also date to the Early Phrygian period. In line with an Early Phrygian date we can note that none

of the step monuments at Dümrek carry an inscription, which may be a further indication that they date to the Early Phrygian period when the Phrygian script had not yet come into use. The earliest datable Phrygian inscriptions we have today are the ones from Tumulus MM at Gordion, with a probable date shortly after ca. 740 BC; the Phrygian script was probably introduced some time during the eighth century BC.[3] Of importance here is to note the complete lack of façades and niches at Dümrek, a good indication that this type of monument did not yet exist when Dümrek experienced its importance as a cult centre during the Early Phrygian period. Dümrek appeared to have been abandoned as a cult centre in the Late Phrygian period, since only a few sherds of this or later periods have been found at Dümrek (Grave, Kealhofer, and Marsh 2005: 155-160, figs. 12-3, 12-4).

---

[3]  For inscriptions of Tumulus MM, see Brixhe and Lejeune 1984: nos. G-105-G-109, and for the date of Tumulus MM see Manning et al. 2001: 2534. No inscriptions have been found in Early Phrygian levels at Gordion (i.e. the pre-destruction layer) or in the destruction layer itself dated to around 800 BC (Berndt-Ersöz 2006a: 126 with n. 287). K. DeVries (2007: 96-97) recently suggested that the Phrygians adopted the alphabet from Semitic speakers around the time of the destruction or slightly earlier, although the earliest conclusive evidence of the Phrygian alphabet are the inscriptions from Tumulus MM.

Vertical section

Elevation

0    100 CM

Plan

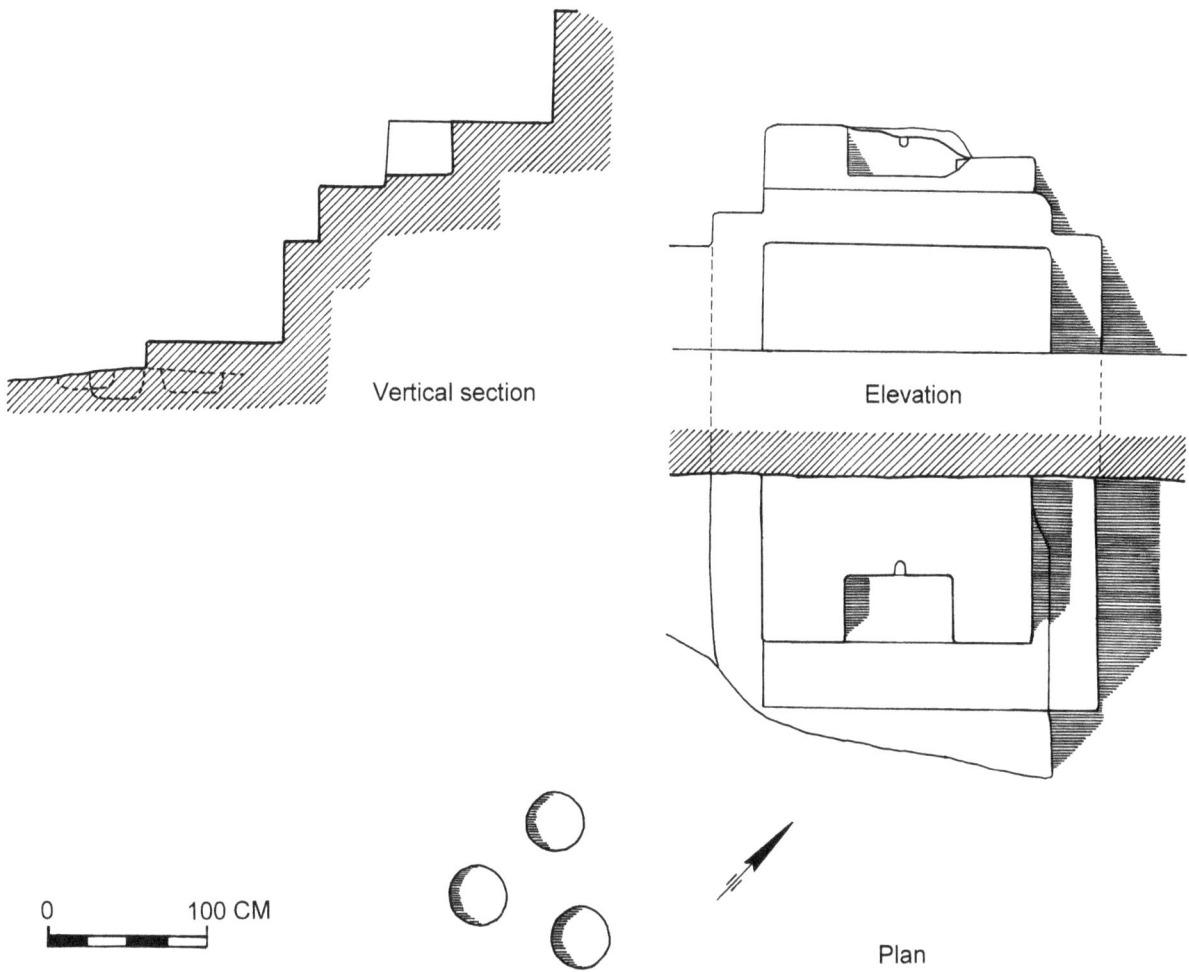

*Figure 2. Step monument at ground level at Midas City (after Haspels 1971: fig. 529:1 & Tüfekçi Sivas 1999: pl. 132b)*

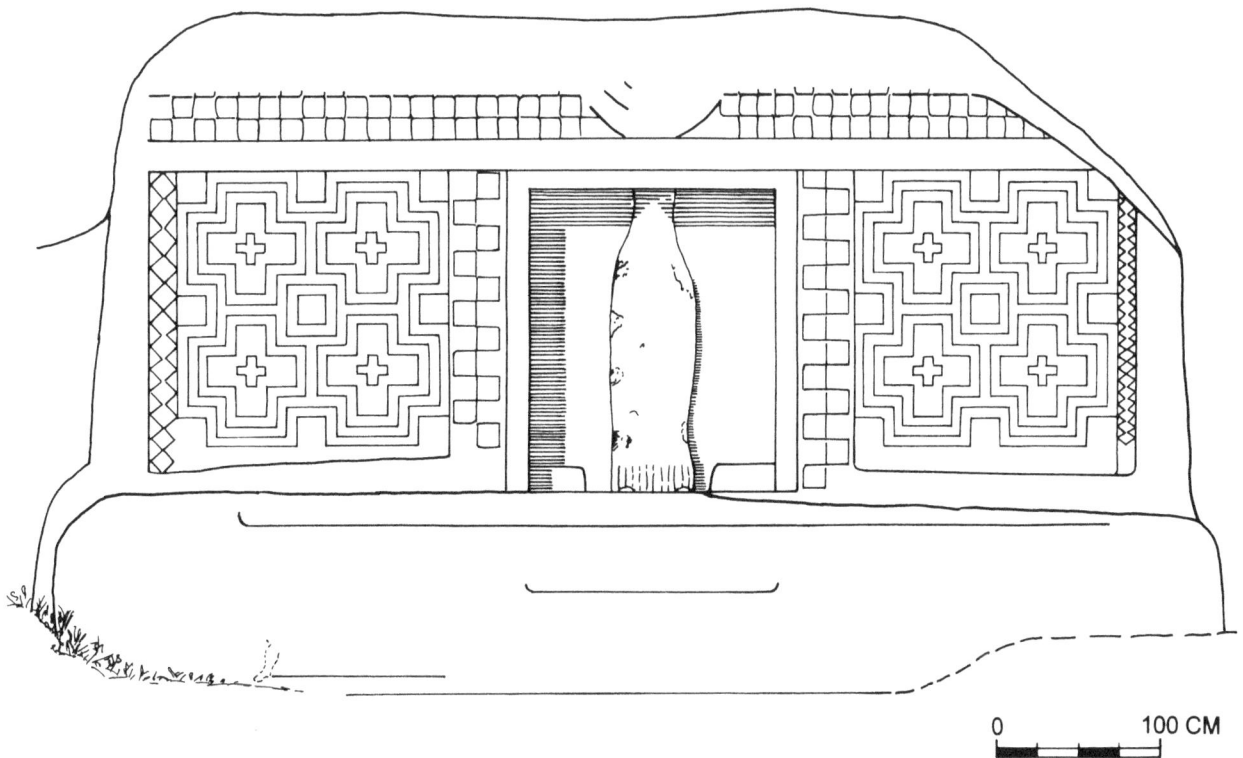

0    100 CM

*Figure 3. The façade Büyük Kapı Kaya at Emre Gölü (after Haspels 1971: fig. 522)*

| Site/ Sacred area | Number of step mon. | Number of façades/niches | Number of idols not being part of a step monument | Inscription | Date of pottery |
|---|---|---|---|---|---|
| **Dümrek** | ca. 15 | -- | -- | -- | EP-MP* |
| **Fındık** | ca. 34 | 1 façade ca. 7 niches | 5? | 1 – façade 1 - niche | ? |
| **Midas City** | ca. 34 | 9 façades ca. 23 niches of various sizes | ca. 24 single idols 1 double idol | 2 - step mon with double idol 1 - step mon ground level 3 - façades | MP-LP |
| **Köhnüş Valley** | 8 | 2 façades >5 niches | 1 triple idol | 1 - step mon ground level 1 - façade | ?-LP |
| **Demirli Köy** | 4 | 2 façades | -- | 1 - step mon | ? |
| **Kümbet** | -- | 1 façade | -- | 1 – façade | LP? |
| **Emre Gölü** | 1 | 4 façades | -- | 1 – façade | ? |
| **Kes Kaya** | -- | 2 façades 1 niche | 1 | -- | LP |

**References**: Dümrek (Berndt-Ersöz 2006a: nos. 101-107; Tamsü 2004: 57-61, nos. 27-38; Grave, Kealhofer, and Marsh 2005), some of the step monuments at Dümrek are unrecorded; Fındık (Berndt Ersöz 2006: 3, n. 27, nos. 2-7, 42-48; Tamsü 2004: 69-81, nos. 53-82; Tüfekçi Sivas and Sivas 2003: pl. 10, nos. I 1-5); Midas City (Berndt-Ersöz 2006a: nos. 30-38, 62-99; Tamsü 2004: 41-56, nos. 1-26; Tüfekçi Sivas 1999: pl 159; Berndt 2002: figs. 35, 46, 93, 94, 99, 103, 111; Berndt 2008:** nos. 3b, 14a-e, 24a, 25a, 29b,c, 31a, 35e,f, 51a, 86a), some of the idols and niches are unrecorded; Köhnüş Valley (Berndt-Ersöz 2006a: nos. 20-25, 54-61; Tamsü 2004: 64-65, no. 43); Demirli Köy (Berndt-Ersöz 2006a: nos. 19, 52-53, 109, 111-112); Kümbet (Berndt-Ersöz 2006a: no. 29); Emre Gölü (Berndt-Ersöz 2006a: nos. 15-18, 50); Kes Kaya (Berndt-Ersöz 2006a: nos. 9-11, 49).

---

* Very small amounts of LP, Hellenistic, Roman and Medieval pottery were recorded.

** I am very grateful to Dietrich Berndt who generously shared his results with me and provided me with an advanced copy of his article prior to publication.

*Table 1. Distribution of different types of rock-cut monuments in sacred areas*

At Fındık we have a large quantity of step monuments (ca. thirty-four in number), but only one small façade and two larger niches and a handful of quite tiny ones (table 1 below; Berndt-Ersöz 2006a: nos. 2-7). It is here of importance to note that in spite of the large number of step monuments compared with façades and niches, none of the step monuments at Fındık carry any inscription while both the façade and one of the two larger niches do (table 1 below; Berndt-Ersöz 2006a: nos. 3, 5). Since no survey has been made at Fındık, we lack chronological data; it therefore has to remain an open question how early the site might be. We have evidence of later Roman and Byzantine occupation at Fındık (Haspels 1971: 194, 243; figs. 216, 563.1, 4), but whether there was a continuous occupation from the Phrygian period until the Roman period is not possible to determine on the basis of present evidence. We can at least conclude that the monuments carrying an inscription (in this case the façade and one large niche) cannot be dated any earlier than the Middle Phrygian period, but the step monuments, at least some of them, may very well be earlier.

At other sites/areas, such as Midas City and the Köhnüş Valley, we have a more equal distribution between the step monuments and the façades/niches. Midas City has both a large number of step monuments and a large number of façades and niches, but here we also find three step monuments with inscriptions (Berndt-Ersöz 2006a: nos.

69, 70, 95). These three step monuments are, however, of a different type than those at Dümrek. All of them are located at ground level and two of them carry a double idol on the back seat. It is possible that this type appeared at a later period than the type of step monument we find at Dümrek. Besides the step monuments with inscriptions there are also three façades with inscriptions at or in the environs of Midas City (Berndt-Ersöz 2006a: nos. 30, 33, 37), in addition to a fourth inscription that was probably intended for a façade that was never cut (Berndt-Ersöz 2006a: 70; Brixhe and Tüfekçi Sivas 2003: 70-71, figs. 6-7).

Midas City was excavated in the 1930s and the excavated settlement belonged to only one period, the Late Phrygian period or the Achaemenian period (Haspels 1971: 141). Since this settlement was built on the bedrock itself there were no remains in situ of any earlier settlements, but excavated material of the eighth and sixth centuries found elsewhere bears witness to an earlier Middle Phrygian settlement (Haspels 1971: 141-142). Pottery and probably fibulae dating to the eighth century were excavated in certain areas (Haspels 1951: 81-85, pls. 20, 33, 41a; 1971: 142-43; Mellink 1993: 153-54; Berndt-Ersöz 2006a: 91). However, none of the eighth century material was found close to any rock-cut monument, with one exception. A few finds possibly dating to the eighth century were found in the area of two step monuments where the Hellenistic

*Figure 4. The Midas Monument at Midas City (after Gabriel 1965: fig. 30)*

shrine of Agdistis or the Mother Goddess was later built, at which time one of the step monuments appeared to have been reused or partly incorporated into the later shrine (Berndt-Ersöz 2006a: 96-98, nos. 76-77). Both these step monuments are of a different type than those at Dümrek, since they are situated at ground level and do not have a semicircular disc above the steps, but another kind of seating arrangement at the uppermost step. Just a few metres in front of the shrine there is a rock with the previously mentioned inscription that was probably intended to be part of a façade that remained unfinished. Whether the excavated material was contemporary with the step monuments is not possible to determine. The step monuments may just as well be earlier than the excavated material as later.

Whether there was a settlement prior to the eighth century at Midas City is unknown. Based on the excavated material it appears that the settlement of the eighth century was period of some significance. It may be of some relevance here to note that a substantial amount of eighth century

pottery was found in connection with two of the so-called concealed staircases, which most probably served as parts of the fortification system (Haspels 1971: 142; Mellink 1993: 154). However, the concealed staircases may not be contemporary with the eighth century pottery found inside them.

So far we can at least conclude that Midas City must have been a site of some importance during the eighth and seventh centuries BC.

Midas City appeared to have experienced a second more prosperous period during the first half of the sixth century BC (Haspels 1971: 142), as witnessed by the imported painted pottery from East Greece and Lydia, the presence of painted architectural terracottas, and architectural fragments such as columns and stone sculptures. The monumental façades at Midas City most probably also date to this period (Berndt-Ersöz 2006a: 89-142). Whether any of the smaller façades and niches at Midas City should be dated any earlier than the sixth century is uncertain, but quite possible.

Let us now turn to the chronology of the remaining relevant settlements. Two of the monuments in the Köhnüş Valley carry inscriptions: one façade with a probable date in the first half of the sixth century and one step monument of the type situated at ground level (Berndt-Ersöz 2006a: nos. 24, 56). The site existed during the Middle Phrygian period but was probably still in use during the Late Phrygian period, since at least the Yılan Taş tomb dates to that period (von Gall 1999; Haspels 1971: 31-32, 58). There are also numerous rock-cut monuments dating to the Roman period, such as tombs and churches (Haspels 1971: 175, 247).

The Köhnüş Valley has an equal distribution between façades/niches and step monuments. There are also two sites where there are no step monuments and for which we have some chronological data based on surface finds. These are Kes Kaya and Kümbet Asar Kale, both dated to the Late Phrygian period based on surface pottery finds (Haspels 1971: 145).[4] At Kümbet there is one façade that has an inscription and at Kes Kaya there are two façades (Berndt-Ersöz 2006a: nos. 9-10, 29). These results give further support for the suggestion that the step monuments appear to have fallen out of use during the Late Phrygian period, at least the type of step monument with a semicircular disc at the back. This is the only type found at Dümrek, a cultic site that was probably no longer in use during the Late Phrygian period.

To conclude, the façade housing the Mother Goddess appeared later than the earliest type of step monument. The majority of the rock-cut façades date to the first half of the sixth century BC. Whether any of the rock-cut façades or niches belong to an earlier period is, however, not possible to determine. However, the concept of a façade with the Mother Goddess existed earlier than the sixth century, as we have stelae, from Central Phrygia, probably dating to the end of the eighth century with such motifs (see below). We may suggest that the façade housing the Mother Goddess was introduced around this time. These images are the first we know that depict a Phrygian deity in human shape. But images of plain façades, i.e. without the Mother Goddess, existed already in the Early Phrygian period, as such drawings are found among the graffiti of Megaron 2 at Gordion (Young 1969: 272).

### *Monumental Façades and Their Occurrence*

We will now examine the other major alteration of Phrygian sacred space. I have already mentioned that during the first half of the sixth century there was a prosperous settlement at Midas City and in connection with this period there

was a sudden emphasis on monumental façades. These monumental façades are, however, confined not only to Midas City but can be found all over the Highlands. The majority of the façades date to a rather short period in the first half of the sixth century. Only a few of them can be dated to the Late Phrygian period, and these tend to be somewhat smaller. Several façades remained unfinished; these can all be dated close to the mid-sixth century, such as the Unfinished Monument, the Areyastis façade, the Burmeç façade, and Arslankaya (Berndt-Ersöz 2006a: 89-142, nos. 34, 37, 18, 16). The most imposing and monumental façade is the so-called Midas Monument at Midas City (fig. 5).

### Can We Relate These Two Transformations of Phrygian Sacred Space With the Historical Development?

I will now discuss these developments of Phrygian sacred space from a historical point of view.

The earliest Phrygian sacred space we know of is probably the one at Dümrek, where only the earlier type of step monument has been found, and as I have earlier suggested, may be connected with a Superior Male god (Berndt-Ersöz 2004; 2007: 33-35). The short geographical distance between Gordion and Dümrek suggests that Dümrek was an important shrine for people coming from Gordion, but perhaps also for a larger area, as pottery from other parts of central Anatolia has also been found here (Grave, Kealhofer, and Marsh 2005: 158-160).

There are no images of the Mother Goddess from Dümrek. The earliest known images of the Mother Goddess have instead been found on stelae from Ankara, with a probable date towards the end of the eighth century (Berndt-Ersöz 2006a: 117-18; Mellink 1983: 359; Roller 1999: 83; cf. Naumann 1983: 294-95, nos. 18, 20). Admittedly we do not have any rock-cut façades that can conclusively be dated that early, but again several of the smaller façades may be dated earlier than the more monumental ones. We would after all expect the larger façades to have had some more modest predecessors.

We may suggest that a major change took place in Phrygian religious iconography around 700 BC or slightly earlier, when the Mother Goddess became visible through the introduction of the façade and the anthropomorphic images of her. The end of the eighth century is the period when the Great King Midas was active (Berndt-Ersöz 2008), and it is tempting to correlate this iconographical development of Phrygian cult with Midas. We can find some support for such a scenario in the later literary accounts, as Midas is intimately connected with the cult of the Mother Goddess in both historical and mythological accounts (Hyg. *Fab.* 191, 274; Plut. *Caes.* 9.3; Pseudo-Hesiod frg. 251 [ed. Rzach 1958]; Diod. Sic. 3.59.8; Arn. *Adv. nat.* 2.73, 5.5-7). We may also note that the largest façade at Midas City was

---

[4]   Haspels writes that possibly the rock of Kümbet was settled for the first time in the Persian period, i.e. the Late Phrygian period. However, an earlier Bronze Age settlement may have existed in the area, since pottery dating to the Hittite period was also noted by Haspels (1971: 286).

dedicated to the King and Leader Midas (Berndt-Ersöz 2006a: no. 30).

Possibly dating to the eighth century is also the growing significance of Midas City as a settlement, and perhaps also as a cultic centre. We know that by the sixth century Midas City had become the main cult centre of Phrygia, but it is uncertain how early this distinction began. It is possible that the anthropomorphic images of the Mother standing in a door-niche may be contemporary with the growing importance or establishment of Midas City as a cult centre. If so, it is possible that the increasing significance of the sacred space at Midas City caused Dümrek slowly to lose its importance as a cult centre, even though it continued as such for some more time.

Midas City probably remained the main Phrygian cult centre at least until the end of the Middle Phrygian period. Probably at some time during the Late Phrygian period Pessinous came to take that position. The most important cult centre of the Mother in Phrygia during the Roman period was the one at Pessinous, but it is uncertain when it became a cult centre of some importance. The earliest archaeological remains from Pessinous date approx. to the fifth century BC (Devreker, Thoen, and Vermeulen 1995: 129-137; Devreker and Vermeulen 1995: 115)[5] and the earliest reference to Pessinous in a written source is in a fourth century fragment of Theopompus preserved by Ammianus Marcellinus (*FGrHist* 115 F 260; Amm. Marc. 22.9.7). It is therefore unlikely that Pessinous during the period of Midas was an important cult centre.

To conclude, the changed iconography of the Mother Goddess, when she became anthropomorphic standing inside a façade, is possibly connected with the growing importance of Midas City as a major cult centre. This change I would like to suggest took place towards the end of the eighth century, when possibly her shrine was located on top of the kale in the area where eighth century material was found, and where she was still worshipped during the later Hellenistic and Roman periods. However, based on present evidence this can only remain a hypothesis.

We will now finally discuss the other major development that can be noticed concerning Phrygian sacred space, i.e. the more or less sudden appearance and emphasis on monumental façades in the Highlands, particularly at Midas City, during the first half of the sixth century BC. The monumental façades appeared at a time when Phrygia had fallen under Lydian control. Several façades remained unfinished when the work was interrupted around the mid-sixth century BC, probably due to the loss of the Lydian empire to the Persians.

Around the same time as the monumental façades appeared in Phrygia, the Lydian king Croesus made huge religious dedications in other subjugated areas of the Lydian empire, such as Ionia and Caria. We know from literary sources that he made substantial dedications at the Artemision in Ephesus and at the Apollo temple in Didyma (Hdt. 1.92, 5.36, 6.19). It has even been suggested that it was Croesus himself who actually financed the temple at Didyma (Parke 1985a: 24-25; 1985b: 60-61, with n. 10).[6] We are familiar with these dedications because of Herodotus's account, but Phrygia was probably geographically too distant to be included in any Greek source. However, just because the Greek sources do not report similar Lydian dedications in other subjugated areas outside the immediate Greek sphere of interest that does not mean that they did not exist. On the contrary, we may rather suspect that Croesus exercised the same religious policy in other conquered areas of the Lydian kingdom, such as Phrygia. Both the Artemision and the Apollo temple were probably chosen because they were the main cult centres of these regions. If we assume a similar policy of Croesus in Phrygia, he will have chosen Midas City for a potential dedication of similar proportions, as this was the main cult centre of Phrygia during this period.

Evidence for such a Lydian policy in Phrygia may indeed be found at Midas City. The dedicator of the most imposing monument at Midas City, the so-called Midas Monument, is named Ates (fig. 4), but Ates is also the name of Croesus's son, at least if we are to believe Herodotus (1.34-43; Berndt-Ersöz 2006b: 26-29).

The date of the Midas Monument, in the first half of the sixth century, conforms with the date of Croesus and his son Ates (Berndt-Ersöz 2006a:130; 2006b). If the identification of the Midas Monument's Ates as being the son of Croesus is correct, then the Midas Monument was a Lydian sponsored monument. We may therefore suggest that the Lydians applied the same religious policy in Phrygia as they did in other subdued areas.

**Conclusions**

The step monument is the earliest type of Phrygian cultic monument we know. The façade housing the anthropomorphic images of the Mother Goddess is a later development and can first be noted in the material record towards the end of the eighth century. Dümrek, a sanctuary north of Gordion, has only the earlier type of step monument, while the rock-cut façade can mainly be found in the Highlands in western Phrygia.

---

[5]   Apart from Late Phrygian material the earliest material is some ash found in a pit hollowed out of earth, which has been dated by carbon 14 to ca. 1500 BC (Devreker et al. 2003; 146). There is, however, no evidence for any continuity between the Bronze Age and the Late Phrygian period at Pessinous.

[6]   The capitals and the figures of the temple have variously been dated to between 550 and 530 BC (Parke 1985b: 61, n. 10 with earlier references). Earlier scholars usually calculated with the date of 547/46 BC as the date of the Persian conquest. However, the date of the Persian conquest of Asia Minor has recently been discussed by several scholars with the conclusion that the fall of Sardis may be as late as 539 BC (Berndt-Ersöz 2008: n. 39, 14, Cahill and Kroll 2005: 605-608; Oelsner 1999/2000: 378-379). A later date for the fall of Sardis increases the possibility that the temple was at least partially financed by Croesus.

The monumental façades found in the Highlands should be dated in a rather short period, in the first half of the sixth century BC, when Phrygia was a subjugated part of the Lydian kingdom. The Lydian religious policy as exercised in other conquered areas may also be found in Phrygia, with the Midas Monument at Midas City being an example of a Lydian royal dedication.

## References

BERAN, T. 1963. Eine Kultstätte phrygischer Zeit in Boğazköy. *Mitteilungen der Deutschen Orient-Gesellschaft zu Berlin* 94: 33-52.

BERNDT, D. 2002. *Midasstadt in Phrygien. Eine sagenumwobene Stätte im anatolischen Hochland.* Mainz am Rhein: Philipp von Zabern.

——2008. Midasstadt: Kleine und kleinste phrygische Felsmonumente, Überlegungen zu einer frühen Besiedlung, in E. Schwertheim & E. Winter (ed.) *Neue Funde und Forschungen in Phrygien* (Asia Minor Studien, 61): 1-32. Bonn: Rudolf Habelt.

BERNDT-ERSÖZ, S. 2004. In search of a Phrygian male superior god, in M. Hutter & S. Hutter-Braunsar (ed.) *Offizielle Religion, lokale Kulte und individuelle Religiosität: Akten des religionsgeschichtlichen Symposiums „Kleinasien und angrenzende Gebiete vom Beginn des 2. bis zur Mitte des 1. Jahrtausends v.Chr.". (Bonn, 20.-22. Februar 2003)* (Alter Orient und Altes Testament, 318): 47-56. Münster: Ugarit-Verlag.

——2006a. *Phrygian rock-cut shrines. Structure, function and cult practice* (Culture and history of the Ancient Near East, 25). Leiden & Boston: Brill.

——2006b. The Anatolian origin of Attis, in M. Hutter & S. Hutter-Braunsar (ed.) *Pluralismus und Wandel in den Religionen in Anatolien im vorhellenistischen Anatolien. Akten des religionsgeschichtlichen Symposiums in Bonn (19.-20- Mai 2005)* (AOAT, 337): 9-39. Münster: Ugarit-Verlag.

——2007. Phrygian rock-cut step monuments: an interpretation, in A. Çilingiroğlu & A. Sagona (ed.) *Anatolian Iron Ages 6. The proceedings of the sixth Anatolian Iron Ages colloquium held at Eskişehir, 16-20 August 2004* (Ancient Near Eastern Studies, 20): 19-39. Leuven: Peeters.

——2008. The chronology and historical context of Midas. *Historia* 57: 1-37.

BRIXHE, C. & M. LEJEUNE. 1984. *Corpus des inscriptions paléo-phrygiennes.* Paris: Editions recherche sur les civilisations.

BRIXHE, C. & T. TÜFEKÇI SIVAS. 2003. Exploration de l'ouest de la Phrygie: nouveaux documents paléo-phrygiens. *Kadmos* 42: 65-76.

CAHILL, N. & J.H. KROLL. 2005. New Archaic coin finds at Sardis. *American Journal of Archaeology* 109: 589-617.

DEVREKER, J., G. DEVOS, L. BAUTERS, K. BRAECKMAN, A. DAEMS, W. DE CLERCQ, J. ANGENON & P. MONSIEUR. 2003. Fouilles archéologiques de Pessinonte: la campagne de 2001. *Anatolia Antiqua* 11: 141-156.

DEVREKER, J., H. THOEN & F. VERMEULEN. 1995. The imperial sanctuary at Pessinus and its predecessors: a revision. *Anatolia Antiqua* 3: 125-144.

DEVREKER, J. & F. VERMEULEN. 1995. Archaeological work at Pessinus in 1993. *Anatolia Antiqua* 3: 113-124.

DEVRIES, K. 2007. The date of the destruction level at Gordion: imports and the local sequence, in A. Çilingiroğlu & A. Sagona (ed.) *Anatolian Iron Ages 6. The proceedings of the sixth Anatolian Iron Ages colloquium held at Eskişehir, 16-20 August 2004* (Ancient Near Eastern Studies, 20): 79-101. Leuven: Peeters.

GABRIEL, A. 1965. *Phrygie: exploration archéologique 4. La Cité de Midas: architecture.* Paris: E. de Boccard.

VON GALL, H. 1999. Der achaimenidische Löwengreif in Kleinasien. Bemerkungen zu dem sog. ‚Zerbrochenen Löwengrab' bei Hayranvelisultan in Phrygien. *Archäologische Mitteilungen aus Iran und Turan* 31: 149-160.

GRAVE, P., L. KEALHOFER, & B. MARSH. 2005. Ceramic compositional analysis and the Phrygian sanctuary at Dümrek, in L. Kealhofer (ed.) *The archaeology of Midas and the Phrygians: recent work at Gordion*: 149-160. Philadelphia: University of Pennsylvania Museum of Archaeology and Anthropology.

HASPELS, C.H.E. 1951. *Phrygie: exploration archéologique 3. La Cité de Midas, céramique et trouvailles diverses.* Paris: E. de Boccard.

——1971. *The highlands of Phrygia: sites and monuments.* Princeton: Princeton University Press.

MANNING, S.W., B. KROMER, P.I. KUNIHOLM & M.W. NEWTON. 2001. Anatolian tree rings and a new chronology for the east Mediterranean Bronze-Iron Ages. *Science* 294: 2532-2535.

MELLINK, M.J. 1981. Temples and high places in Phrygia, in A. Biran (ed.) *Temples and high places in Biblical times. Proceedings of the colloquium in honor of the centennial of Hebrew Union College-Jewish Institute of Religion, Jerusalem, 14-16 March, 1977*: 96-104. Jerusalem: Hebrew Union College-Jewish Institute of Religion.

——1983. Comments on a cult relief of Kybele from Gordion, in R.M. Boehmer & H. Hauptmann (ed.) *Beiträge zur Altertumskunde Kleinasiens. Festschrift für Kurt Bittel*: 349-360. Mainz am Rhein: Philipp von Zabern.

——1993. Midas-Stadt, in *Reallexikon der Assyriologie* 8: 153-156. Berlin: Walter de Gruyter.

NAUMANN, F. 1983. *Die Ikonographie der Kybele in der phrygischen und der griechischen Kunst* (Istanbuler Mitteilungen Beiheft, 28). Tübingen: Ernst Wasmuth.

OELSNER, J. 1999/2000. Review of *Herodots babylonischer Logos*, by R. Rollinger. *Archiv für Orientforschung* 46/47: 378-379.

PARKE, H.W. 1985a. *The oracles of Apollo in Asia Minor.* London: Croom Helm.

——1985b. The massacre of the Branchidae. *Journal of Hellenic Studies* 105: 59-68.

ROLLER, L.E. 1999. *In search of god the mother: the cult*

*of Anatolian Cybele*. Berkeley: University of California Press.

Sams, G.K. 1997. Gordion and the kingdom of Phrygia, in R. Gusmani, M. Salvini & P. Vannicelli (ed.) *Frigi e Frigio. Atti del 1° simposio internazionale, Roma, 16-17 ottobre 1995*: 239-248. Roma: Istituto per gli Studi Micenei ed Egeo-Anatolici-CNR.

Seeher, J. 1999. Die Ausgrabungen in Boğazköy-Hattuša 1998 und ein neuer topografischer Plan des Stadtgeländes. *Archäologischer Anzeiger*: 317-344.

Tamsü, R. 2004. *Phryg kaya altarları (Eskişehir-Afyonkarahisar-Kütahya illeri yüzey araştırması ışığında)*. Unpublished MA thesis, Anadolu Üniversitesi, Eskişehir.

Tüfekçi Sivas, T. 1999. *Eskişehir-Afyonkarahisar-Kütahya il sınırları içindeki Phryg kaya anıtları*. Eskişehir: Anadolu Üniversitesi.

Tüfekçi Sivas, T & H. Sivas. 2003. Eskişehir, Kütahya, Afyonkarahisar illeri yüzey araştırması arkeolojik enventar raporu. *TÜBA-TÜKSEK Kültür envanteri dergisi/Journal of cultural inventory* 1: 2-32.

Young, R.S. 1957. Gordion 1956: preliminary report. *American Journal of Archaeology* 61: 319-331.

——1958. The Gordion campaign of 1957: preliminary report. *American Journal of Archaeology* 62: 139-154.

——1969. Doodling at Gordion. *Archaeology* 22: 270-275.

# THE MEANING OF SHAPE: POTTERY INNOVATIONS AND TRADITIONS IN THE SANCTUARY AT BRONZE AGE MILETUS[1]

## Ivonne Kaiser

This paper will discuss the peculiarities of the pottery produced and used in the sanctuary in Miletus phase IV (Niemeier 2005: col. pl. 1; Niemeier 2007a: 5-6), which is contemporary with the Neopalatial period in Crete, the period when Milesian ties with Crete were at their greatest intensity. Excavations in the area of the later temple of Athena in Miletus (Kleiner 1968: 36-40; Weber 2007: appendix 3), conducted by Wolf-Dietrich and Barbara Niemeier from 1994 to 2004, have yielded a great deal of evidence for actual Cretan/Minoan presence on the site (Niemeier and Niemeier 1999: 543-553) for which the locally produced ceramics are only one indicator, but a very strong indicator. When a mudbrick altar was found in 1999, Niemeier argued that the sanctuary forming the architectural frame for the altar is of Minoan character too (fig. 1; Niemeier 2005: 6-7; col. pl. 1, quadrant 315/590).

### Introduction to the History of the Site and its Landscape

According to ancient sources, Miletus was founded by Sarpedon of Crete (brother of King Minos) who had led settlers from the Cretan city of Miletus (Milatos) to Asia Minor where they named the new city after the Cretan predecessor (Prinz 1979: 107). Much discussion in the field of ancient history has since followed. The main discussion focuses on the question of whether the ancient sources bear a trace of the truth (Niemeier 2007a: 3). Leaving the historical tradition aside, the archaeological arguments are sufficient to support the thesis that Cretans, or people from the so-called Minoan world, and thus referred to as Minoans in this paper, settled in this place. In describing the Milesian topography below, it will become obvious what the so-called "pull factors" (Sonnabend 2006: 105) for the Minoan settlers were and why they chose this site

to establish their settlement. In contrast, we know nothing of the "push factors," the reasons why the people left their home island in the first place.

Neither the landscape of ancient Miletus nor the limits of the ancient city are easy to see nowadays. Over the centuries the Maeander River has slowly brought so much debris that Miletus now lies approximately 8 km further inland from the seashore than in antiquity, as the studies by the geographer Helmut Brückner have shown (Brückner 2003: 123, fig. 1). Today the most prominent feature in the city is the theater. Situated in a flat landscape, Miletus is surrounded by a range of hills called "Stephania" to the south and, to the east, another range nowadays known as the Latmos Mountains, or, in Turkish, "Beş Parmak Dağları," the "Five Finger Mountains." This range rises to a height of 1400 m. In antiquity, the waters of the open sea reached up to the Latmos Mountains and formed the Latmian Gulf where today the Bafa Gölü is situated. Consequently, this means that Miletus was a harbor town in antiquity and was laid out on a prominent peninsula. To the north, the Maeander valley is closed by the mountain range called "Mykale." To reach Miletus by sea one had to pass the island of Lade which lies to the northwest and the Zeytin Tepe which lies to the east (Brückner 2003: 128, fig. 3). In historical times the city had four harbors: the Harbor of Athena, situated in a wide natural bay; the Theater Harbor; the Lion Harbor, which became most important during the historical phases of the city; and the Harbor of Humei Tepe in the northeast. The later peninsula that lay between the Theater Harbor and the Harbor of Athena to the southwest was originally an island (Weber 2007: 342, fig. 12), as geoarchaeological research has revealed (Brückner 2003: 129). It is here that we find the oldest settlement of Miletus.

Excavations in this part of the ancient city were undertaken as early as 1906/1907 by Theodor Wiegand who reached the latest Mycenaean level in this area (von Gerkan 1925: 52; 73-77). When Carl Weickert resumed excavations in

[1] I would like to thank the organizers of the symposium for the interesting and stimulating conference and Wolf-Dietrich and Barbara Niemeier for letting me study the Milesian period IV local pottery.

21

*Figure 1. Miletus Phase IV site map*

1938, continued in 1955, he found two preceding phases, an earlier Mycenaean phase and a Minoan phase before that. He called the Minoan architectural remains "building period 1" (Schiering 1959/60: 4-8). Whereas the excavations of the 1930s and 1950s (Weickert 1955: 102-103) focused directly around the foundations of the temple of Athena (Schiering 1959/60: 4 with appendix 2), the work resumed by the Niemeiers in 1994 concentrated a little bit further to the south of the temple of Athena in an area approximately 25 x 35 m (Niemeier and Niemeier 1997: 209-241), where Wiegand had done only an east-west test trench.

But when was Miletus first inhabited? The excavations by Walter Voigtländer and Berthold Weber in the 1980s showed that the earliest settlement on the grounds of the later city dates to the late Chalcolithic period. Hermann Parzinger, who studied and published the pottery excavated by Weber, called this phase Miletus I (Parzinger 1989: 428). Excavations conducted by the Niemeiers have produced more material for this phase and for the following Miletus II phase which coincides with the Early Bronze Age II and III (Niemeier 2005: 2-3). For this period the Niemeiers' excavation yielded finds showing contacts with the Aegean region, e.g. a head of a marble figurine of the Keros-Syros

culture of the Cyclades (Niemeier 2005: col. pl. 3). The succeeding Middle Bronze Age, called Miletus III, shows the first Cretan and further Cycladic impact on the site as the studies by Wolf-Dietrich Niemeier (Niemeier 2005: 3-4) and Amy Raymond (Raymond 2001: 19) have made clear. Of special interest here is the imported fine Kamares pottery but, despite its appearance, the main character of the site was, according to Raymond, Anatolian, which manifested itself in a majority percentage of red-slipped ceramics and Anatolian vase shapes (Raymond 2005: 69-70; 92, table 3.3). It seems that the transition from Miletus III to Miletus IV was a slow process in which Miletus III shapes were produced in Miletus IV fabrics and vice versa.[2] Once the Miletus IV settlement was established, its overall character became truly Minoan (Niemeier 2005: 4-10). Miletus IV, which is the former "building period 1" of Weickert, correlates to the time period from MM III to LM I B or the Neopalatial period on Crete. Because of the Minoan character of the remains we use terms such as Middle or Late Minoan. When, in this paper, I use the term "Minoan," I mean pottery imports such as vases with ripple pattern, running spirals, and marine style decoration (Niemeier 2005: col. pl. 10); luxury items and Minoan style wall

---

[2]  This is work in progress conducted by Amy Raymond and the author.

painting (Niemeier 2005: col. pls. 14-18); local imitations of Minoan fine pottery; seals and sealings of Minoan style (Niemeier 2005: col. pl. 19); and Linear A signs inscribed on pottery (Niemeier 2005: 8, fig. 20).

The best indicator for the thoroughly Minoan-ness of the site, however, is the locally produced coarse or domestic ware, 90% of which consists of Minoan shapes. The most prominent shapes are tripod cooking pots, conical cups, bridge spouted jars, semi-globular and straight-sided cups, storage jars, amphorae, ewers, and fire stands (Niemeier 2005: col. pl. 11). Most of the material, mainly pottery, excavated from 1994 to 2004, has been examined. A few ceramic assemblages from the years 2002 and 2004 have yet to be sorted. But my impression is that the percentage given above will not change dramatically with further study although ongoing work on the Bronze Age sites of the Çeşme peninsula, the publication of the Iasos material (Momigliano 2006: 81-90), and the new excavations since 2006 on Tavşan Adası will increase our knowledge of the period and their remains and might give us new insights.

**The Sanctuary**

Since up until the 1999 season we thought we were excavating a settlement site, the unearthing of a mudbrick altar with four different phases belonging to Miletus IVa or, in other terms, MM III/LM I A, was a surprise (fig. 1). The area around the altar was paved with schist slabs and the altar was probably situated in a court with a small side chamber to the west (Niemeier 2005: 6-7, fig. 16). In addition to locally produced pottery, which will be described in a moment, numerous animal bones bearing cut marks were found in heaps next to the altar. Unfortunately, the latest phase of the altar was cut away by the sounding trench Wiegand did in this area. Furthermore, we could not excavate deeper in the adjacent area to the north because a Miletus V wall and two Mycenaean circular pottery kilns were found at this location (Niemeier 2005: col. pl. 1, quadrant 315/590). A phenomenon linking the altar area with Crete was a group of conical cups which were placed upside down next to the altar (Rutkowski 1986: 44; 146). To the south of the altar was a storage area where a pithos was found as well as a rounded plastered offering table (Niemeier 2005: 6 col. pl. 12). To the east stood a second room containing the carbonized remains of wood interpreted by W.-D. Niemeier as a chair (Niemeier 2005: 7, fig. 18). A number of interesting items found in the area together with the chair were a small coarse ware askos (Niemeier 2005: 6, fig. 13), several tumblers and conical cups (Niemeier 2005: 7, fig. 19), a fragment of a conical rhyton with appliqué representation of a lioness running (Niemeier 2005: 6, col. pl. 13), and in addition the top part of a coarse ware conical rhyton (Kaiser 2005: pl. 47 f). Rhyta, especially, are associated with cultic activities. The shape of the conical rhyton is well known in Late Minoan Crete as depictions in wall paintings and actual finds make clear (Koehl 1981: 183-186). Furthermore, a nearly complete fire-box was found (Kaiser 2005: pl. 47 e) which has parallels on Crete, Kythera (Coldstream and Huxley 1972: pl. 35 no. 55), and Keos (Georgiou 1986: pl. 15, no. 66) and elsewhere in the Aegean. All in all fragments of eleven fire-boxes have been found in the excavated area. The assumed function for fire-boxes was to create pleasant smelling scents from oil and petals or incense that were laid around the rim while the object was heated from the bottom (Georgiou 1986: 8-11). Traces of charcoal found on our example, as well as on other fire-boxes found in the Aegean, support this theory.

The area from the west to the east wall (south of the altar, fig. 1) was covered by a thick layer of domestic pottery. This pottery layer was found in the first year of the excavation and was already published in the first preliminary report from 1997 under the heading "kitchen ceramics" (Niemeier and Niemeier 1997: 229-232). At this early stage of excavation it was not obvious that this must have been the debris from a storage room or from a dining hall on an upper floor of the building that had actually collapsed into the sanctuary or was deposited there on purpose after the sacred space went out of use (Gesell 1985: 20). The debris contained three complete cooking pots and thirty-four cooking pot legs. The explanation for such a vast amount of cooking pots became obvious after the altar was excavated: They were used for preparing ritual meals in the sanctuary following rites performed at the altar. That these rites consisted of sacrificing animals is made plausible by the bones that were found adjacent to the altar area. Their zooarchaeological analysis has shown that they belonged to sheep, goat, and cattle, all of which were typical Minoan sacrificial animals according to the reference material from Crete (Marinatos 1986: 11-14; Hamilakis 2008: 10). A possible explanation for the great amount of tripod cooking pots can be that they were used to cook a stew from the meat and vegetables, as studies by Tzedakis and Martlew have shown (Tzedakis and Martlew 1999: 89, no. 55; 90, no. 57; cf. criticism of method: Hamilakis 2008: 14-15).

Compared to the later Greek or the contemporary Egyptian or Near Eastern world, evidence for canonical architectural buildings where ritual action took place is scarce in the Bronze Age Aegean. In the Minoan world ritual action was performed in open air shrines, in house shrines, in specially designed rooms in the palaces or in architectural complexes which are not easy to understand for the archaeologist (Privitera 2008: 159-194). Furthermore the altars where animals were sacrificed are not built units as in later Greek sanctuaries, but were movable objects (Marinatos 1986: 15; cf. Long 1974: fig.86). Although we don't know exactly what kind of building to reconstruct from the architectural remains of Miletus IV, it seems possible, nevertheless, that our sanctuary fits in the categories described by Gesell for the Neopalatial period of Minoan Crete (Gesell 1985: 19-33). In addition to the finds of rhyta, askoi, and fire-boxes, the huge amounts of coarse ware pottery, occurring in a variety of domestic shapes, indicate more than simply private usage. Moreover, it is no coincidence that we find more open shapes in the area under discussion. In sanctuaries mostly open vase shapes are to be found; in contrast, in settlements the percentage between open and closed shapes is more even, while graves contain more closed than open shapes.

**Ceramic Items as Proof for Minoan Presence**

All the ceramics which are described below were made from the local, micaceous clay and have at first sight no religious relevance. We have found part of a locally-produced potter's wheel (Niemeier 2005: 6, fig. 15) which has an exact parallel at the site of Ayia Triada in southern Crete. Installations for pottery production aside from this single find, such as kilns, workbench, or puddling floor have not been found in Miletus IV. The only possible remains of a potter's kiln comes from the south part of our excavation where we uncovered a patch of a clay feature that was heavily damaged by later activities on the site and which dates to the Miletus IVa phase (Niemeier 2005: col. pl. 1 quadrant 320/575). The rest of the feature might belong to a bench of a channel type kiln as we see in Crete, the kiln from Kommos where the benches are still intact. The Kommos example also dates to the LM I A period (Shaw et al. 2001: fig. 6).

The most frequently found ceramic shape is the conical cup, a sure indicator of Minoan presence when they appear in huge quantities (Gillis 1990: 1; 14, fig. 4-5) but not necessarily an indicator for cultic action – unless they are deposited, as in our case, upside down next to an altar. By now we have reached the mark of over 600 complete cups and countless fragments (Niemeier and Niemeier 1997: 234, fig. 67) and comparisons can be made with examples from almost every Cretan and many Aegean sites (Hatzaki 2007: 5.16, no. 4); the similarities are evident in their conical bodies and solid bottoms. The Milesian cups are well fired with an average height between 3.5 and 4.2 cm.

Another strong indicator that we have a "Minoan-style kitchen" is the tripod cooking pot. These pots made their first sporadic appearance in Miletus III and continued well into Mycenaean times (Miletus V and VI). In the Miletus IV phase, the cooking pots can be identified by the following features which essentially form a fingerprint: a straight lip, horizontal handles, an imitation of a metal rivet opposite a small spout and legs which have a rounded cross-section (Niemeier and Niemeier 1997: 235, fig. 68-9). Again we find the best *comparanda* on Crete (Martlew 1986: 422). Further examples of household ceramics from Miletus are bridge-spouted jars, ewers, and amphorae (Niemeier 2005: 6, fig. 12); a preference for open shapes is obvious. Aside from a standardized amount of bowls and plates there are two main cup shapes: the semi-globular cup (fig. 2) and the straight-sided cup (fig. 3) with the handle attached outside. Both are again provided with parallels on Crete (Knappett and Cunningham 2003: 125-127, fig. 12-4).

*Figure 2. Miletus semi-globular cup AT98.103.020 (photo: Franz Galle)*

*Figure 3. Miletus straight-sided cup AT98.839.001 (photo: Franz Galle)*

The last shape to mention in discussing household assemblages should be the so-called fire-stand, grill-stand, or spit-rest, as they are named in archaeological publications (Georgiou 1983: 78-80). This is a shape widely known in the Aegean and on Crete, but there are also examples from western Asia Minor as a fire stand from Aphrodisias testifies (Kadish 1969: pl. 27). They usually are rectangular in shape with a broader bottom than top and present a triangular cross-section and semi-circular depressions on the top (fig. 4). Furthermore they can be equipped with a horizontal or vertical handle. Hara Georgiou, in her publication of examples from Keos, has related them to the working of lead (Georgiou 1986: 23). The Kean fire-stands show traces of burning. If we assume that these items were used in an industrial process in combination with fire, it is remarkable that none of the Milesian examples show any traces of burning and that no remains of metal working have been found in the excavated area in Miletus. A possible solution is that the Milesian spit-rests were used in another industrial or domestic process or in a cultic context. But nevertheless the question still remains why they were found in such large quantities at the different sites. Miletus has yielded over twenty individual pieces, one of which is decorated with a protome on one end; the other end is broken (Kaiser 2005: pl. 47 c). If we follow Marinatos's explanation that the animals were not slaughtered and grilled in the

*Figure 4. Miletus fire-stand AT95.108.002 (left) and AT94.159.109 (photo: W.-D. Niemeier)*

*Figure 5. Miletus ledge-rim plates AT97.359.036 (left) and AT97.386.001 (photo: W.-D. Niemeier)*

small enclosures identified by the excavators for religious purposes but somewhere outside (Marinatos 1986: 17-18; Sakellarakis 1970: 164; Hamilakis 2008: 7-8), then the spit rests in our case might have been used for offerings of pieces of meat at the altar.

Another group of stands has appeared in the excavations; we call them "horned-stands." They are round, hollow, and have two prominent, massive horns. Between the horns a handle is applied (Kaiser 2005: pl. 47 d). Until now, I have not found an exact parallel for these stands. On display in the Pamukkale Museum is an object from the Beycesultan excavations that is roughly similar in shape to our horned stands. In one of the Milesian assemblages three horned-stands have been found close to one another. This leads to the thought that they might possibly have served as some sort of pot holder. If you place two or three of them together you can put a pot or a baking tray on the horns. Another provoking thought is that they are cult symbols comparable

to the so called horns of consecration known from Crete (cf. Long 1974: pl. 31). It is interesting to note that like rhyta, fire boxes, and spit rests, they only appear in the Miletus IV period, whereas other shapes from the domestic pottery assemblage, even if modified, continue at least into the beginning of the Miletus V period (LH III A 1-2), e.g. conical cups, cooking pots, lipless bowls, jugs and ewers.

**Anatolian Remains**

So far we have evidence for a Minoan sanctuary furnished with the utensils necessary for performing a Minoan ritual. As stated above, the locally produced Minoan shapes comprise about 90% of the total coarse ware pottery. In the same contexts that have been described so far we have found pottery variants which are not of Minoan type as well as the horned stands which we have already mentioned. About 5% of the pottery from each context belongs to another type, the so-called red-wash ware. The paste for these vessels was local, as the petrographical analyses have shown, but the red coating and the shapes are unusual for Crete. The wash was often rather carelessly applied to the vessels and flakes off easily. The red-wash pottery consists mostly of open shapes, as the ledge rim plates show, and a few closed shapes, as a spout testifies. Some bowl shapes occur in both the red-wash and in the usual Milesian fabric without any coat or wash applied. The same is true for the ledge rim plate (fig. 5). For these shapes there are parallels in the material neither from Beycesultan which is, although 230 km away to the west, one of the few published Anatolian sites which can be used for comparisons, nor from the rest of the Aegean. To my present knowledge these shapes seem, therefore, to derive from the people who inhabited the place before the arrival of the new wave of Minoan settlers at the beginning of the Miletus IV phase.

A similar origin likely explains and applies to one of our cooking pots, which displays an elongated spout and basket handles (Kaiser 2005: pl. 47 b). Usually the horizontal handles are attached beneath the rim; on this particular example, however, the handles rise above the rim. Basket handles, in fact, seem to be a frequent motif of the Beycesultan material (Lloyd and Mellaart 1965: 120, fig. P.24, nos. 36-8); the assumption that this feature might derive from an Anatolian rather than an Aegean setting is thus quite plausible. However, other than in the Middle Bronze Age or in the following Mycenaean period, no really good parallels have yet been found in the Anatolian material. I suggest, instead, that what seems Anatolian in terms of decoration and shape was simply a continuation of the features established in Miletus III. Between Miletus III and Miletus IV no destruction level has been found and thus there was no catastrophe at the end of Miletus III. Therefore, maybe the people of Miletus III, who were already accustomed to Minoan objects brought by traders or even to Minoans living there in a small group, welcomed the new settlers. For the sanctuary as such, this means that perhaps, side by side with the Minoan rituals, rites of a more Anatolian manner were performed.

**Conclusion**

Miletus had contacts with Aegean culture as early as the Early Bronze Age. Those contacts were intensified in the earlier part of the Middle Bronze Age when a relationship between Miletus and the Old Palace Period of Minoan Crete was established. The reasons for this might have been commercial (Niemeier 2007b: 45). At the site of Miletus, imports of fine Kamares pottery and other Minoan objects began to arrive. Later, at the beginning of the New Palace Period a group of people from Crete arrived on the Western coast of Asia Minor and actually settled there. The settlement is to be seen in the wider spectrum of sites south of the Mykale ridge yielding Minoan remains. So far the relationship between the sites of Miletus, Tavşan Adası, Akbük, and Iasos is not understood. The newcomers brought with them their own traditions concerning pottery

production, as attested by the find of a potter's wheel, and religious practices. The place they settled was probably chosen because of the favourable location with the open sea to the west and the Maeander River valley to the east. The settlement easily accessible from the sea with good harbors favored commercial activities with the Aegean and with the cultures of inner Anatolia. In case of a crisis people could board their boats and leave the settlement rapidly. What the finds from the sanctuary made obvious is that despite the new environment, the settlers pursued their own religious traditions in the enclosure. They seem to have used the same equipment as at home to perform rites even though we only have a few material remains to judge from. Furthermore the pottery finds show there was no special set of dishes used in the sanctuary. We have no idea if the ceramics were used just once or many times in the rituals. But it seems that the production process took place right next to the sanctuary. The huge amount of conical cups indicates that a common shape was used to consume the meals that were presumably cooked in the tripod cooking pots. The standardized size of the conical cups provokes the thought of a uniform distribution of the food among the feasting participants. The cup shapes can be interpreted as a receptacle for liquids. In terms of standardization the cup and bowl shapes offer a greater variety than the conical cups. As the cooking pot with basket handles or the red wash ledge rim plates suggest, the use of Anatolian shapes or Anatolian decoration might be explained by the Minoans either adopting parts of the Anatolian behavioral patterns or hybridizing them with their own.

**References**

BRÜCKNER, H. 2003. Delta evolution and culture – aspects of geoarchaeological research in Miletos and Priene, in G.A. Wagner et al. (ed.) *Troia and the Troad. Scientific approaches*: 121-142. Berlin & Heidelberg: Springer.

COLDSTREAM, J. N. & G. L. HUXLEY (ed.). 1972. *Kythera. Excavations and studies*. London: Faber and Faber.

GEORGIOU, H. 1983. Coarse wares and technology, in O. Krzyszkowska & L. Nixon (ed.) *Minoan society*. Proceedings of the Cambridge Colloquium 1981: 75-92. Bristol: Bristol Classical Press.

——1986. *Keos VI. Ayia Irini: specialized domestic and industrial pottery*. Mainz: Philipp von Zabern.

GESELL, G. C. 1985. *Town, palace, and house cult in Minoan Crete*. Göteborg: Paul Aström.

GILLIS, C. 1990. *Minoan conical cups. Form, function and significance*. Göteborg: Paul Aström.

HAMILAKIS, Y. 2008. From feasting to an archaeology of eating and drinking, in L. Hitchcock, R. Laffineur & J. Crowley (ed.) *DAIS. The Aegean feast*, Proceedings of the 12th International Aegean Conference, University of Melbourne, 25-29 March 2008. *Aegaeum* 29: 3-19. Eupen: Université de Liège.

HATZAKI, E. 2007. Neopalatial (MM IIIB-LM IB), in N. Momigliano (ed.) *Knossos pottery handbook. Neolithic and Bronze Age (Minoan)*: 151-196. London: The British School at Athens.

KADISH, B. 1969. Excavations of prehistoric remains at Aphrodisias, 1967. *American Journal of Archaeology* 73: 49-65.

KAISER, I. 2005. Minoan Miletus. A view from the kitchen, in R. Laffineur & E. Greco (ed.) *Emporia. Aegeans in the central and eastern Mediterranean*. Proceedings of the 10th International Aegean Conference, Italian School of Archaeology at Athens, 14-18 April 2004. *Aegaeum* 25/1: 193-198. Eupen: Université de Liège & University of Texas at Austin.

KLEINER, G. 1968. *Die Ruinen von Milet*. Berlin: De Gruyter.

KNAPPETT, C. & T. F. CUNNINGHAM. 2003. Three Neopalatial Deposits from Palaikastro, East Crete. *Annual of the British School at Athens* 98: 107-187.

KOEHL, R. B. 1981. The functions of Aegean Bronze Age rhyta, in R. Hägg & N. Marinatos (ed.) *Sanctuaries and cults in the Aegean Bronze Age*. Proceedings of the First International Symposium at the Swedish Institute in Athens, 12-13 May 1980: 179-87. Stockholm: Paul Aström.

LLOYD, S. & J. MELLAART. 1965. *Beycesultan II. Middle Bronze Age architecture and pottery*. London: William Clowes and Sons.

LONG, C. R. 1974. *The Ayia Triadha sarcophagus. A study of Late Minoan and Mycenaean funerary practices and beliefs*. Göteborg: Aströms Förlag.

MARINATOS, N. 1986. *Minoan sacrificial ritual. Cult practice and symbolism*. Stockholm: Aströms Förlag.

MARTLEW, H. 1986. Domestic coarse pottery in Bronze Age Crete, in E. B. French & K. Wardle (ed.) *Problems in Greek prehistory*: 421-24. Bristol: Bristol Classical Press.

MOMIGLIANO, N. 2006. The relationship between Crete and Caria in the Bronze Age, in *Pepragmena 9. Diethnous Kritologikou Synedriou 1.-6. Oktobriou 2001. A4*: 82-90. Herakleion: Etairia Kritikon Istorikon Meleton.

NIEMEIER, B. & W.-D. NIEMEIER. 1997. Milet 1994-1995. *Archäologischer Anzeiger* 1997: 189-248.

——1999. The Minoans of Miletus, in P. Betancourt, V. Karageorghis, R. Laffineur & W.-D. Niemeier (ed.) *Meletemata. Studies in Aegean archaeology presented to Malcolm H. Wiener as he enters he 65th year. Aegaeum* 20: 543-54. Liège and Austin: Université de Liège & University of Texas at Austin.

NIEMEIER, W.-D. 2005. Minoans, Mycenaeans, Hittites and Ionians in western Asia Minor, in A. Villing (ed.) *The Greeks in the East*: 1-36. London: British Museum.

——2007a. Milet von den Anfängen menschlicher Besiedlung bis zur Ionischen Wanderung, in J. Cobet, W.-D. Niemeier & V. von Graeve (ed.) *Frühes Ionien. Eine Bestandsaufnahme*. Panionion-Symposium Güzelçamlı 26. Sept. – 1. Okt. 1999: 3-20. Mainz: Philipp von Zabern.

——2007b. Westkleinasien und Ägäis von den Anfängen bis zur Ionischen Wanderung: Topographie, Geschichte und Beziehungen nach dem archäologischen Befund und den hethitischen Quellen, in J. Cobet, W.-D. Niemeier & V. von Graeve (ed.) *Frühes Ionien. Eine Bestandsaufnahme*. Panionion-Symposium Güzelçamlı 26. Sept. – 1. Okt. 1999: 37-96. Mainz: Philipp von Zabern.

PARZINGER, H. 1989. Zur frühesten Besiedlung von Milet. *Istanbuler Mitteilungen* 39: 415-431.

PRINZ, F. 1979. *Gründungsmythen und Sagenchronologie*. Munich: Beck.

PRIVITERA, S. 2008. *Case e rituali a Creta nel periodo neopalaziale*. Venezia: Università "Ca'Foscari".

RAYMOND, A.E. 2001. Kamares ware (and Minoans?) at Miletus. *Aegean Archaeology* 5: 19-26.

——2005. *Miletus in the Middle Bronze Age and Minoan presence in the eastern Aegean*. PhD Dissertation, University of Toronto.

RUTKOWSKI, B. 1986. *Cult places of the Aegean*. Bibliotheca Anica 10. Warsaw: Polish Academy of Sciences.

SAKELLARAKIS, J. A. 1970. Das Kuppelgrab A von Archanes und das kretisch-mykenische Tieropferritual. *Prähistorische Zeitschrift* 45: 135-219.

SCHIERING, W. 1960. Die Ausgrabung beim Athena-Tempel in Milet 1957. I. Südabschnitt. *Istanbuler Mitteilungen* 9/10: 4-30.

SHAW, J.W., A. VAN DE MOORTEL, P.M. DAY & V. KILIKOGLOU. 2001. *A LM IA ceramic kiln in south central Crete*. Hesperia Supplement 30. Princeton: American School of Classical Studies at Athens.

SONNABEND, H. 2006. Herodot und die Auswanderung der Lyder nach Italien im Licht moderner Migrationsforschung, in E. Olshausen & H. Sonnabend (ed.) *„ Trojaner sind wir gewesen" – Migrationen in der antiken Welt*. Stuttgarter Kolloquium zur Historischen Geographie des Altertums 8, 2002: 104-7. Stuttgart: Franz Steiner.

TZEDAKIS, Y. & H. MARTLEW (ed.). 1999. *Minoans and Mycenaeans. Flavours of their time*. Exhibition Catalogue, Athens National Archaeological Museum 12 July – 27 November 1999. Athens: Greek Ministry of Culture.

VON GERKAN, A. 1925. *Kalabaktepe, Athenatempel und Umgebung*. Milet I 8. Berlin: Schoetz.

WEBER, B. 2007. Der Stadtplan von Milet, in J. Cobet, W.-D. Niemeier & V. von Graeve (ed.) *Frühes Ionien. Eine Bestandsaufnahme*. Panionion-Symposium Güzelçamlı 26. Sept. – 1. Okt. 1999: 327-362. Mainz: Philipp von Zabern.

WEICKERT, C. 1955. Die Ausgrabung beim Athena-Tempel in Milet 1955. *Istanbuler Mitteilungen* 7: 102-132.

# Epigraphy versus Archaeology: Conflicting Evidence for Cult Continuity in Ionia during the Fifth Century BC[1]

## Anja Slawisch

The epigraphic and archaeological evidence document a flourishing economic and cultural life in Ionia during Archaic times (Cobet et al. 2007). Not least, its prosperity is witnessed by the foundation of many secondary cities across the Mediterranean and Black Sea by colonizers from Ionian cities. Citizens of Miletos, for example, were responsible for around fifty colonies and secondary foundations (Ehrhardt 1983: 96). However, the scene changed dramatically – at least with respect to politics – when the Ionian cities were conquered by the Persians in 546/5 BC. Among other things, the new powers obliged the conquered cities to pay levies to the Persian state and to provide soldiers for its army. There is significant controversy among scholars of ancient history whether or not the outbreak of the Ionian revolt in 498 BC may be attributed to an economic decline caused by these sorts of Persian intervention (Murray 1988; Georges 2000). However, it is beyond any doubt that the Ionian revolt, and in particular the defeat of the Ionians in 494 BC, marks a decisive event for practices of both cult worship and everyday life, as well as for the nature of political or administrative organization in the entire region. Oswyn Murray has described the situation in Ionia as follows: "The failure of the Ionian revolt marks the end of Ionian history: that group of cities which dominated the trade of Mediterranean and Black Sea from Spain to south Russia, and which had created Greek poetry, philosophy, science and history, did not regain its economic prosperity or cultural eminence until half a millennium later in the very changed conditions of the high Roman empire" (Murray 1988: 490).

Recent excavations and the resultant new finds have created doubts about this cataclysmic picture of fifth century Ionia. Increasingly, scholars have begun to focus on the question of continuity versus disjunction during this key period (Osborne 1999; Carlson 2003), but the evidence needs careful assessment. This short paper is not, of course, the place to discuss every aspect of the development of Ionian cities during the fifth century BC. Instead, it will focus on one particular case – Miletos, the most famous Ionian city, and its nearby oracle-sanctuary of Didyma/Branchidai – in order to illustrate the complexities of the problem.

## Cult Continuity? The Epigraphical Evidence of the Molpoi Statutes

One consistently cited example of cult continuity after the failure of the Ionian revolt is from the so-called Molpoi Statutes, an inscription which was found in 1903 during the German excavation in the Milesian Delphinion (Kawerau and Rehm 1914). This epigraphic text is concerned with the regulation of cult activities during the New Year festival period and the procession from the Delphinion to the Didymeion – along the 16 km long Sacred Way from Miletos to Didyma – organized by the so-called Molpoi, a cultic association. All the scholars who have studied this inscription agree that it was not inscribed before 200 BC and that it cites a much earlier document which refers, most probably, to a document from the second half of the sixth century BC, but at least to the time when Philtes, Son of Dionysos, was the Aisymnet, and therefore the Eponymous of Miletos, during the years 450/49 BC (Herda 2006: 15–20). Fortuitously, a list of Milesian Eponyms was uncovered the same year from the same location as this Molpoi inscription. The list starts, in fact, with the year 525/24 BC, but the shape of the letters and the design of

[1] This paper emerges from a wider project I am currently undertaking, "Ionia in the Classical Age," kindly supported by a Feodor Lynen Fellowship from the German Humboldt Foundation and undertaken at Bilkent University from October 2006 to September 2008. I would also like to thank my mentors Prof. Dr. A. E. Furtwängler (Martin Luther University, Halle-Wittenberg) and Doç. Dr. Y. Ersoy (Bilkent University, Ankara) for their support and instructive discussions. Furthermore I am thankful to all my colleagues from the Department of Archaeology and History of Art at Bilkent University and my friends B. Hürmüzlü, E. Maloney, and T. C. Wilkinson, who all made my stay both pleasant and stimulating. I would also like to thank T. C. Wilkinson who corrected the English text which would not have been half as readable without his help.

the lines indicate that, here again, we have a transcription of an older text most probably written down during the years 334/3 BC when Alexander the Great was Stephanephoros in Miletos. Together with over twenty-five other inscriptions, the blocks were reused in late Roman times as a pavement to prevent groundwater from flooding the Delphinion area. Following Georg Kawerau and Albert Rehm, who first published the inscriptions, Alexander Herda in his recent book *Der Apollon-Delphinios-Kult in Milet und die Neujahrsprozession nach Didyma* argues that these inscriptions must have been on public view during the Hellenistic and early Roman times, initially freestanding and later as part of the walls of the Delphinion complex (Herda 2006: 27–30). From the epigraphic evidence, then, Kawerau, Rehm, and Herda all take the Molpoi Statutes as evidence for a general cult continuity and, in particular, a maintenance of the procession from Miletos to Didyma, during the fifth century BC. Can the archaeology from the area support this idea by providing firm evidence for continuity?

**Archaeological Evidence: the Delphinion**

From the stations mentioned in the Molpoi Statutes where offerings were given to particular gods or rituals performed, as yet only a few places have been identified on the ground, even though the general route of the Sacred Way is known (Schneider 1987; Herda 1996). The first of these is the Delphinion, where the processions are said to have started. This complex, first excavated between 1903 and 1905 under the direction of Theodor Wiegand, is situated in the southeast of the so-called Lion's Harbor. Most of the architectural remains visible today are from the Hellenistic and Roman periods. As an unpublished sounding undertaken in the Delphinion in 1973 showed, however, there is also an Archaic level with a destruction level attributed to the Ionian defeat (Herda 2005: 243–245; Müller-Wiener 1986: 95–100). The excavated complex consisted of halls and a courtyard with altars and votives of different dates and types which are to some extent identifiable in the inscriptions and which – according to Herda – show four main phases: late Archaic, early Classical, early Hellenistic, and Roman (Herda 2005: 259). Unfortunately, the relevant small finds, ceramics, and sculpture from these periods have not been published, so we cannot be certain of the dating of these architectural features and votive offerings.

According to Wölf Koenigs, however, the architectural decoration of the altar of Apollo Delphinios derives from two different phases: a late Archaic and an early Classical (Koenigs 1980: 69ff., 75ff.) and that the latter replaced the former, which had been destroyed during the war. The replacement is said to have been built as soon as Miletos was freed: in other words, immediately after 479 BC. As justification for the early Classical dating of the corner acroteria, Koenigs refers to the special shape of the leaves, parallels to which were found on a column neck from the Polykrates temple at Samos and, according to him, from

the chronologically later anta capital from Didyma. But the latter is definitely not to be dated after the Persian destruction, as Berthold Weber demonstrated (Weber 1999). We will come back to this point when speaking about the Temple of Apollo at Didyma.

Even if Koenigs is correct in identifying different phases of construction in the Delphinion, the stylistic similarity of the corner acroteria can be interpreted in a number of different ways. It is possible, for example, that the Milesians simply repaired the altar to their main goddess immediately after their liberation. Equally the corners might also represent two phases of the late Archaic period. The problem is, we cannot be certain of the actual date of construction: both could have been built before 479 BC, or even before 494 BC.

**The Archaic Cult Complex**

Approximately halfway from Miletos to Didyma an Archaic cult complex, the *Kultbezirk an der Heiligen Straße*, was unearthed during the years 1985 and 1986. This architectural complex was surrounded by perimeter walls, which enclosed an area with at least two buildings and a large terrace where the well-known sphinx sculptures were once placed. On the basis of its position in the landscape, the architecture, and the large amount of discarded storage, eating, and drinking vessels, the excavators interpreted this complex as a location where people took part in cultic symposia within some sort of cult for heroes, a founder, or family (Tuchelt 1996: 231–241). Even if we cannot identify this cult site with one of the named stations we know from the Molpoi inscription, it would appear close enough to the Sacred Way that any annually recurring event on the scale described should have left behind some residues.

In the final publication the excavators report that this complex was in continuous use from the second half of the sixth century BC until its destruction in the fourth century BC (Tuchelt 1996: 225–229). This is at odds with the suggestion made in some earlier reports where the destruction was dated to the early fifth century, probably attributed to the Persians (Schattner 1989: 204; Herda 2006: 329 f.). From over 4800 potsherds 495 pieces were classified as significant for dating but unfortunately, all of these were ultimately from the same depositional context, one which was seriously damaged by the later agricultural use of this area. The revised chronology for the final publication is thus surprising and inexplicable. The roof tiles, the sculpture, and most of the ceramics are without any doubt late Archaic, a fact which is also highlighted by the authors themselves (Tuchelt et al. 1996: passim). The next finds we are able to date are coins of the fourth century BC (Baldus 1996: 217–223), and a few potsherds from the second half of the fourth century. From the forty-four fragments published as being of fifth century date, not one is indisputably from this period. Indeed, the author himself obviously had some doubts when he provided parallels for the ceramics in question from both the late sixth and the fourth centuries, but nevertheless concludes that the ceramics show the continuity of occupation in this place (Schattner 1996: 163–216 esp. 213–215). Leaving aside this questionable evidence of continuity, there also remains the need to find a plausible reason for the building's destruction and abandonment during the fourth century, if indeed this is the case, something for which there has been no convincing explanation so far (Tuchelt 1996: 240).

**The Sanctuary of the Nymphs**

Another site on the way to Didyma has been identified with the "Sanctuary of the Nymphs," on the basis of the discovery by Wiegand in 1901 of a seated female figure with a votive inscription (Bumke et al. 2000: 59). This site is situated in an isolated, natural landscape where a spring emerges from a rock, around 9 km from Miletos. A surface survey followed by some limited soundings, carried out in 1994, brought to light a few architectural structures as well as a wide range of ceramics. The survey team suggested that there was an uninterrupted occupation at the site from the Archaic to the early Byzantine period, with a notable concentration of material from the Hellenistic period. But their graph of ceramic frequency by period gives a misleading impression of the occupation in different periods. The "pre-Hellenistic" bar might easily be taken to mean fifth century occupation, but in fact it means late Archaic – as the authors indicate elsewhere in the text (Bumke et al. 2000: 64). The soundings in the area of the spring gave a more detailed picture, which was nevertheless interpreted the same way: as continual use from the Archaic to the late Roman/early Byzantine period. But two periods with a remarkable decrease in quantity of ceramics are mentioned: the fifth and the first half of the fourth century BC and the Roman Imperial period (Bumke et al. 2000: 69ff.). Thus it seems that there was – according to the details of the archaeological finds – no significant activity at this place during the fifth century BC.

**The Branchidai Statues**

During the first expedition of the "Society of Dilettanti," which took place in 1765, its explorers came across the now well known seated statues of the "Branchidai." In the following years, and even recently, further examples have been found. The general consensus is that these should be attributed to the Archaic period, although the precise decade is debated. But as Hubert Knackfuß pointed out in his comprehensive study of the architectural remains of the Didymeion in 1941, all of these statues were found without a base or foundation, suggesting, as is now universally accepted, that this find spot was not their primary location. This is further indicated by the inscription on the seat of Chares, which reads: "I am Chares, son of Klesis, ruler over Teichiosa, gift to Apollo" (Knackfuß 1941: 156; Tuchelt 1970; Herda 2006: 327). Thus this statue must have stood,

in the first instance, within the temenos of the temple, and not somewhere outside along the Sacred Way.

The statues are mentioned in the Molpoi Statutes as the last station among a short list of seven enumerated places where a *Paion* was to be sung by participants of the procession (cf. lines 28–30). Before starting these cultic rituals, two holy stones had to be placed, one next to Hekate, "who stood outside the doors," the second stone, "outside the doors of Didyma" (cf. lines 26–28). Herda interprets these lines as implying that all the stations, including the statues, lay outside the temenos of Apollo (Herda 2006: text p. 10, comments on pp. 327–332), but the inscription does not state this explicitly. Indeed it is easily possible that these statues were merely moved from one area within the temenos to another, rather than transferred to outside the temenos, given the prohibition against removing votive offerings from a sacred space. Our view of the full ancient extent of the sanctuary is still overly influenced by the modern wall built around the Hellenistic temple. This sometimes has led us to forget that the ancient temenos could have extended much further towards the Sacred Way to Miletos.[2]

The alternative explanations for this discrepancy between primary and secondary position of the statues, and the description in the Molpoi Statutes, are much more complex. Herda gives multiple dates for lines 30 and 31, from which the phrase "at the statues of Chares" comes. Those parts dealing with seasonal descriptions, he says, were added around the year 200 BC while the rest must be the residues of the late Archaic text. The statues were – according to his interpretation – displayed in a kind of a family cult site during the Archaic period which was dedicated to Apollo and was outside the temple because he also needs to explain the inscription on the Chares statue (Herda 2006: 315–319, 349ff.). This is rather a complex and tortuous explanation for something which could be otherwise explained much more simply. If the statues were indeed moved from an initial position to the new location alongside the Sacred Way but still within the temenos, the descriptions in the Molpoi Statutes are unlikely to refer to the Archaic procession, since the statues would not yet have been there. The most probable time for the displacement of the statues would have been the time when the new and larger temple was in construction and the ground required for its expansion needed to be cleared of its contents: in other words during the second half of the fourth century BC.

During the 1980s, under the direction of Klaus Tuchelt, trenches were dug along the Sacred Way which showed a cumulative sequence of depositions representing paths at different periods with ceramics from the seventh or sixth century BC to the first century AD (Tuchelt 1984: 220ff.; Herda 2006: 371). The first recognizable roadway was, according to the ceramics, built during the second half of

2   I am grateful to Andreas E. Furtwängler who pointed out this problem and discussed the issue with me in some detail.

the sixth century: a date that accords with the estimated date when the New Year's procession from Miletos to Didyma was first held and Apollo's marble temple was built. This 6.4 m wide street was apparently built with curb stones on both sides and a gravel surface. It seems that there were no changes to this basic structure until the fourth century BC. The ceramics from the Archaic, through the Classical, up to the early Hellenistic period have recently been published by Thomas Schattner (Schattner 2007). According to this publication, there was no indisputably fifth century material – to be precise: no material which can definitely be dated from the time when the Persians were said to come to Didyma through to the second half of the fourth century. Schattner dates a few potsherds to the fifth and early fourth century. But when we look at the given contexts, the sherds all appear to be mixed with either late Archaic or Hellenistic/Roman material (Schattner: 2007: 19, 23, 28, 33, 473ff.). There is not one stratigraphically assured high Classical context. So again we see an absence of archaeological data for our period in question.

## The Temple of Apollo at Didyma

The procession ended in Didyma, at the temple and the altar of Apollo Didymeus. Much has been written about the temple and its assumed destruction as a consequence of the Persian seizure in the year 494 or 479, the year when Xerxes escaped. In his study of 1988, Tuchelt noticed the difficulties in finding a real destruction level or any traces of a battle or pillage. Only the hall in which offerings were kept was apparently destroyed by fire. In contrast, the remains found of the Archaic temple do not show any particular signs of burning. A few architectural fragments show a slightly damaged surface which might have been caused by a fire.[3] It looks increasingly likely that although the temple structure remained, it fell into general disuse because of the lack of priestly organization, as reported by the written sources. If these sources are correct, the priests were deported to and resettled in Sogdiana. The ancient sources report that the oracle also stopped working: the fountain ran dry and only returned when Alexander the Great entered the historical arena. Of course – as Herda underlines – for the New Year's procession, no oracle was needed in the first place (Herda 2006: 360ff.), but it would be much harder to perform the rites correctly without the temple priests.

Walter Hahland, in his frequently discussed article of 1964, used the suggestion of cult continuity from the Molpoi Statutes as support for the idea that some of the architectural anta capitals from Didyma were early Classical copies of the late Archaic one. The best parallel he cites is a late Archaic capital from Samos (Hahland 1964; Voigtländer 1972). Given Weber's article of 1999, however, with his new stylistic classification of a fragment from the late

Archaic temple of Athena at Miletos, it seems that a dating of the Didyma capitals to the Classical period is most unlikely (Weber 1999: 436).

Even if we are not sure that the temple itself was needed to perform the New Year's ritual, an altar certainly was vital. The identification of the round structure in front of the Hellenistic temple with the altar of Apollo Didymeus has been contentious, and the arguments complex. But as Tuchelt and Herda have already argued, the soundings made by Florian Seiler in 1991 and 1992 which uncovered ash, ceramic, small bronze finds, and animal bones, make it probable that we do in fact have an altar-like structure. It seems very likely to me that this is the altar in question, but one which was not used during the fifth century. The majority of the material appears to be late Archaic (including the ceramics, arrowheads made from bronze, and other typical Archaic metal objects) but, as far as I know, there is almost no fifth century material (Tuchelt 2000: 337; Herda 2006: 356–358).

In addition, the material from the excavations in the temple area since 2004 shows the same spectrum of finds (Furtwängler 2005, 2006). The latest ceramics can be dated to the first quarter of the fifth century BC. A subsequent gap in the material ends only with the first datable finds from the second half of the fourth century BC. If we are to assume that any ritual took place here we would need to explain the complete absence of datable material. One problem is our lack of knowledge concerning the development of local ceramics during the fifth century. It is possible that local shapes did not change when the Persians entered the area and late Archaic forms had a much longer period of usage than is normally appreciated. But as soon as imports from Attica disappear from the record we feel unable to date the local material. Otherwise, the lack of small finds and ceramics could also be due to a comprehensive change of cult activities and a breach of votive tradition as a result of the economic decline of the whole region after the years of war and destruction: in effect, a discontinuity.

## Revising the Epigraphical Interpretation

If, as it increasingly seems to me, it is most probable that there was no New Year's procession to Didyma during this period, how can we explain the implication of continuity given by the Molpoi inscription? It should not be forgotten that this inscription was not engraved before 200 BC, but refers to an older document most probably from the late Archaic period. Since the name Philtes, son of Dionysos, is indicated, the inscription – they say – must be evidence for the continuity of the procession during the fifth century. In this regard, all the epigraphists are in agreement (Sokolowski 1955: 129–135; Ehrhardt 2003: 12; Herda 2006: 15–20).

On the other hand, disagreement prevails when it comes to the dating of particular lines and their exact meaning

---

[3]   For this interesting information I am thankful to Uta Dirschedl (DAI Berlin), who has comprehensively studied the architectural remains of the Archaic temple at Didyma.

(Kawerau and Rehm 1914: 277–284; Herda 2006: 226). Lines 8–10, 23–25, 30–31, 34–37, 43–45 have been alternatively assigned to the late Archaic period, the Hellenistic, or even later Hellenistic times. This shows the confusing range of possibilities for dating the different parts of this particular inscription (Herda 2006: 426, table 1). Lines 1–6 and 40–42 are the ones that, according to the epigraphists, are most likely to be firmly datable. As mentioned before, there is no debate about Philtes, who was Stephanephoros in 450/49 BC according to the List of Milesian Aisymnetai. But for the second individual mentioned, Charopinos, two dates are possible, because no patronymic is given for him and there are two different Charopinoi in the List: one in 479/78 and one in 352/51 BC. The reason why both Rehm and Herda favor the early dating is the phrase in line 40: ἔαδε Μολποῖσιν, instead of ἔδοξε Μολποῖσιν in line 4 when Philtes is mentioned (Herda 2006: 404ff.). The latter is the chronologically later one, they argue. In dating the Charopinos mentioned in the Molpoi statutes in the years 479/78 BC, the years when Miletos was freed from the Persian occupation, Herda says: "Die Molpoi-Satzung ist somit Kronzeuge der sofortigen Wiederaufnahme von Neujahrsfest und Prozession nach Didyma" [The Molpoi Statutes are the chief witness for an immediate renewal of the New Year's festival and the procession to Didyma] (Herda 2006: 405).

But what if the older phrases in this inscription were intentionally used rather as a conscious reinvention of the nearly forgotten cultic traditions of Archaic times, when Miletos was one of the most prosperous cities with an active cultic life? Given that another significant Ionian cultic festival, the Panionia, was not celebrated after the defeat of the Ionian revolt and only restarted in the fourth century BC (Schipporeit 1998: 230ff.), are we witnessing a reinvention rather than continuity?

The Lists of Aisymnetai were compiled during the time of Alexander the Great, earlier than the Molpoi Statutes. One purpose of compiling the list of names was surely to create a long and unbroken history of the town visible to everyone. Later, both inscriptions were set up together at the Delphinion, where they were found in the early nineteenth century. It would not have been difficult at the time when the Molpoi Statutes were put in stone to use the names given in the List to create a continuous tradition. And it would not be the first example of a city reconstructing its own continuous history with the help of invented cultic events or myths, as the Parian Marbles demonstrate (Jacoby 1904; *FGrH* 239; Scheer 1993: 65). The archaeological evidence that we have discussed earlier suggested a renewal of the procession not before the fourth century BC. Later in this century the temple was re-planned and in the course of these activities the Statues of Chares were transferred to the Sacred Way, where they stood when the Molpoi Statutes were engraved. At the same time this date would also align remarkably well to the time when the second Charopinos mentioned was in charge, during the years 352/1 BC.

## Conclusions

The Molpoi Statutes appear to have been a Hellenistic inscription referring to an Archaic or late Archaic tradition. The historic names they cite were also published on the early Hellenistic List of Aisymnetai. The name Charopinos is found twice in this list and based on the argument above is unlikely to be dated 479/78 but rather 352/51 BC. The latter date fits better with the archaeological evidence. It is possible that the inscription was composed – using the names from the List of Aisymnetai – to refer back to a late Archaic tradition and to renew Milesian claims on the Didymeion.

In the past, the architectural remains from the Delphinion and the Didymeion have been dated to the early Classical period mainly on the evidence of the Molpoi Statutes. In contrast, the latest material from the Sacred Way and the Didymeion does not show any obvious activity after the Persian victory and during the fifth century. According to the excavated material a reactivation of the procession seems not to have started before the fourth century BC. The displacement of the Statues of Chares most probably took place when space was required for the new and larger temple in construction during the second half of the fourth century BC.

In contrast to the original arguments from the epigraphical analysis of the Molpoi Statutes, the archaeological material suggests there was no cult activity along the Sacred Way from Miletos to Didyma during the fifth century BC. Rather it seems that the cited inscription refers to an older tradition, interrupted early in the fifth century and renewed during the Hellenistic period. The inscription was made to recall, explain, and tie into a lost tradition. But despite the evidence from this case study, our ability to assess the extent of continuity or disjuncture is hampered by our difficulty to recognise fifth century BC material (architectural decoration, ceramics, etc.). We still do not know exactly how to identify the local material from this period. More studies will thus be required to untangle the question of wider cultural continuity in this Ionian landscape.

## References

Baldus, H.R. 1996. Die Münzfunde, in Tuchelt et al. 1996: 217–223.

Bumke, H., A. Herda, E. Röver & T.G. Schattner. 2000. Bericht über die Ausgrabungen 1994 an der Heiligen Straße von Milet nach Didyma. Das Heiligtum der Nymphen? *Archäologischer Anzeiger*: 57–97.

Carlson, D.N. 2003. The Classical Greek shipwreck at Tektaş Burnu, Turkey. *American Journal of Archaeology* 107: 581–600.

Chandler, R. 1769. *Ionian antiquities*. London: Spilsbury & Haskell.

Cobet, J., W.-D. Niemeier & V. von Graeve (ed.). 2007. *Frühes Ionien: Eine Bestandsaufnahme. Akten des*

*Symposions Panionion (Güzelçamlı), 26. September bis 1. Oktober 1999.* Milesische Forschungen Bd 5. Mainz: Philipp von Zabern.

EHRHARDT, N. 1983. *Milet und seine Kolonien.* Frankfurt am Main: Lang.

——2003. Milet nach den Perserkriegen: Ein Neubeginn? in E. Schwertheim (ed.) *Stadt und Stadtentwicklung in Kleinasien.* Asia Minor Studien 50: 1–19. Bonn: Habelt.

FURTWÄNGLER, A.E. 2005. Didyma 2004. *Kazı Sonuçları Toplantısı* 27/2. Ankara: 205–212.

——2006. Didyma 2005. *Kazı Sonuçları Toplantısı* 28/2. Ankara: 405–418.

GEORGES, P.B. 2000. Persian Ionia under Darius: the revolt reconsidered. *Historia* 49: 1–39.

HAHLAND, W. 1964. Didyma im 5. Jahrhundert v. Chr. *Jahrbuch des Deutschen Archäologischen Instituts* 79: 142-240.

HERDA, A. 1996. Von Milet nach Didyma. Eine griechische Prozessionsstraße in archaischer Zeit, in F. Bubenheimer et al. (ed.) *Kult und Funktion griechischer Heiligtümer in archaischer und klassischer Zeit. 1. Archäologisches Studentenkolloquium, Heidelberg, 18.–20. Februar 1995*: 133–152. Mainz: Deutscher Archäologen-Verband.

——2005. Apollon Delphinios, das Prytaneion und die Agora von Milet. Neue Forschungen. *Archäologischer Anzeiger*: 243–294.

——2006. *Der Apollon-Delphinios-Kult in Milet und die Neujahrsprozession nach Didyma. Ein neuer Kommentar der sog. Molpoi-Satzung.* Milesische Forschungen Bd. 4. Mainz: Philipp von Zabern.

JACOBY, F. 1904. *Das Marmor Parium.* Berlin: Weidmann.

KAWERAU, G. & A. REHM. 1914. *Milet I.3: Das Delphinion in Milet.* Berlin: Königliche Museen/G. Reimer.

KNACKFUSS, H. 1941. *Didyma I: Die Baubeschreibung.* Berlin: Staatliche Museen/Gebr. Mann.

KOENIGS, W. 1980. Bauglieder aus Milet II, in Milet 1978–1979. *Istanbuler Mitteilungen* 30: 56–91.

MÜLLER-WIENER, W. 1986. Bemerkungen zur Topographie des archaischen Milet, in Müller-Wiener, W. (ed.) *Milet 1899–1980: Ergebnisse, Probleme und Perspektiven einer Ausgrabung. Kolloquium Frankfurt am Main 1980.* Istanbuler Mitteilungen Beiheft 31: 95–119. Tübingen: Wasmuth.

MURRAY, O. 1988. The Ionian revolt. *Cambridge Ancient History* IV²: 461–490.

OSBORNE, R. 1999. Archaeology and the Athenian empire.

*Transactions of the American Philological Association* 129: 319–332.

SCHATTNER, T.G. 1989. Didyma. Ausgrabungen an der Heiligen Straße 1985 und 1986. Die Fundkeramik. *Archäologischer Anzeiger*: 201–204.

——1996. Die Fundkeramik, in Tuchelt et al. 1996: 163–216.

——2007. *Didyma IV: Die Fundkeramik vom 8. bis zum 4. Jahrhundert v. Chr.* Mainz: Philipp von Zabern.

SCHEER, T.S. 1993: *Mythische Vorväter: zur Bedeutung griechischer Heroenmythen im Selbstverständnis kleinasiatischer Städte.* Munich: Edition Maris.

SCHIPPOREIT, S. 1998. Das alte und das neue Priene. Das Heiligtum der Demeter und die Gründung Prienes. *Istanbuler Mitteilungen* 48: 193–236.

SCHNEIDER, P. 1987. Zur Topographie der Heiligen Straße von Milet nach Didyma. *Archäologischer Anzeiger*: 101–129.

SOKOLOWSKI, F. 1955. *Lois sacrées de l'Asie Mineure.* Paris: E. de Boccard.

TUCHELT, K. 1970. *Die Archaischen Skulpturen von Didyma: Beiträge zur frühgriechischen Plastik in Kleinasien.* Istanbuler Forschungen 27. Berlin: Gebr. Mann.

——1984. Didyma. Bericht über die Arbeiten der Jahre 1980–1983. Mit Beiträgen von H. R. Baldus, J. Bossneck, A. v. d. Driesch, K. B. Gödecken, W. Schiele, P. Schneier und U. Wintermeyer. *Istanbuler Mitteilungen* 34: 193–344.

——1988. Die Perserzerstörung von Branchidai-Didyma und ihre Folgen - Archäologisch betrachtet. *Archäologischer Anzeiger*: 427–438.

——1996. Chronologie. Zur Bestimmung des Bezirks, in Tuchelt et al.1996: 225–241.

——2000. Der Vorplatz des Apollontempels von Didyma und seine Umgebung. Eine Rekonstruktion von Befund, Prozess und Gestalt. *Jahreshefte des Österreichischen Archäologischen Instituts* 69: 311–356.

TUCHELT, K., P. SCHNEIDER, T.G. SCHATTNER & H.R. BALDUS. 1996. *Didyma III.1: Ein Kultbezirk an der Heiligen Straße von Milet nach Didyma.* Mainz: Philipp von Zabern.

VOIGTLÄNDER, W. 1972. Quellhaus und Naiskos im Didymaion nach den Perserkriegen. *Istanbuler Mitteilungen* 22: 93–112.

WEBER, B.F. 1999. Die Bauteile des Athenatempels in Milet. *Archäologischer Anzeiger*: 415–438.

# Vision and the Ordered Invisible: Geometry, Space, and Architecture in the Hellenistic Sanctuary of Athena Nikephoros in Pergamon

*John R. Senseney*

Sacred landscapes of the past are creations of both the (pre) historical subjects that perceived them and the modern subjects that perceive them anew. Natural and human-made features of cultic importance gain coherence as components of sacred spaces through the cognition of some sense of order that unites them. To access this order requires our recourse to the beliefs, collective memory, knowledge, and practices that conditioned the sensory perception of landscapes. Of course, this perceptional dimension need not have reflected the original intentions of the people (patrons, architects or masons and sculptors, etc.) who physically shaped the relationships of built and natural forms. On the other hand, evidence for such intention during a given period may point to the cultural tendencies that guided the ways in which contemporary subjects viewed their environments. In other words, visuality – the practices of seeing inseparable from the cultural and social background that conditions vision (Jay 1988: 16-17; Bryson 1988: 91-92; Elsner 2007: xvii) – may be revealed by intention in design process because such intention must itself be determined by certain ways of seeing the world.

This paper will examine evidence from Hellenistic sanctuaries in Asia Minor and Kos in order to evaluate the possibility of a geometric underpinning in the Sanctuary of Athena Nikephoros at Pergamon (Doxiadis 1972: 104-105; Coarelli 1995: 37-43). In doing so, I will explore the question of intentional use of geometry in design process in order to build upon John Onians's ideas concerning the invisible presence of geometry as a culturally based ordering principle in the perception of spatial interrelationships in natural and architectural landscapes (Onians 1979: 164-166). As a mode of perception dependent upon education rather than natural (and therefore universal) cognitive functions, this proposed geometry would have inscribed the viewer as a member of the learned elite, simultaneously providing his sense of subjectivity and modifying his reading of the sacred landscape. While the only documented

perception of the geometry underlying the Pergamene sanctuary is that of the modern scholars who propose it, a key consideration for determining the possibility of similar ancient perceptions will be demonstrable parallel evidence for geometry as an invisible ordering feature in Hellenistic architecture.

## The Sanctuary of Athena Nikephoros in Pergamon

The Sanctuary of Athena Nikephoros on the Pergamene acropolis (figs. 1A, 1B) originated in the 320s BC with the Doric temple built by Philetairos and dedicated to Athena (Bohn 1885; Berve and Gruben 1978: 128; Gruben 1986: 425-429; Schalles 1985: 83-84), to which Attalos I added the epithet Nikephoros – "Bringer of Victory" – following his victory over the Gallic tribe of the Tolistoagii in 233 BC. The great battle with the Tolistoagii took place in the Kaikos River valley at the Teke Bayır, upon which Attalos I's soldiers likely erected their trophy (Coarelli 1995: 41). As a monument to his victory and as a thank offering to Athena Nikephoros, Attalos built a circular base (height ca. 2.48 m, lower diameter 5.25 m, upper diameter excluding cornice 3.15 m – see figs. 1A, B), upon which was placed a group of bronze sculptures representing the defeated Tolistoagii. Julius Caesar later had marble copies of these sculptures taken to Rome (Coarelli 1995: 8, 10-16), and these monumental, over life-size works survive today as the famous Suicide Gaul in the Palazzo Altemps (fig. 1C) and the Dying Gaul in the Capitoline Museums (fig. 1D). As John Marszal has demonstrated, the long base near the south side of the sanctuary upon which most recent studies place the location of these works could not have supported statuary larger than life-size (Marszal 2000: 207-208). Nor will the unprotected Nikephorion serve as a plausible alternative location for the Hellenistic originals, since this sanctuary was destroyed twice, in 201 and 156 BC, by Philip V of Macedon and Prousias II of Bithynia, respectively (Marszal 2000: 206). Short of the more radical

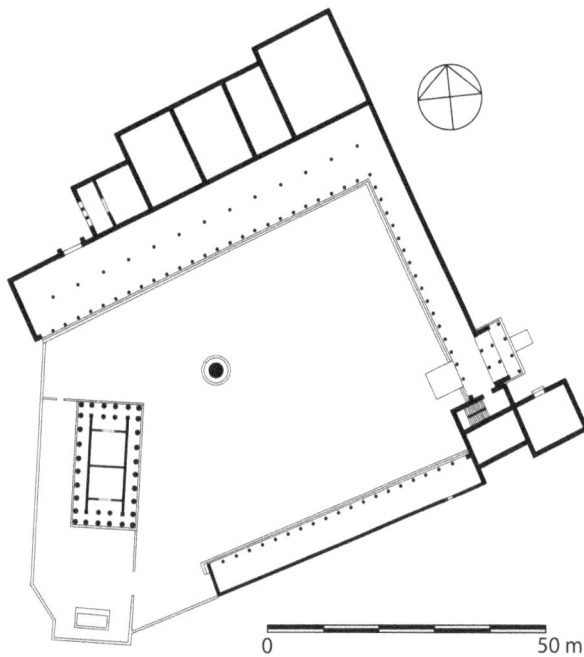

A. Restored plan of Sanctuary of Athena Nikephoros at Pergamon. After Bohn 1885: pl. 40.

B. View of Sanctuary of Athena Nikephoros looking west toward Teke Bayır

C. Suicide Gaul group, Roman copy of Hellenistic Pergamene original, Palazzo Altemps, Rome

D. Dying Gaul, Roman copy of Hellenistic Pergamene original, Capitoline Museums, Rome

*Figure 1*

proposal of moving the original location of these works to a large base in front of the Stoa of Attalos I at Delphi (Marszal 2000: 206; Stewart 2004: 210-212), this discovery may lead us to return the group to the circular base in the Sanctuary of Athena Nikephoros as proposed in the classic restoration. Deliberately erected in view of the Teke Bayır as the site of the original trophy of the victory, this monument thereby bound the sanctuary to this important feature of the landscape, emphasizing the connection

between the goddess, the battle, and Attalos I. In the 180s and 160s BC, Eumenes II added the stoas to the north and east, along with a monumental propylon to the southeast now restored in Berlin, and finally the stoa to the south.

A principal concern of design for this new scheme may have been to frame a single field of vision for Attalos's monument and the Teke Bayır (fig. 1A), created by the edges of the temple and the new northern stoa when viewed from the perspective of the sanctuary's southeastern entryway (Coarelli 1995: 38-41). This idea emerges from a twentieth century scholar's analysis of a geometric underpinning (fig. 2A), wherein conceptual lines, both straight and curvilinear, interconnect the privileged viewing point with architectural features (Doxiadis 1972: 104-105). The proposal for an invisible linear network intentionally ordering buildings and landscape in a Hellenistic environment is fascinating, but very difficult to substantiate. Simply put, this type of analysis rests upon the highly imprecise practice of drawing on modern small-scale restored plans and positing estimated measurements for relevant dimensions. Even if one were to subject actual measurements to analytic geometry, we would still have to contend with the question of a plausible control for establishing tolerances for ancient surveying methods proposed to have followed theoretical patterns over large-scale distances.

## Orthogonal Underpinnings in Hellenistic Architecture

Rather than addressing the perhaps unanswerable question of whether the proposed conceptual linear ordering at Pergamon was intentional, it may be more methodologically responsible and even more interesting to ask whether this analysis is consistent with Hellenistic habits of viewing. To answer this question, we might turn to other Hellenistic examples to confirm whether the very premise of a conceptual linear ordering existed in architectural design. One analysis (Hoepfner 1990: 18-19) reveals a geometric interrelationship of features found between the agora of the early fourth century BC at Magnesia-on-the-Maeander and the temples of Zeus and Artemis (fig. 2B) added by the celebrated architect Hermogenes in the late third century BC (Humann et al. 1904: 107-111, 130-141; Wycherley 1942: 25-26; Bean 1976: 554-557; Coulton 1976: 253; Kreeb 1990). Accordingly, the quartering of the southern half of the agora establishes the location of the temple of Zeus while the long central axis of the Artemision aligns with the agora's conceptual center. Of course, this proposal suffers from the same limitations of verifiability as that related to the Pergamene sanctuary, but Hermogenes's Artemision itself provides a more secure analysis. Unlike the case with a vast space like a sanctuary or agora, the interconnected masses of the temple building itself control how elements relate orthogonally. Hermogenes's Artemision follows a similar grid-like linear network as that found in the temple of Athena Polias in Priene of the fourth century BC by the architect Pytheos (fig. 2C). The systematic grid-based alignment of external with internal features, a quality not found in earlier Greek temples,[1] suggests an awareness of space that is ordered according to invisible lines.

Accounting for this linear organization of space in temples involves complexities of interpretation. John Onians

suggests this tendency toward the grid may have been stimulated by new thinking in the field of geography, as in Eratosthenes's map of the third century BC that conceives of the earth in terms of orthogonal lines of latitude and longitude (Onians 1979: 151). Yet if this relationship to the Hellenistic intellectual environment is valid, we might counter that the direction of influence may in fact be the reverse: that geographers may have grasped the notion of orthogonally organized space from architecture. After all, the grid-iron character of "Hippodamian" planning long preceded even Hippodamos himself (Ward-Perkins 1974: 22-33). In any case, whether we consider Ionic temples like those of Pytheos and Hermogenes or an entire city such as Miletos, this evidence for the intentional design of architecture according to conceptual lines across space is relevant to whether Hellenistic viewers may have perceived the proposed invisible geometry within the Sanctuary of Athena Nikephoros at Pergamon. Still, it is the degree of relevance of these comparisons that we might scrutinize. The temples and city plans in question involve networks of straight lines that are obvious even at the level of casual observation. The proposed geometry of the Pergamene sanctuary, on the other hand, involves curved lines across the void in a manner that is neither obvious nor, strictly speaking, akin to Hippodamian planning or Ionic grid-based temples. If the case for geometric vision at Pergamon is to be made, we must directly confront the question of curvilinear geometry in architectural space during the Hellenistic period.

## Curvilinear Geometry in Hellenistic Asia Minor

The play of circles was not unknown to Hellenistic architecture, as witnessed in the working drawings, like fig. 2D shown here, which were discovered on the walls of the adyton in the temple of Apollo at Didyma (Haselberger 1991: 102-103). For the sanctuary at Pergamon, there is a more relevant example: the shield of the Dying Gaul, which preserves a drawing executed with far less assuredness and precision than that seen at Didyma (figs. 3A, B, D). Here, the individual circumferences are broken and of inconsistent diameter, and do not always coincide with the lines with which they are intended to intersect. As has been reasonably explained, these imperfections likely result from having been transferred to the marble copy by means of a tracing device, followed with the application of a compass by a copyist who did not understand the subtleties of the figure's geometry (Fincker 1995: 49). The actual geometric figure that was copied from the Pergamene original demonstrates a circumscribed pentagon and the related construction of a circumscribed star dodecahedron, generated by the pentagon's five equal angles of 72° that are given graphic emphasis as radial lines (fig. 3B). Filippo Coarelli proposes that the principal axes of this geometric form guided the composition of the sculptural group of the Dying and Suicide Gauls (fig. 3C) that stood together on the circular monument of Attalos I in the Sanctuary of Athena Nikephoros (Coarelli 1995: 29-31). Coarelli

---

[1]  I distinguish this later systematic approach to alignment from the "rule of the second column" commonly found in the fifth century BC in which the centers of the second and third columns on the fronts and sides of a temple align with the side of the cella wall and the front of the antae; see Korres 1994: 88 and fig. 38.

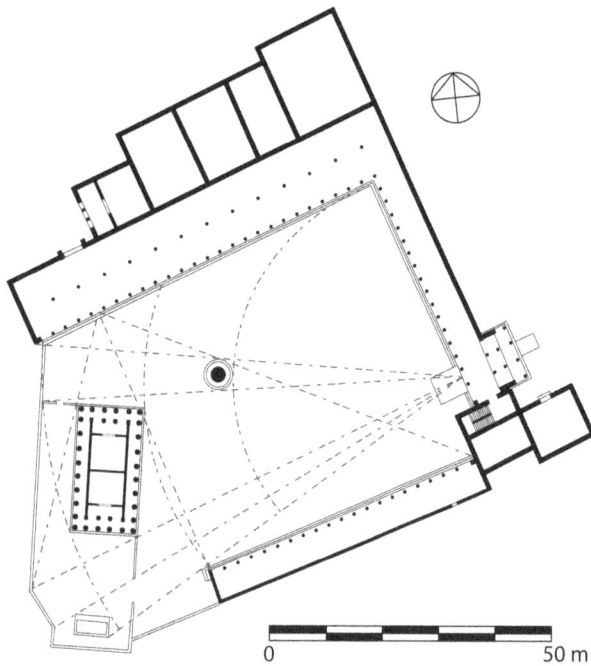

A. Plan of Sanctuary of Athena Nikephoros at Pergamon showing proposed geometric underpinning. After Doxiadis 1972: 107, Figure 61

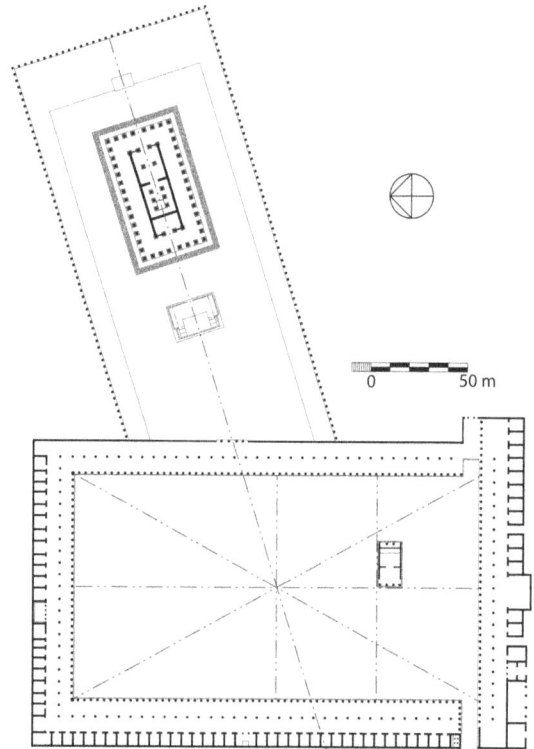

B. Plan of Artemision and agora at Magnesia-on-the-Maeander showing proposed geometric underpinning. After Hoepfner 1990: 19, Figure 29

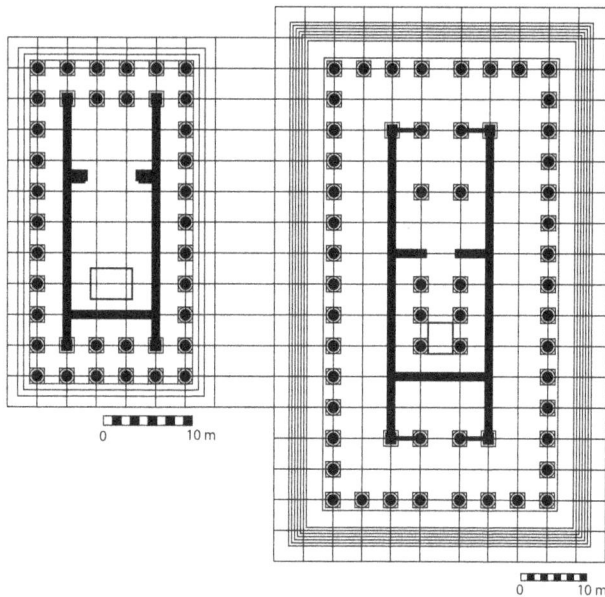

C. Restored plans showing the grid systems of Pytheos' Temple of Athena Polias, Priene (left) and Hermogenes' Artemision, Magnesia-on-the-Maeander (right). After Coulton 1988: 70, Figure 23.

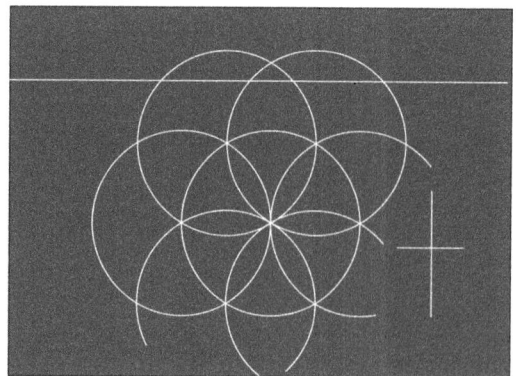

D. Restored incised drawing from the walls of the adyton at the Didymaion. After Haselberger 1991: 103, Figure 4.

*Figure 2*

A. Dying Gaul, Roman copy of Hellenistic Pergamene original, Capitoline Museums, Rome. Arrow points to location of incised geometric drawing.

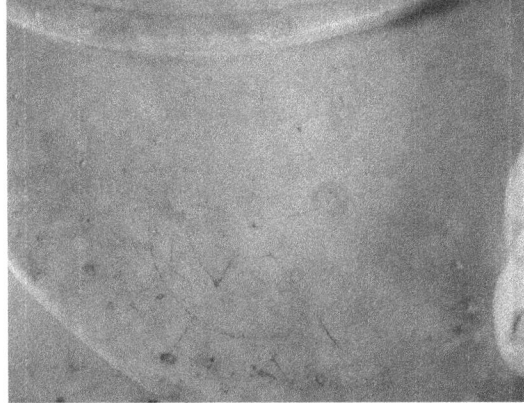

B. Incised geometric drawing on the Dying Gaul, Roman copy of Hellenistic Pergamene original, Capitoline Museums, Rome

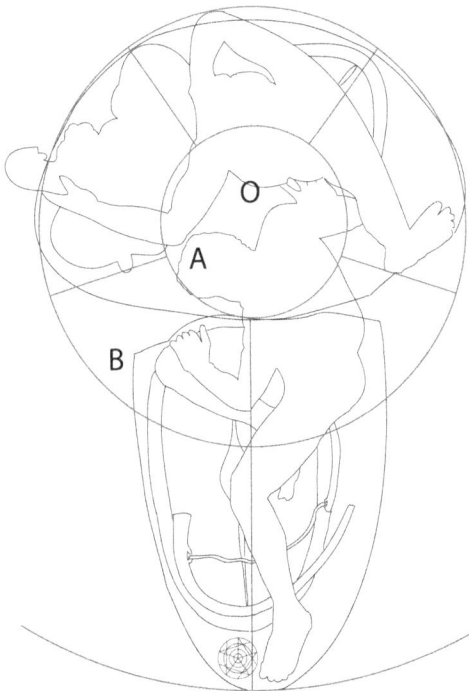

C. Restored sculptural composition of the Dying and Suicide Gauls viewed in plan with geometric underpinning proposed by Filippo Coarelli. The lowest arc indicates the outer edge of the upper surface of the circular base on which the group stood (see Figures 1A and 1B). After Coarelli 1995: 59, Figure 9.

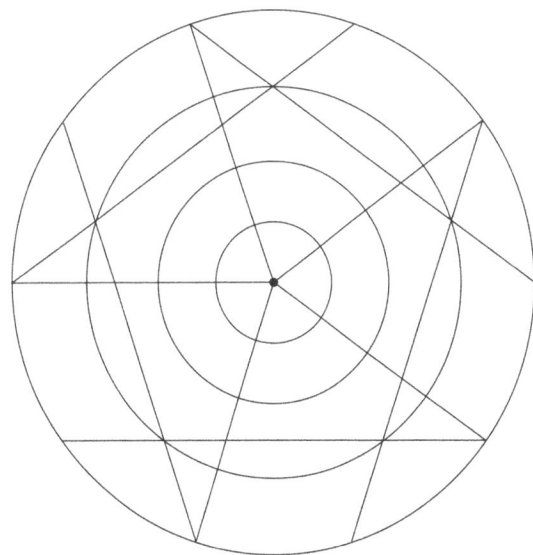

D. Restored geometric drawing incised on the shield of the Dying Gaul (see Figures 3A, 3B, 3C). After Coarelli 1995: 84, Figure 57.

*Figure 3*

furthermore argues that the same geometry may have governed the architectural composition of the sanctuary as a whole (Coarelli 1995: 37-41). According to this theory, the base of the sculptural group upon which the drawing appears becomes the circumcenter where the main axis leading from the propylon bifurcates at an angle of 72°, just as in the geometric construction on the shield of the Dying Gaul. From this center the invisible axes project to interconnect the main entrance, the center of the temple, and the secondary entrance of the sanctuary (fig. 4A). In this way, the ordering principle of space is not just a conceptual linear network, but also an underlying Euclidian geometric idea.

Support for this proposal may be found in Vitruvius's description of Greek theaters (5.7.1-2), where the circumscription of a set of three squares placed at 30° angles establishes the radial pattern of aisles (fig. 4B). Not limited to theory alone, this geometry and its variations has been demonstrated in actual Hellenistic theaters (Isler 1989: 141-150). Hellenistic theaters thereby provide a parallel for both the curvilinear quality and Euclidian character of geometry proposed for Pergamon.

Yet again, however, we must be rigorous in our assessment of such comparisons. In doing so, we might acknowledge that the planar quality of Greek theaters renders the spatial interrelationships of essential elements like the orchestra, *skene*, and aisles visible and even obvious. It is difficult to overlook that this kind of organization does not precisely parallel the Pergamene sanctuary's interrelationship between the center of the temple – a location that is itself invisible from any perspective within the open air of the sanctuary – and the center of a doorway in the rear wall of a stoa, which is based on an angle of 72° that establishes the invisible axes generated by a theoretical circumscribed pentagon. While theaters may provide evidence for the use of curvilinear Euclidian geometry in their designs, this intention of design may securely indicate that Hellenistic theatergoers perceived geometry in space, but not necessarily that the same viewers may have perceived geometry in the less obvious case of a sacred landscape of human-made and natural features like that experienced on the acropolis at Pergamon. Our supporting parallels therefore must include an example in which intentional geometry in design process relates to spatial relationships whose rationale appears far from obvious.

### The Temple of Dionysos at Teos

The advantage of seeking out possible parallels from individual temples is that their structurally unified character obviates problems of measurement and survey over large intervening voids within a complex like a sanctuary or agora. Initially, this aim of identifying temples that feature intentional uses of geometry appears promising. Going back well before the Hellenistic period, several examples of geometric-based designs in Greek architecture have been

proposed. But what we require are proposals that, firstly, do not rely upon arbitrarily selected locations within plans and, secondly, can be verified with analytic geometry.

One intriguing possibility is J.J. de Jong's analysis of Hermogenes's temple of Dionysos at Teos (de Jong 1989: 110-113), according to which the architect's design of the naos, pronaos, and opisthodomos deliberately features irrational proportions based on the application of the compass and straightedge (figs. 4C, D). De Jong suggests a geometric process of design that transcends the gridded underpinning of Ionian temples associated with the tradition of Pytheos and Hermogenes. He thus presents the fascinating scenario of Hermogenes as master geometer, working with irrational proportions in the manner of an architect of the Roman Imperial era. It would also appear to show that Hellenistic design process works in ways that are not easily discernable to the viewer, thereby providing a parallel for the proposed geometry of the Sanctuary of Athena Nikephoros at Pergamon. Beginning with a square $ABCD$ with sides equal to one module, the diagonal of the square, equal to $\sqrt{2}$, establishes the width of the temple with a simple pivot of the compass to $E$. With the compass centered at $E$, the distance to diagonal to $D$, equal to $\sqrt{3}$, establishes the extent of the cella at $F$. Centering the compass at $G$ found along a straight line from $F$, the distance to $B$ establishes the extent of the pronaos at $H$. Finally, the extent of the opisthodomos at $I$ is found by the distance to $A$ with the compass centered at $E$.

My use of analytic geometry to study the actual dimensions of Hermogenes's building does not support this argument, however. Instead, discrepancies of more than 15 cm and 3% between actual and theoretical measurements represent major departures that do not plausibly reflect constructional errors and adjustments to an irrational geometric scheme that is, to begin with, uncharacteristic of Hellenistic design process. The premise of de Jong's analysis is a module of 8.216 m, which establishes the length of the sides of square $ABCD$. The diagonal of this square, found as the square root of the product of 2 x 8.216², equals 11.619 m for the width of the naos including the wall, expressible as $CE$. For purposes of checking de Jong's proposal, this calculation reverses his method for finding the module. We may now establish a quadrant with $C$ at the origin 0, 0 and $E$ at 11.619. $EF$ will equal $ED$, which is the square root of 8.216² + 11.619², or 14.230, establishing the shared x ordinate for $F$ and $G$. The distance $GD$ is therefore 14.230 − 8.216, or 6.014. $GB$, equal to the square root of 8.216² + 6.014,² is 10.182, which should be equal to $GH$. Theoretically, therefore, $H$ should be located at the sum of $CG$ and $GH$ (14.230 + 10.182), and therefore at 24.412. De Jong, however gives respective measurements for the lengths of cella and pronaos as 14.25 m and 10.01 m, equal to 24.26 m. The difference of 15.2 cm between the theoretical and actual measurements is difficult to explain away. Similarly, de Jong shows the length of the opisthodomos as established by an arc, in my drawing corresponding to

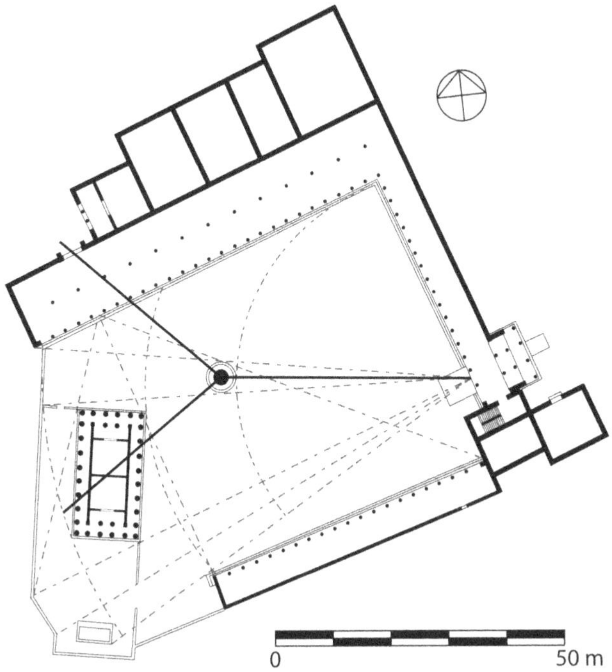

A. Restored plan of the Sanctuary of Athena Nikephoros at Pergamon, showing Coarelli's addition of three axes to Doxiadis' proposed geometry. After Coarelli 1995: 59, Figure 10.

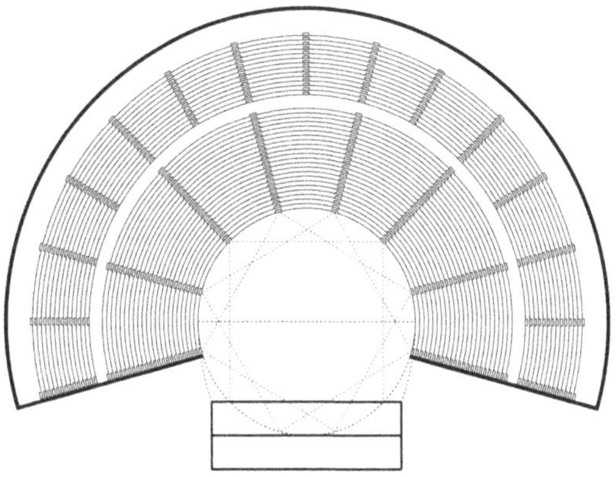

B. The Greek theater and its geometric construction based on three circumscribed squares as described by Vitruvius.

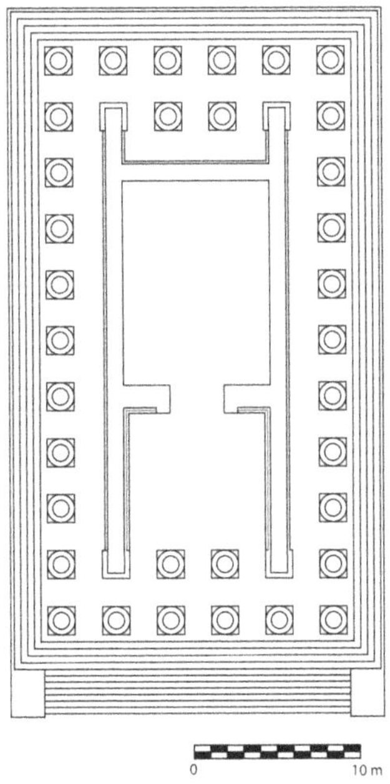

C. Restored plan of Hermogenes' Temple of Dionysus at Teos. After Duran Mustafa Uz in Hoepfner and Schwandner 1990: 52, Figure 1.

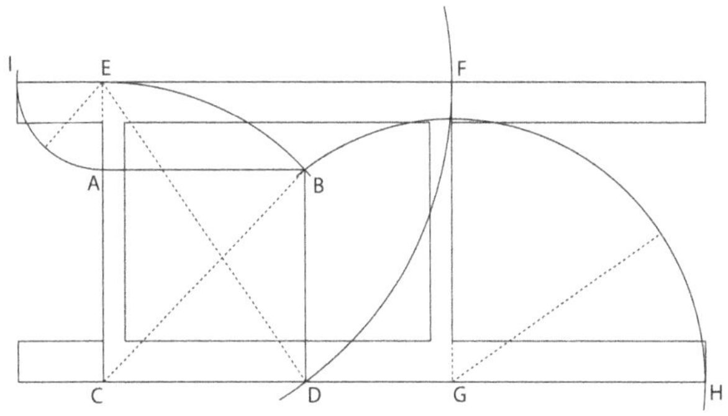

D. Geometric analysis of Hermogenes' Temple of Dionysus at Teos according to J.J. de Jong. After de Jong 1989: 111, Figure 10.

*Figure 4*

*A* and *I*, which are equidistant from *E*. *EA* is 3.403 m, as given by *EC – AC*, or 11.619 – 8.216. Yet de Jong gives the width of opisthodomos as 3.52 m, a difference of 11.7 cm over a relatively short distance, an error that exceeds 3%. Of course, the error of +15.2 cm in the pronaos and -11.7 cm in the opisthodomos balance out to only 3.5 cm, which going by the numbers is acceptable. De Jong's proposed proportions, however, are a strikingly unpractical 1:1.125 x √3 for the ratio of the length of the cella to the total length of the naos. In order to demonstrate a plausible correlation to the practice of drawing with the compass and straightedge, these unwieldy proportions must at least adhere to each of the actual dimensions in the opisthodomos, cella, and pronaos. Clearly, this last consideration of showing how this proposed geometry works at the level of drawing is the purpose of the illustration that de Jong provides, which I have redrawn here (fig. 4D). The lack of conformity between the calculations given here and the illustration of the procedure of geometric drawing, however, calls into question the merit of the proposal concerning the intentional design of the temple at Teos. We must therefore look elsewhere for a credible example of invisible geometry in the design of a Hellenistic temple.

**Temple A at Kos**

Although the proposal for intentional geometry in the preceding temple does not hold up to mathematical rigor, there is fortunately one other example that may better substantiate the possible reliance on geometry in designing Hellenistic sanctuaries. More relevant to Pergamon than the temple at Teos is the Asklepieion on the island of Kos. The Attalid monarch Eumenes II gave money for the expansion of this sanctuary (Hansen 1971: 291, 466), which began around 170 BC and featured an axially symmetrical arrangement on its upper terrace with a pi-shaped stoa and a temple axially aligned with a grand staircase (fig. 5A). The Koan arrangement of stoas and terraces certainly recalls the architecture of Pergamon (Hansen 1971: 291). In addition, the choice of the outmoded Doric order for the temple of the upper terrace (Temple A) represents an archaizing tendency that further connects this environment with Pergamon and its Doric temple of Athena. In terms of their Attalid funding and architectural features, therefore, the Pergamene and Koan sanctuaries share noteworthy connections.

As I have demonstrated through analytic geometry and AutoCAD, Temple A at Kos is ordered through a geometric underpinning that transcends visual experience (Senseney 2007: 574-581). Although the temple is rectilinear, invisible circumferences govern the interrelationships of its main features (fig. 5B). The guiding form is a circumscribed Pythagorean triangle *ABC*, the center of whose hypotenuse is the center of two circumferences sharing a whole number 3:5 ratio, which together establish the outer corners of the cella and pronaos. Despite the experiential orthogonal relationship of forms in the completed temples, this geometry makes sense at the level of drawing which, during the Hellenistic period, was a markedly interdisciplinary practice. Long before the common use of the T-square, Greeks established accurate perpendicular and parallel lines through circumferential intersections produced with the compass and rule. As seen here (fig. 5C), circumferences of four and five units centered respectively on the ends and center of a baseline *x* of three units produce intersections that establish the extent of the Pythagorean triangle as well as the outer lines of the plan, with the extent of the pronaos determined by the larger circumference.

In a general way, this kind of drawing recalls the Greek *analemma* (fig. 5D), the drawing that allows for the laying out of sundials. It is Vitruvius who describes the algorithm for drawing the Greek *analemma* (9.7.2-7), underscoring the habits of drawing shared by astronomers and architects in the Hellenistic world (Senseney 2007: 564). More importantly, the application of the compass and rule in the creation of large scale built form suggests an awareness of space as characterized by unseen linear and curvilinear networks that order visual interrelationships. Whether it is the paths of the stars or the masses of a building that describes space, the character of space as a linear network gives it a positive identity that becomes the basis for visible forms. In describing the harmony of forms in temple buildings, Vitruvius gives the analogous example of the well-shaped human body that is described by the circle and the square (3.1.3). For Vitruvius, therefore, both the body and the temple are characterized by an underpinning that is emphatically geometric, as geometric as the circumscribed triangle that underlies Temple A at Kos and the circumscribed pentagon on the Roman copy of the Dying Gaul from the Sanctuary of Athena Nikephoros in Pergamon. Both of these, furthermore, emphasize concentric circles that relate to polygons and follow Euclidian norms. In the case of the Koan temple, the circumscription of a right triangle relates to Thales's theorem (Euclid, *Elements* 3.31). In the case of the Pergamene drawing, the drawing relates to the construction of a circumscribed pentagon (Euclid, *Elements* 4.11). In summary, Temple A at Kos strongly supplements the less complete parallels offered above (Ionic grid-based temples, orthogonal city plans, and theaters) by mathematically demonstrating the intentional application of geometry in a form where that geometry is not easily apprehended. As I stated at the outset of this paper, such intention in the design of architecture is predicated upon the cultural practice of seeing environments in ways that are not readily apparent. In turn, both the practice of designing such spaces and the dissemination of such methods of design through architectural theory likely reinforced tendencies toward geometric vision in buildings, cities, and landscapes.

**Geometry and Experience at Pergamon**

The Euclidian geometric underpinning at Kos is arguably characteristic of the intellectual environment at Pergamon. In the home of the Attalid court, the same monarchical

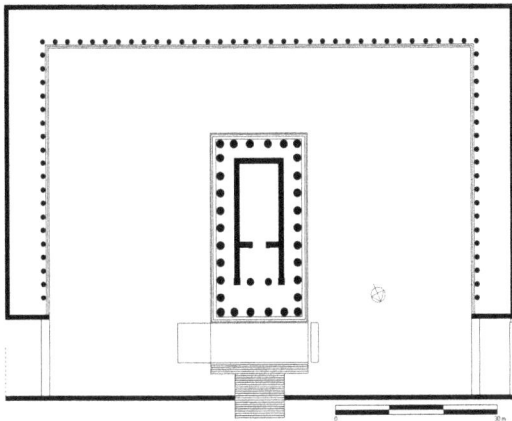

A. Plan of Temple A and the upper terrace complex of the Asklepieion at Kos

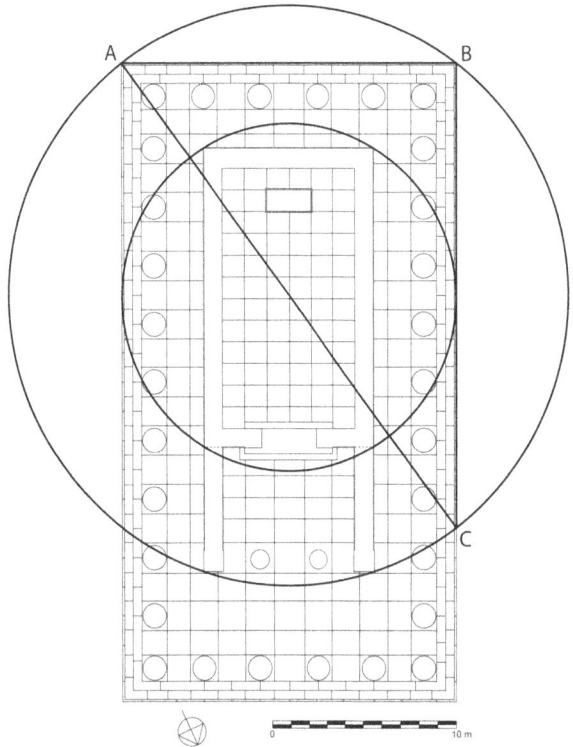

B. Plan of Temple A of the Asklepieion at Kos with its proposed geometric underpinning as demonstrated with analytic geometry and AutoCad. The theoretical geometry consists of 3:4:5 Pythagorean triangle ABC and two circumferences sharing a 3:5 relationship in diameter and establishing the locations and extents of the naos and pronaos.

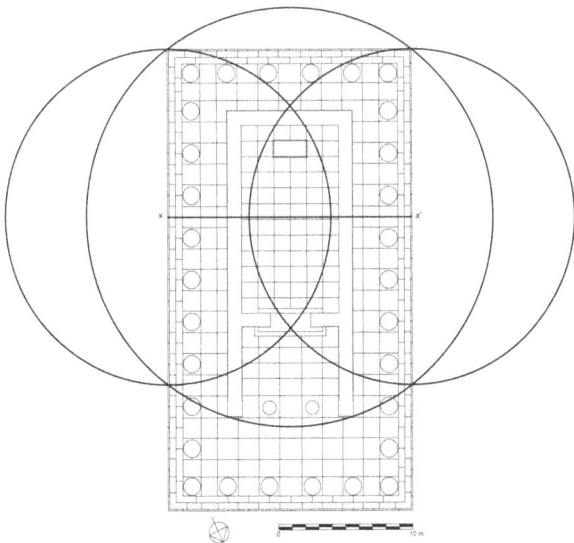

C. Plan of Temple A of the Asklepieion at Kos showing compass-and-straightedge-based construction of the proposed theoretical Pythagorean triangle that generates the locations and extents of features in plan.

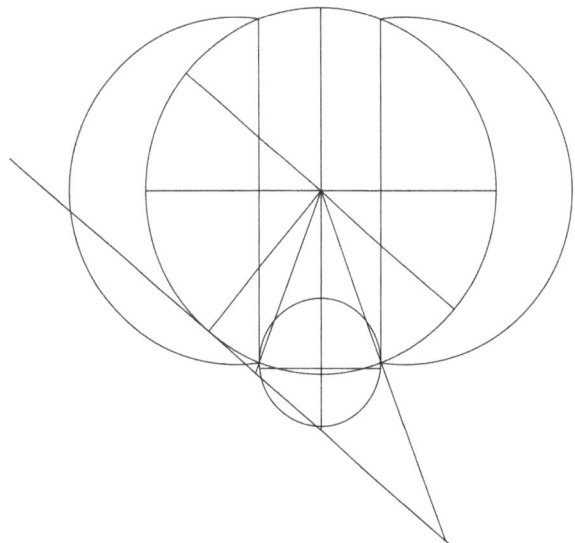

D. The analemma as described by Vitruvius

*Figure 5*

sponsorship of geometry, optics, and geography funded the production of architecture and sculpture. Significantly, Antigonos the Karystian, the sculptor whom the Elder Pliny connects with Attalos I's sculptures celebrating his victories over the Gauls (*HN* 34.84), was known to be a serious student of mathematics (enesiusDiog.Laert. 4.29, 39, 43, 44; Hansen 1971: 399). Based on the related evidence emerging from my analysis of Temple A at Kos, combined with the prevalence of geometry in Attalid Pergamon and even the mathematical interests of sculptors in Pergamon, I do *not* argue that the design of the sculptural group and architecture of the Sanctuary of Athena Nikephoros intentionally followed the form of the circumscribed pentagon on the Dying Gaul. What I do argue is that the Attalid sponsorship of scholarship made for an intellectual environment where readings of space like Coarelli's modern interpretation were possible and even likely. In further support of this idea, this evidence from an Attalid-sponsored monument at Kos shows the Hellenistic understanding of architecture specifically to relate to a governing geometric underpinning, even when that geometry is invisible to the casual viewer.

An important difference between these complexes is the axial symmetry of the upper terrace at Kos (fig. 5A), which was made possible by a unified building campaign that did not incorporate diverse monuments built over more than a century as in the case at Pergamon (fig. 1A). The design at Kos, therefore, could create a conception that was not possible on the Pergamene acropolis. Now, the geometry of ascending planes created through terracing becomes experiential through the symmetrical frame and governing central axis. In this way, the Temple of Asklepios becomes the visual focus of the healing sanctuary. Lying at an oblique angle in relationship to the stoas and the entering visitor, the Temple of Athena at Pergamon lacks this sense of focus, and even seems pulled away from its function as the shrine of a sanctuary focused on the theme of victory that was applied to it at a later date in its history.

On the other hand, there are a number of levels at which meaning could unfold for the contemplative, educated Hellenistic viewer, and it may be worth speculating on one possible reading of the Sanctuary of Athena Nikephoros according to the ancient experience. Upon entering the sanctuary, the visitor's vision would be dominated not by the temple as in the case of an axially symmetric composition like that at Kos. Instead, the temple and north stoa would frame the relationship between the sculptural monument to victory over the Tolistoagii and the Teke Bayır as the dominant rising feature of the landscape of the Kaikos River valley. The interrelationship between this landscape, the concept of victory, and its sacred connotation are then revealed by the inscription on the sculptural monument, where Attalos I offers his thanks to Athena for the victory beside the Kaikos River (Hansen 1971: 31-32). Next, upon ascending the steps of the base of this monument, the visitor would look down to find the form of the circumscribed

pentagon and the prominent axes that radiate from the central circle (figs. 3A, B, D).

It is arguable that, in next asking the meaning of this form, the Hellenistic viewer had a greater tendency to relate geometry to vision than does the modern observer who proposes this possibility. A written passage attributed to Attalos I that appears in Strabo, quoting Demetrios, may be particularly instructive in this regard. Attalos describes a particular tree as follows:

> *Its circumference is twenty-four feet; and its trunk rises to a height of sixty-seven feet from the root and then splits into three branches equidistant from one another, and then contracts again into one head, thus completing a total height of two plethra and fifteen cubits (Strabo 13.1.44, translated by Jones 1929: 89).*

Clearly, it is not only the tree that Attalos sees, but also the geometry that gives the tree its sense of order. This mode of vision is consistent with the philosophical interests of the kings of Pergamon. Before and after Attalos I, the Attalids provided generous support to the Academy in Athens. Four separate philosophers from Pergamene territory, in fact, became heads of the Academy (Hansen 1971: 396) and thereby stewards of Platonic thought.[2] In the traditions of Platonic idealism, it is not the sensible and experiential that is valued, but rather the transcendent, eternal truth that forms the ultimate reality underlying what can be seen. Geometry in particular is posited as a truth that goes beyond embodied experiences, underscoring the necessity of reason in the apprehension of reality. Understood in this way, the visible masses of a tree or an architectural environment may be less privileged than the invisible element that provides its sense of order.

In this mindset, furthermore, a contemplation of the Dying Gaul's incised geometry with its axes radiating from a circle would likely not be far off from an equation of this circle with the circle on which the viewer stands, and the radiating axes of the geometry with the invisible axes that unite the sanctuary's entrances with the central axis of the temple (fig. 4A). In this way, the temple is pulled into the conceptual center of the complex and aligned with the idea of victory and Athena's divine intervention in the Kaikos valley. The sacred landscape as such is not just one that is shaped by visible order in the manner of the axial symmetry found at Kos, but rather one that only the mind can grasp, and which in the traditions of Plato would arguably be a landscape of a higher order. To put it another way, it is the Form or the Idea, in Greek *ideia*, that underlies the mimesis that the eyes see. It is perhaps this notion that best approaches the significance of Vitruvius's observation (1.2.2) that Greeks called their architectural drawings *ideiai*

---

2    These philosophers include the founder of the Middle Academy Arkesilaos from Pitane, Telekes from Phokaia, Evander from Phokaia, and Hegesinos from Pergamon.

(Haselberger 1997: 77, 92-94; Senseney 2007: 560). The idea that architectural drawing follows geometry, while the built form of the sanctuary merely reflects that perfect Idea, may be a concept that could only have come into being in an environment where the patronage of philosophy and geometry on the one hand, and architecture and sculpture on the other hand, were one and the same. Upon coming into being as a theory, it could then be put into practice in subsequent architectural projects.

## Acknowledgements

I would like to thank Charles Gates, Jacques Morin, Oya Pancaroğlu, and Thomas Zimmermann for organizing and inviting me to participate in the Sacred Landscapes Symposium. A Scholars Travel Fund from the Campus Research Board of the University of Illinois at Urbana-Champaign funded my attendance at Bilkent University. A fellowship from the American Research Institute in Turkey funded my research at the sites in Turkey mentioned in this paper. A Beata Inaya Research Fellowship funded my research at Kos and a grant from the Alain K. and Leonarda F. Laing Endowment of the History and Preservation Unit of the School of Architecture at the University of Illinois at Urbana-Champaign allowed me to study the Ludovisi Gauls at the Capitoline Museums and Palazzo Altemps in Rome. This paper is dedicated to the memory of Toni Cross, who as a friend and advisor was instrumental in facilitating my research in Turkey and introducing me to the scholarly community of Ankara. All drawings and photographs are my own.

## References

BEAN, G.E. 1976. Magnesia-on-the-Maeander, in R. Stillwell (ed.) *The Princeton Encyclopedia of Classical Sites*: 554-557. Princeton: Princeton University Press.

BERVE, H. & G. GRUBEN.1978. *Tempel und Heiligtümer der Griechen*. Munich: Hirmer.

BOHN, R. 1885. *Das Heiligtum der Athena Polias Nikephoros*. Berlin: Spemann.

BRYSON, N. 1988. The gaze in the expanded field, in H. Foster (ed.) *Vision and visuality*: 87-114. Seattle: Bay Press.

COARELLI, F. 1995. *Da Pergamo a Roma: i Galati nella città degli Attalidi*. Rome: Quasar.

COULTON, J.J. 1976. *The Architectural development of the Greek stoa*. Oxford: Clarendon Press.

DE JONG, J.J. 1989 Greek mathematics, Hellenistic architecture and Vitruvius' *De Architectura*, in H. Geertman & de Jong, J.J. (ed.) *Munus Non Ingratum: proceedings of the international symposium on Vitruvius' De Architectura and the Hellenistic and Republican architecture, Leiden, 20-23 January 1987*: 100-113. Leiden: Stichting Bulletin Antieke Beschaving.

DOXIADIS, C.A. 1972. *Architectural space in ancient Greece*. Cambridge, MA: M.I.T. Press.

ELSNER, J. 2007. *Roman eyes: visuality and subjectivity in art and text*. Princeton: Princeton University Press.

FINCKER, M. 1995. Il diagramma inciso sul plinto del Galata Morente, in Coarelli, F., *Da Pergamo a Roma: i Galati nella città degli Attalidi*: 49-52. Rome: Quasar.

GRUBEN, G. 1986. *Die Tempel der Griechen*. Darmstadt: Wissenschaftliche Buchgesellschaft.

HANSEN, E. 1971. *The Attalids of Pergamon*. 2nd ed. Ithaca: Cornell University Press.

HASELBERGER, L. 1991. Aspekte der Bauzeichnungen von Didyma. *Revue Archéologique*: 99-113.

—— 1997. Architectural likenesses: models and plans of architecture in classical antiquity. *Journal of Roman Archaeology* 10: 77-94.

HOEPFNER, W. 1990. Bauten und Bedeutung des Hermogenes, in Hoepfner, W. & E.-L. Schwandner (ed.) *Hermogenes und die hochhellenistische Architektur*: 1-61. Mainz-am-Rhein: Philipp von Zabern.

HUMANN, C., J. KOHTE & C. WATZINGER. 1904. *Magnesia am Maeander: Bericht über die Ergebnisse der Ausgrabungen der Jahre 1891-93*. Berlin: G. Reimer.

ISLER, H.P. 1989. Vitruvs Regeln und die erhaltenen Theaterbauten, in Geertman, H. & J.J. de Jong (ed.), *Munus Non Ingratum: proceedings of the international symposium on Vitruvius' De Architectura and the Hellenistic and Republican architecture, Leiden, 20-23 January 1987*: 141-153. Leiden: Stichting Bulletin Antieke Beschaving.

JAY, M. 1988. Scopic regimes of modernity, in H. Foster (ed.) *Vision and visuality*: 3-23. Seattle: Bay Press.

JONES, H.L., transl. 1929. *The geography of Strabo*. vol. 6. Loeb Classical Library. London: William Heinemann.

KORRES, M. 1994. The architecture of the Parthenon, in P. Tournikiotis (ed.) *The Parthenon and its impact in modern times*: 54-97. Athens: Melissa Publishing House.

KREEB, M. 1990. Hermogenes – Quellen und Datierungsprobleme, in Hoepfner, W. & E.-L. Schwandner (ed.) *Hermogenes und die hochhellenistische Architektur*: 103-113. Mainz-am-Rhein: Philipp von Zabern.

MARSZAL, J. 2000. Ubiquitous barbarians: representations of the Gauls at Pergamon and elsewhere, in De Grummond, N.T. & B.S. Ridgway (ed.) *From Pergamon to Sperlonga: sculpture and context*: 191-234. Berkeley: University of California Press.

ONIANS, J. 1979. *Art and thought in the Hellenistic age: the Greek world view 350-50 BC*. London: Thames and Hudson.

SCHALLES, H.-J. 1985. *Untersuchungen zur Kulturpolitik der Pergamenischen Herrscher im dritten Jahrhundert vor Christus*. Tübingen: Ernst Wasmuth.

SENSENEY, J.R. 2007. Idea and visuality in Hellenistic architecture: a geometric analysis of Temple A of the Asklepieion at Kos. *Hesperia* 76: 555-595.

STEWART, A. 2004. *Attalos, Athens, and the Akropolis: the Pergamene "Little Barbarians" and their Roman and Renaissance legacy*. Cambridge: Cambridge University Press.

*John R. Senseney*

WARD-PERKINS, J.B. 1974. *Cities of ancient Greece and Italy: planning in classical antiquity*. New York: George Braziller.

WYCHERLEY, R.E. 1942. The Ionian Agora. *Journal of Hellenic Studies* 62: 21-32.

# CULT AND LANDSCAPE AT PERGAMON

## Soi Agelidis

The acropolis hill of Pergamon is a 330 m high andesite massif that rises in the Kaikos River (Bakır Çay) valley. Though situated only 26 km from the coast, Pergamon's landscape is determined by the surrounding mountains, Pindasos (Kozak) to the north and Aspordenon (Yünd Dağ) to the south. The city of Pergamon was, at the time of its foundation, limited in extent to the top of the acropolis hill. In the course of time it expanded down the slopes and, finally, in Roman times, across the lowlands to the west.[1] Due to the particular geography of Pergamon, sanctuaries within and outside the city often have remarkable locations, for example the sanctuaries of Dionysos, on a narrow elongated terrace on the west slope, and Athena, on its wide terrace on the upper acropolis hill. Some cults, though, were causally connected to the site of worship because of significant natural formations which were essential for the cult. This paper will examine three such sanctuaries in which the relationship between landscape and cult seems especially strong: the Asklepieion, not far from the city, and two sanctuaries of Meter, both located some distance away, one at Mamurtkale, the other at Kapıkaya.

### The Asklepieion

The Asklepieion is situated about 2 km southwest of the acropolis in the lowlands towards the sea. The centre of the sanctuary was a 50 m long and 40 m wide rock outcrop with a spring, around which the first known buildings were set and the first widely distributed cult in late Classical and Hellenistic times was established (fig. 1). The initial founding of a cult in this area cannot, however, be exactly dated. The earliest building remains have been assigned to the late fifth century BC (Ziegenaus and De Luca 1968: 10–11), although pottery and terracotta figurines found in this site date back to the sixth century BC (Boehringer 1959: 163–164; Ziegenaus and De Luca 1975: 61, 65, 86).

These finds from the middle as well as from the northern and western part of the later sanctuary suggest strongly that the area was settled at the latest in the Archaic period.[2] With a settlement situated around the significant formation of the rock outcrop and the spring, the assumption stands to reason that a deity had been worshipped at that site (see also: Ziegenaus and De Luca 1975: 92, 145; Scheer 1993: 103, 108–109). The lack of built structures is not a valid argument against this supposition, for on the one hand, buildings are not required for worship; on the other hand, if structures did exist, they could be completely lost if built out of impermanent materials on rock.

According to textual sources, the cult of Asklepios was brought from Epidauros to Pergamon. Pausanias testifies that Archias, after experiencing healing from a grave wound in Epidauros, brought this cult to his homeland (Pausanias 2. 26, 8–9; Habicht 1969: 1). Inscriptions found in Epidauros and Pergamon verify this incident, which is placed in the early fourth century BC (Allen 1983: 162–163; Scheer 1993: 130–131; Radt 1999: 220). This dating of the cult's founding fits more or less the dating of the first building remains in the sanctuary.

The Archias story attests that the person who established the Asklepios cult in Pergamon was not a ruler but a private citizen. The worship had at that point been modest and private, as findings of pottery as well as the remains of buildings suggest (Ziegenaus and De Luca 1968: 10–29, 96–111). Nevertheless, grave reliefs and funerary or dedicatory buildings found along the sacred way suggest that the cult had a certain importance at least for a particular group of people (Ziegenaus and De Luca 1975: 50–53, pls. 34–36, 38–39, 84; De Luca 1984: 135–142, pls. 62–64, 69).

Though building activity in the sanctuary was constant from

---

[1]  For the geographical position of Pergamon and its surroundings, see Radt 1999: 19, fig. 4. For the development of the city, see Radt 1999: 57, fig. 11; 58, fig. 12.

[2]  Excavations in the area west of the later Asklepieion yielded pottery and building remains documenting settlement activity dating back to the Bronze Age.

*Figure 1. Pergamon, Asklepieion. View of the rock bar from the south-west (photo: the author)*

the fifth century BC, a change took place in the second half of the third century BC. Around mid century the southern part of the temple forecourt was raised, the incubation building and also the existent southern altar were enlarged, and a new altar, the middle altar, was built (Ziegenaus and De Luca 1968: 29–31, 111–115). This sudden expansion is to be connected with the advancement of the cult by Attalos I, which led to the promotion of Asklepios worship to a state cult. Beside the extension of the sanctuary's buildings, further evidence for this development includes the assignment of a nameable sculptor, Pyromachos, to create the cult statue of the god and the appearance of Asklepios for the first time on the city's coins (Habicht 1969: 2; Voegtli 1993: 28, no. 35–115; pl. 1). Together they all document the first great bloom of Asklepios's cult.

After the destruction of the Asklepieion by Philip V of Macedonia in 201 BC, the sanctuary was rebuilt on an even much larger scale. The courtyard was doubled to the south and closed by porticoes, the temple was restored in a different, more modern style, and the incubation building as well as the altar were also enlarged. The sanctuary attained its largest dimensions ever. The expansion to the south with the porticoes enclosing a much bigger courtyard and the

enlargement of the incubation building suggest a massive growth in the numbers of worshippers (Ziegenaus and De Luca 1968: 39–47, 125–134).

In the following centuries, until the decline of the Hellenistic sanctuary in the first century AD, the southern part of the complex experienced repeated destruction and rebuilding. The best known incident was the destruction of the sanctuaries located outside Pergamon's walls, including the Asklepieion, by Prusias, king of Bithynia, in 155 BC (Ziegenaus and De Luca 1968: 47–76, 134–169). A brief period of importance came with Attalos III. According to an inscription found in the sanctuary, the king determined after a glorious victory to erect a statue of himself in the temple of Asklepios Soter, thus making himself the god's cult associate. A yearly feast held for both Attalos and Asklepios would remind everyone of the king's victory (Fränkel 1890: 153–159, no. 246; Boehringer and Krauss 1937: 3; Nilsson 1950: 164–165).

The next heyday was to come with Hadrian, who probably initiated the renewal of the Asklepieion in his first journey to Pergamon in AD 124. Many members of the city's high society, persons of a certain intellectual standard like the

*Figure 2. Pergamon, Asklepieion. Model (by H. Schleif) of the sanctuary in the mid second century BC, view from the west (DAI Istanbul reproduction 82/9,2)*

emperor himself attended to this assignment and created a remarkable new site (fig. 2). The courtyard was newly framed by porticoes on all sides except the western where the new propylon and temple, and later a library, were built. The ensemble was symmetrically constructed with the entrances onto the sanctuary of both propylon and temple corresponding in their appearance (Deubner 1938: 40–43; Habicht 1969: 9–14, 103–106, no. 64; Le Glay 1976: 368–371; Radt 1983: 457–458; Radt 1984: 437–439). Although the surrounding buildings were renewed in an elaborate manner, the northeastern corner of the sanctuary with the old temples, altars, and spring on and around the rock outcrop maintained their old, comparably modest form and setting. This was the part of the sanctuary that preserved the old cult, continuing the centuries-old tradition (Ohlemutz 1940: 145–146; Ziegenaus and De Luca 1968: passim; Ziegenaus and De Luca 1975: 5–17). The modern complex, however, with its big temple, a library, and an odeion had a completely different character and was addressed to an entirely different circle of people, basically identical with the donors of the new buildings (Habicht 1969: 13–14, 15–17; Le Glay 1976: 371). For the ordinary people the Asklepieion was a place of healing; for the upper class it was a venue in which they could enjoy intellectual amusement combined with baths and some mystic cult activity. Significant for the side by side existence of two different concepts around one god are his names in the two temples: in the old one he was Asklepios Soter, the healing god, whereas in the new one he was called Zeus Asklepios

Soter, a construct for the intellectual stratum (Ohlemutz 1940: 157).

The worship activity in the area of the Asklepieion can be summarized as follows: at a distinctive site with a rock outcrop and a flowing spring, a modest cult to an unknown deity was probably created. Later, Asklepios and his believers took over the site to establish a new cult. Initially more a matter of a small, private group, the adoration of the healing god from Epidauros attracted in the course of time more and more worshippers. The consequence was a repeated modest extension of the sanctuary, particularly of the incubation buildings. At that point Attalos I, who seems to have recognized a chance to appear as a benefactor to a large part of his people, initiated the first major enlargement of the sanctuary, commissioned Pyromachos to create a cult statue, and struck the first coins with Asklepios's image. The motivation of Hadrian to boost again the cult of Asklepios is, on the contrary, not clear. In any case he stimulated a concentrated action of the rich who created a new, elaborate complex and donated to this cult. The interest of the emperor brought the emergence of a new circle of worshippers and of a novel worship which, however, did not replace the old healing cult but existed parallel to it.

## The Sanctuary of Meter at Mamurtkale

For the cult of Meter the landscape is even more important. She was worshipped at various points in Pergamon. The Megalesion and possibly an additional sanctuary on the

*Figure 3. Mamurtkale, Meter sanctuary. Plan after the excavation (after Conze and Schazmann 1911: pl. 1)*

highest point of the acropolis were situated within the city, but her most important shrines lay in the surrounding mountains, at Mamurtkale and Kapıkaya (Ohlemutz 1940: 181–191; Roller 1999: 206–209, 209–212).[3]

The sanctuary of Meter at Mamurtkale lies ca. 30 km to the southeast of Pergamon at over 1000 m height in the Yünd Dağ. This mountain range consists of two peaks connected by a saddle. The lower peak is connected to a terrace on which the sanctuary was built. Our evidence about the early appearance of this site is marginal, the visible remains

dating to early Hellenistic times when Philetairos created a whole new complex in the sanctuary of Meter (fig. 3) (Conze and Schazmann 1911: 20; Allen 1983: 15–16; Schalles 1985: 26–31; Schmidt-Dounas 2000: 9–10). A 67 x 67 m square courtyard is lined on three sides by porticoes leaving the southeastern side open. The northeastern portico is about 22 m longer than the opposite on the southwest in order to keep the harsh winds from blowing over the courtyard. The northwestern portico is interrupted by the temple that was built in Doric style on a four-stepped krepis, and had two columns in antis and a pronaos almost as deep as the cella. In the front a staircase descends to a paved way which leads to the altar. Beyond it a further paved way

---

[3] Concerning the cult of Meter in Phrygia, see the essays of L. E. Roller and S. Berndt-Ersöz in this volume.

on the axis of temple and altar led to the southeast; due to its poor preservation its end remains unknown (Conze and Schazmann 1911: 14–35; Bringmann and von Steuben 1995: 293–295).

The evidence for a cult practiced before this quite monumental setting of the sanctuary is provided inside the temple and the altar. The cult image framed by an aedicula stood inside the temple. Its base lies significantly about 1 m below the ground of the temple; hence it stood there some time before the building of the temple. The second place hiding prehellenistic remains is the altar: here we find inside the structure of the third century BC a smaller earlier altar (Conze and Schazmann 1911: 28–30, 31, pl. II, X 1). The finds of terracotta figurines in the sanctuary dating back to the fifth century BC, in combination with the situation of the cult image and the altar, suggest the existence here of a cult of Meter at least since Classical times, though we cannot know how long before that time the goddess was worshipped at this location by her first followers (see also Schalles 1985: 26. 27–28; Roller 1999: 210–211). The greatest flourishing of the worship documented by architecture and finds can be dated into the third and second centuries BC. This popularity was followed by a sudden decline in the first century BC, a time which left no archaeological evidence at all. Findings from Roman times are minimal – some coins but not even one terracotta figurine (Conze and Schazmann 1911: 37–44; Nohlen and Radt 1978: 77–90).

A fragment of a big ceramic vessel bearing the relief of a flute player and the inscription ATTIN attests that as in many other Meter sanctuaries, her young shepherd companion was also worshipped here (Conze and Schazmann 1911: 41 pl. 8 no. 4). Although this fragment is the only indication for the Attis cult at Mamurtkale, it can only derive from this location and due to the inscription is a convincing piece of evidence.

The orientation of the cult image and the altar are of particular interest. The aedicula faced towards Pergamon in the southeast, whereas the altar, standing perpendicular to the temple, is orientated to the northeast. Since the altar is the most important element for the cult, it should be the first structure to have been built, being initially used for worship with a simple, aniconic cult image. When the aedicula was added, the wish to allude to Pergamon led to the different, henceforth decisive, orientation for the sanctuary. Later on Philetairos retained and emphasized this orientation by situating the cult image in the temple and surrounding the precinct by the porticoes, but leaving the southeast side open in order not to disturb the visual contact with Pergamon. The connection with his city of residence was further underlined by the use for the temple of certain design elements characteristic of Pergamene buildings, for example, the three-metopes system known from the Athena temple. The Meter sanctuary had, according to coin finds, already in the fifth century BC a supraregional importance.

Hence Philetairos's benefaction affected not only the rural population in the direct surroundings of Pergamon but also the people of cities like Aigai, Pitane, and Adramytion (Conze and Schazmann 1911: 42–43; Allen 1983: 16; Schalles 1985: 27–30).

## The Sanctuary of Meter at Kapıkaya

The Meter sanctuary at Kapıkaya is located in the mountains 10 km northwest from Pergamon (figs. 4–5). At a height of over 60 m lies a grotto formed by a massive boulder which has fallen from a higher level on top of an open cavity in the rock (Conze and Garbrecht 1912: 128). In this already remarkable natural formation a spring flowed, too. Such a site was predestined for the cult of the Great Mother, goddess of the mountains and the wild nature who was said to have been born out of a stone and often was adored in the form of a rock (Hepding 1903: 118; Nohlen and Radt 1978: 70). The rise of her cult at this place cannot be dated, but we suppose at the beginning it consisted of a modest worship by shepherds and travelers (Nohlen and Radt 1978: 69). The earliest finds are dated to the third century BC; the majority of the material, however, comes from the second and first centuries BC. Numerous terracotta figurines, lamps, pottery, and coins document the heyday of the sanctuary in the middle and late Hellenistic period (Nohlen and Radt 1978: 32–68). The finds suggest that the cult was addressed not only to Meter but also to Attis, her shepherd companion (Nohlen and Radt 1978: 33, 35, 72–73 ). In Roman times a remarkable change took place. It is likely that Meter was still adored here but Mithras became the main deity. His cult was practiced until the fourth century AD, with a certain flowering recorded for the second and third centuries when the cooking ware is well represented (Nohlen and Radt 1978: 73–76).

Although the sanctuary was in continuous use at least from the third century BC to the fourth century AD, its setting remained modest. The central point of cult and sanctuary was the natural grotto with the spring inside. We suppose that initially this natural situation was adequate for the practice of the cult, but in the third century BC at the latest, when bigger crowds started visiting, the site was at some points modified. Inside the grotto the rock was carved in order to create a water basin, and a bench and niches for dedications and lamps (Nohlen and Radt 1978: 6–8). Directly at the front of the entrance to the south and southwest a terrace was carved out of the rock. It is limited to the north by the high rising rock with carved niches in its face and a bench attached at its base and, to the west by another rock-cut bench with a back rest towards the steep slope. The terrace was extended south and east, beyond the outcrop, but the wall retaining this part has collapsed and the fill spilled down the slope. The central niche in the northern rock face carried the cult statue made of wood (Nohlen and Radt 1978: 8–10). Further to the east remains of walls and rock carvings suggest the existence of further water installations across the whole sanctuary

*Figure 4. Kapıkaya. View from the southeast, with the Meter sanctuary marked (photo: the author)*

(Nohlen and Radt 1978: 11–12). Finally, the path leading to the sanctuary was broadened by straightening the rock, with some niches – originally occupied by reliefs with the image of the goddess – marking the path as the access to the cult site of the deity (Nohlen and Radt 1978: 4–6). We see that despite the efforts to gratify the needs of the growing number of followers, the setting remained natural and humble. We have to assume that during the feasts for the goddess, which partly took place at night, the worshippers camped around the temenos.

The only stone building was erected in Roman times when the cult itself had changed significantly: Meter was probably still adored but the emphasis of worship lay now on Mithras. The grotto was still in use, but for specific acts within the Mithraic cult this new building was necessary (Nohlen and Radt 1978: 14–15).

Although at Kapıkaya we find no evidence of a ruler's influence on the sanctuary or the cult, it is notable that there are no remains of a cult practice there before the third century BC when Philetairos promoted the cult of Meter at Mamurtkale. Therefore it has been suggested that Philetairos's promotion of the Meter cult led to the founding or development of the cult at Kapıkaya as well (Schalles 1985: 31). Nevertheless the heyday of Meter's sanctuary at Kapıkaya can clearly be dated to the second

and first centuries BC, that is during the reign of the last three Attalid kings and the subsequent early Roman period. We cannot exclude the possibility that modest worship took place before the time of Philetairos, but, if this were the case, it left no traces. A certain influence of the first Attalids at Kapıkaya is likely, although it seems not to have been significant.

The sanctuaries of Meter on Mamurtkale and Kapıkaya were established at an indeterminable time by unknown people. In Mamurtkale the monumentalisation of the sanctuary undertaken by Philetairos led to a form of ennoblement of the actually nature-connected cult. The lack of a natural feature adaptable to cult such as the grotto on Kapıkaya may have allowed this urban-oriented remodeling of the site which probably even included the pavement of the road to the sanctuary. Nevertheless the cult on Mamurtkale did not outlast Hellenistic times but was essentially abandoned already in the first century BC, with some sporadic visitors in Roman times. In Kapıkaya the attraction of more and more worshippers led to a modification of the site, though leaving its natural character untouched. The constant tight connection to nature was not disturbed after the adoption of the Mithras cult and the erection of a stone building for it, since the grotto was still in use and its surroundings remained unchanged.

*Figure. 5. Kapıkaya, Meter sanctuary. Grotto and terrace, view from the east (photo: E. Steiner, DAI Istanbul 71/70,9)*

## Conclusion

The examination of the three sanctuaries around Pergamon has shown different developments even though all three started in a similar manner. In each site the initial cult was established at an unknown date by worshipping a deity at a remarkable natural formation. The rock outcrop with spring in the Asklepieion and the grotto likewise with a spring at Kapıkaya are quite obvious landmarks. The motivation for founding a cult at Mamurtkale, however, should be sought in the overall landscape situation in these mountainous heights. In the Asklepieion and at Kapıkaya the growing number of devotees led to a modification of the setting, in the first instance by the erection and enlargement of functional buildings, in the second by carving the bedrock into benches, water installations,

and pathways. The more monumental furnishing of the Asklepieion was the achievement of Attalos I, a ruler who saw in the advancement of the cult an opportunity to appear as a benefactor to a large part of the public. This effort is even more obvious due to the issuing of coins struck with the image of Asklepios at the same time as the rebuilding of his sanctuary. At Mamurtkale the connection to the ruler seems to have been even stronger. Before the renewal stimulated by Philetairos, the sanctuary was very modest and sporadically frequented. Its heyday came only after the enlargement. At Kapıkaya, in contrast, the cult flourished without the benefit of a ruler; the increase of the worshippers' community was not an achievement of one person but a more spontaneous action carried out by private citizens. This trend remained unchanged into Roman times. The sanctuary stayed in use and even switched cult, yet

53

always without the intervention by a ruler. The Asklepieion shows the same tendency. The major conversion of the sanctuary under the patronage of Hadrian produced a new focus but left the old cult untouched. The buildings around the rock outcrop were still the center of the worship of Asklepios as a healing god, as in the centuries before.

The exercise of cult in the Asklepieion and at Kapıkaya continued over centuries, though not for the same deity over the entire duration of worship. The constant factor at both sites was the concentration of the cult at all times around a distinctive topographical feature. The change of cult – at the Asklepieion early with the change from the unknown deity to Asklepios, at Kapıkaya quite late with the shifting of the cult from Meter to Mithras – proves that the natural site was the point of attraction, used by the people for varying cults depending on their current needs. This distinctive quality of the landscape can be termed as the genuine religious character of the site, which allowed the changing of cults as long as the location remained sacred. The patronage of rulers, in contrast, had a comparatively brief effect in the numbers of worshippers but not an enduring effect on the retention of cults.

## References

ALLEN, R.E. 1983. *The Attalid kingdom. A constitutional history*. Oxford: Clarendon Press.

BRINGMANN, K. & H. VON STREUBEN (ed.). 1995. *Schenkungen hellenistischer Herrscher an griechische Städte und Heiligtümer, Teil 1. Zeugnisse und Kommentare*. Berlin: Akademie Verlag.

BOEHRINGER, E. 1959. Pergamon, in E. Boehringer (ed.) *Neue deutsche Ausgrabungen im Mittelmeergebiet und im vorderen Orient*: 121–171. Berlin: Mann.

BOEHRINGER, E. & F. KRAUSS. 1937. *Das Temenos für den Herrscherkult*. Altertümer von Pergamon IX. Berlin: De Gruyter.

CONZE, A. & G. GARBRECHT. 1912. *Stadt und Landschaft*. Altertümer von Pergamon I 1. Berlin: De Gruyter.

CONZE, A. & P. SCHAZMANN. 1911. *Mamurt-Kaleh. Ein Tempel der Göttermutter unweit Pergamon*. Jahrbuch des Kaiserlich Deutschen Archäologischen Instituts. 9. Ergänzungsheft. Berlin: De Gruyter.

DE LUCA, G. 1984. *Das Asklepieion 4. Teil. Via Tecta und Hallenstraße. Die Funde*. Altertümer von Pergamon XI 4. Berlin: De Gruyter.

DEUBNER, O. 1938. *Das Asklepieion von Pergamon*. Berlin: De Gruyter.

FRÄNKEL, M. 1890. *Die Inschriften von Pergamon*. Altertümer von Pergamon VIII 1. Berlin: De Gruyter.

HABICHT, C. 1969. *Die Inschriften des Asklepieions*, Altertümer von Pergamon VIII 3. Berlin: De Gruyter.

HEPDING, H. 1903. *Attis. Seine Mythen und sein Kult*. Gieszen: Ricker.

LE GLAY, M. 1976. Hadrien et l'Asklépieion de Pergame. *Bulletin de Correspondance Hellénique* 100: 347–372.

NILSSON, M. P. 1906. *Griechische Feste von religiöser Bedeutung mit Ausschluss der attischen*. Leipzig: Teubner.

NILSSON, M. P. 1941. *Geschichte der griechischen Religion* 1. Munich: Beck

NILSSON, M. P. 1950. *Geschichte der griechischen Religion* 2. Munich: Beck.

NOHLEN, K. & W. RADT. 1978. *Kapıkaya. Ein Felsheiligtum bei Pergamon*. Altertümer von Pergamon XII. Berlin: De Gruyter.

OHLEMUTZ, E. 1940. *Die Kulte und Heiligtümer der Götter in Pergamon*. Würzburg: Triltsch.

RADT, W. 1983. Pergamon. Vorbericht über die Kampagne 1982. *Archäologischer Anzeiger* 1983: 455–469.

——1984. Pergamon. Vorbericht über die Kampagne 1983. *Archäologischer Anzeiger* 1984: 431–452.

——1999. *Pergamon. Geschichte und Bauten einer antiken Metropole*. Darmstadt: Wissenschaftliche Buchgesellschaft.

ROLLER, L. E. 1999. *In search of god the mother: the cult of Anatolian Cybele*. Berkeley: University of California Press.

SCHALLES, H.-J. 1985. *Untersuchungen zur Kulturpolitik der pergamenischer Herrscher im dritten Jahrhundert vor Christus*. Istanbuler Forschungen 36. Tübingen: Wasmuth.

SCHEER, T. S. 1993. *Mythische Vorväter. Zur Bedeutung griechischer Heroenmythen im Selbstverständnis kleinasiatischer Städte*. Munich: Edition Maris.

SCHMIDT-DOUNAS, B. 2000. Geschenke erhalten die Freundschaft. Politik und Selbstdarstellung im Spiegel der Monumente, in K. Bringmann & H. von Streuben (ed.) *Schenkungen hellenistischer Herrscher an griechische Städte und Heiligtümer, Teil 2. Historische und archäologische Auswertung, Band 2*. Berlin: Akademie Verlag.

VOEGTLI, H. 1993. *Die Fundmünzen aus der Stadtgrabung von Pergamon*. Pergamenische Forschungen 8. Berlin: De Gruyter.

ZIEGENAUS, O. 1981. *Das Asklepieion 3. Teil. Die Kultbauten aus römischer Zeit an der Ostseite des Heiligen Bezirks*. Altertümer von Pergamon XI 3. Berlin: De Gruyter.

ZIEGENAUS, O. & G. DE LUCA. 1968. *Das Asklepieion 1. Teil. Der südliche Temenosbezirk in hellenistischer und frührömischer Zeit*. Altertümer von Pergamon XI 1. Berlin: De Gruyter.

——1975. *Das Asklepieion 2. Teil. Der nördliche Temenosbezirk und angrenzende Anlagen in hellenistischer und frührömischer Zeit*. Altertümer von Pergamon XI 2. Berlin: De Gruyter.

# THE GODS OF THE LATMOS: CULTS AND RITUALS AT THE HOLY MOUNTAIN FROM PREHISTORIC TO BYZANTINE TIMES

*Anneliese Peschlow-Bindokat*

The Latmos Mountains, along the east shore of Lake Bafa, occupy the hinterland of Miletos. Named in Turkish Beşparmak, Five Fingers, to describe their characteristic serrated silhouette, with their wildly rugged gneiss rocks these mountains dominate the landscape even from afar (Peschlow-Bindokat 2007: 162). For most archaeologists and tourists the perception of the Western coast of Turkey comes from the Classical past of this area. But within the typical Mediterranean appearance of the land with its smooth contours, the ragged ridges of these mountains have their distinct, "other" appearance, and according to the weather, can loom downright menacing and hostile, for example during an approaching thunderstorm.

Lake Bafa originally was part of the Aegean Sea, such that the Latmos was part of the coast; today it lies at the foothills of the mountains (Peschlow-Bindokat 2003: 10-13, figs.1a-5). The lake formed the southeastern and most backwards portion of the Gulf of Latmos. Beginning in Roman times it was cut off from the sea by the silt accumulated by the Maeander River and became a landlocked, brackish lake (Müllenhoff 2005: 180).

## The Weather God

The Latmos was one of the holy mountains of Asia Minor. Its highest peak, Turkish Tekerlekdağ, climbing to nearly 1400 m and visible from all sides, was the home of an old stone and rain cult (Peschlow-Bindokat 2003: 9-17). Here the Anatolian weather god was venerated as early as the Neolithic period. In Classical times the Greeks replaced the old weather god with their own weather god Zeus. The archaeological proof is a little temple on the back side of the main mountain range, situated in a romantic valley amidst a pine forest. This small building is oriented towards the peak and was dedicated to Zeus Akraios (Peschlow-Bindokat 2003: 9, 15, figs. 9 a-c).

During Medieval times the Latmos was still considered a holy mountain like Mount Athos in northern Greece. The mountains then were a center of monastic life and thirteen monasteries and a great number of hermits' caves are documented (Peschlow 1993: 651-716; 2005: 162-201). The most important was the monastery of Saint Paul the Younger, who lived here in the tenth century. In his Vita, written a few years after his death, one finds an interesting episode: at the time of Saint Paul processions were still sent up to the mountain's peak during periods of severe drought to pray for rain (Wiegand 1913:116). We still know the route of the pilgrims in the tenth century. They followed the ancient paved road from Myus up to Bozalan, from there to the monastery of Saint Paul (Arapavlusu) and further on to the peak (fig. 1). At several locations along the way they painted inscriptions and crosses into the rocks.

At the highest point lies a big stone which is said to have been holy for all eternity. This stone is nothing other than the peak, a natural rock which looks like a big isolated stone, a meteor (Peschlow-Bindokat 2003: 14, fig. 7-8). This natural rock was the main cult place of the region. The Christians erected a cross on it to demonstrate their dominance over the old pagan cult. The stone also possessed healing power, it was believed, and gave enlightenment to the monks coming here.

In sum, the peak of Latmos was indeed a fertile place for cult, in use continuously from Neolithic times through the Classical period and into the Middle Ages.

## The Mountain God

Besides the weather deity, an indigenous mountain god was worshipped in the Latmos. This god, who arose from the rocky landscape of the mountains with its innumerable caves, was also represented by the peak, because it was at the same time the location of an old stone cult. The power

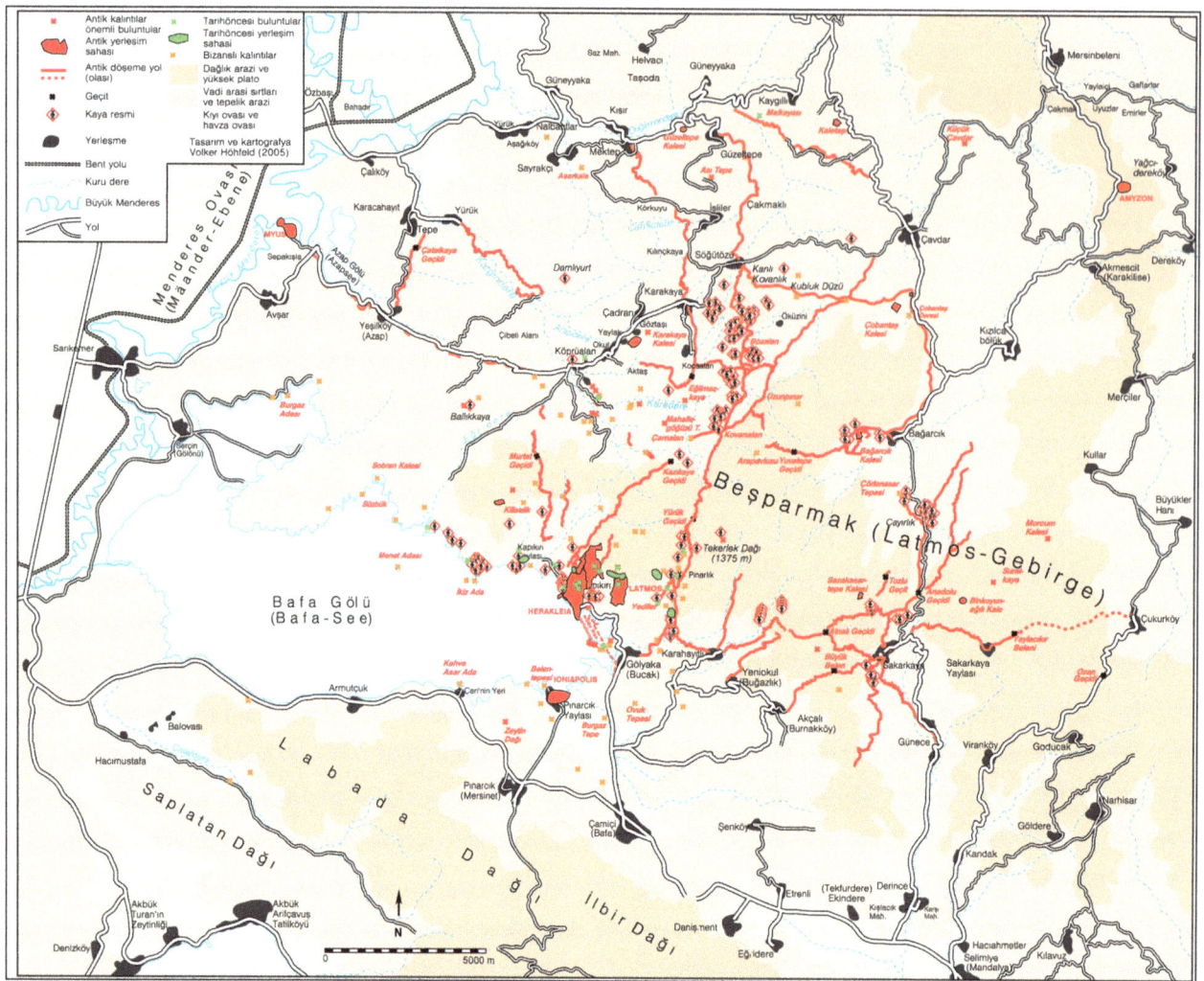

*Figure 1. Distribution map of the rock paintings*

of this god becomes visible in the weathering structures of the gneiss which are of unusual prominence throughout the Latmos (Philippson 1936: 16). Sometimes their fascinating forms look like demons, or wild or fantastic animals such as reptiles or turtles (fig. 2).

This local mountain god lived on in Greek mythology as Endymion, the young shepherd and lover of the moon goddess, Selene; this myth was a popular motif on Roman sarcophagi (Peschlow-Bindokat 2003: 9, 16, fig. 10). Endymion was the local hero of the Latmos. He was considered the founder of Herakleia and can be understood as a personification of the mountains. The foundation legend of Magnesia describes the city as situated opposite Endymion, meaning the Latmos (Peschlow-Bindokat 2005a: 22-23).

Endymion also died in the Latmos, where still in Roman times his tomb was visited (Strabo 14.636); it may be identified with the chamber tomb in the agora of the city of Latmos (Peschlow-Bindokat 2005a: pl. 48, 1-2). According to Pausanias (5.1.5) the hero also had an adyton in the mountains. Perhaps the structure northwest of the agora,

which was rebuilt in Byzantine times as a little monastery, was this adyton (Peschlow-Bindokat 2005a: 23-25, pls. 49-52). Adyta generally are places which were not open for the common people; sometimes they were underground, such as caves. Under the chapel lies a cave with beautiful Byzantine paintings with Christ Pantokrator in the center (Peschlow 2005: 170). Here too Christians changed an old local cult according to their needs into a sanctuary of Christ.

In this context belongs also the so-called Christ Cave in the valley north of the city of Latmos, where people settled in prehistoric times and later again in Byzantine times when the cave served as a prayer room for the hermits living in the area (Peschlow 2005: 197; Peschlow-Bindokat 2006a: 90-91, figs. 90 a-c). The cave was decorated with frescoes showing scenes of the life of Christ. This cave, which differs from the other ones nearby in that it is more spacious and gives the impression of a regular rectangular building, was also a holy place in prehistoric times. Because in the northeast corner different prehistoric objects were found, among them a small vessel with a human face which would not have been a common object, but must carry a ritual meaning (Peschlow-Bindokat 2006a: 91, figs. 90 d-e), I

*Figure 2. Weathering forms of the Latmos: "turtle"*

suggest that this cave was the prehistoric sanctuary of the mountain god.

In Herakleia Endymion also had a sanctuary, which tried to copy a natural cave (Peschlow-Bindokat 2005b: 118-119). Even if constructed, in form it is a cave. The cave seems to have been a characteristic mark of the mountain god.

Weather and mountain deities were generally closely interrelated throughout Anatolia ever since prehistoric times. At some sites they were worshipped together; sometime they were even considered to be one and the same (Haas 1982: passim). Perhaps the most impressive document for a relationship between these two deities is the famous rock relief of Yazılıkaya near the capital of the Hittite empire, Hattusha, where the weather god is standing on the necks of the mountain gods (Peschlow-Bindokat 2003: 17, fig. 12). In the Latmos the situation is more or less the same, with the difference that the mountain itself stands for the mountain god, while his peak represents the seat of the weather god. This old Anatolian tradition was taken over by the Greeks who simply substituted for him their own weather god, Zeus. For the mountain god one encounters a different situation. Perhaps this has something to do with the fact that in Greece mountain gods did not play as important a role as in Anatolia. Anyhow, the Greeks changed the appearance of this god from an old bearded man in the Anatolian iconography to a young shepherd and

hunter sleeping in a cave of the Latmos and being loved by the moon goddess, Selene.

This motif appears for the first time in Greek Archaic literature in the poems of Sappho (Lobel and Page 1955: frg. 149). It seems doubtful that this romantic love story is of Anatolian origin; rather it may be a Greek invention, deriving from the moon rising above the Latmos which is, indeed, an extraordinary spectacle of nature in this rocky landscape. The main argument for this interpretation is the fact that here in Caria as well as throughout the Near East the moon deities are male and *not* female (Laumonier 1958: passim). Maybe we have here the birth place of a Greek myth?

**Prehistoric Rock Paintings**

No doubt, the Latmos was a "ritual" landscape. The weather and the mountain gods, both local phenomena, were its main deities. Both personify local powers, namely the sky and the mountains, which are seen in symbiosis. There is no other region in the entire Mediterranean where one can study the influence of landscape and climate on religious ideas of the population and upon their expressions in art as well as in the Latmos. The most impressive examples for this influence are the prehistoric rock paintings.

The first painting was discovered in 1994; today their

number has grown to over 170 (Peschlow-Bindokat 2003; 2005b: 51- 76; 2006a; 2007: 162-165). These paintings are unique in style and subject. They are undoubtedly related to the mountains. This is seen in two ways: first they relate to the peak, because they are placed around it (fig. 1); some of them are also oriented directly towards the peak. This suggests a relation between the paintings and the cult of the peak. In this context it is also worth pointing out that most of the sites with paintings are located above a brook or a spring. Water is, as we know, the basis of all life.

The second aspect that confirms a relation can be read from the special kind of rock formations of the Latmos with their typical weathering spots in which the power of the mountain god is manifested. The "painters" were careful to use the weathered spots of the gneiss as painting ground, while employing skillfully their edges as frames. One of the most impressive examples of this procedure graces the cave of Kovanalan where three different forms of the weathering of the gneiss can be studied together. The rock from outside has a rounded shape, termed "Wollsackverwitterung" in German (Peschlow-Bindokat 2003: 31-32, figs. 25-27b); when the interior of a rock is completely hollowed, it is called a "Tafoniverwitterung." Standing inside the cave, one has the impression of looking at a living organism. The weathered surface of a rock's interior is called "Wabenverwitterung"(bee-hive structure). And these hollows are painted.

Before discussing the subject of the paintings, some remarks concerning their date are in order. The schematic style, the small size of the figures, the iconography of the female figures with their buttocks protruding far behind them, also the ornaments and signs give an indication for a date of creation between the Neolithic period and the Bronze Age.

A real base for the chronology, however, could be determined only from the context. Thanks to discoveries made in recent years, such as marble idols and animal figurines (Peschlow-Bindokat 2005b: 79-81; 2006a: 85, fig.77; 86, fig.78; 93, fig. 92), and pottery of the late Neolithic and Chalcolithic periods, that is of the sixth and fifth millennia BC, a first frame of reference has been established (Peschlow-Bindokat 2006a: 86-89, figs. 79-80a, 81-85, 88-89b). This pottery shows close relations to the Neolithic-Chalcolithic pottery of Tigani on Samos (Gerber 2003: 204-210). The Latmos was at this time part of the southeastern Aegean culture.

As a rule the rock paintings present only one theme: the human figure. Besides this motif, various ornaments, signs, and symbols appear. Representations of animals are very rare. The representations of humans do not focus upon the individual, but instead show people in their social existence. Consequently pictures of single figures are rare. The multi-figured images usually show both sexes which appear in varying groupings. The majority deals with representations of women and men as couples (Peschlow-Bindokat 2003: 39-49). The principal themes appear to be the relation

*Figure 3. İkizada, copy of the rock painting with wedding scene*

between the sexes and the family. These subjects are completely new in rock art. In the context of this article only three sites with rock paintings will be discussed: İkizada, Göktepe, and Balıktaş.

A key for understanding the numerous family scenes of the Latmian paintings is the site of İkizada at the north shore of the lake (Peschlow-Bindokat 2006a: 53-54, figs. 40 a-e). The picture in question fills exactly the width of the ceiling of a "cave," a space closed by different rocks (fig. 3). The painting is well preserved and shows fourteen human figures, most of them women, and some ornaments.

This picture seems very well composed. In the center a big couple, a man and a woman, are framed by smaller dancing women to the right and sitting women to the left in a kind of *sacra conversazione*. The imagery seems to be quite clear. What can it represent if not a wedding scene? In this case it would constitute the earliest known representation of a wedding scene anywhere.

When we found the first rock painting in 1994 near Göktepe, which is one of the most important paintings, we proposed as an interpretation a wedding scene, but with a big question mark. Today, after knowledge of the İkizada painting, this question mark seems much less warranted.

The location of the Göktepe painting encompasses a small courtyard, framed by rocks, that gives the impression of a little nature sanctuary (Peschlow-Bindokat 2003: 51-57, figs. 42-47, 49). The pictures were placed onto the weathered underside and back side of the rock's brow at the east side of the courtyard. They show an assembly of numerous human figures, among them several couples and a group of dancing figures. Its borders have been worked, giving it a frame which was set in red. The center of this picture seems to be a hollow in the lower zone that was painted. Due to the effects of weathering, the actual motif can no longer be recognized, but it may have shown a couple. The imagery of the Göktepe painting is more or less the same as that of İkizada.

The site of Balıktaş can also be understood as a little nature sanctuary. It looks like a "rock house" consisting of a big rock lying on two others, with the entrance at the south side and a rock bench along the western face. The ceiling block is weathered on its under side in many little hollows like a coffered ceiling (Peschlow-Bindokat 2003: 22-23, figs. 16a-17f). Each hollow has its own picture with different motifs: humans, ornaments, and hands. The most fascinating paintings are located in two neighboring hollows near the entrance side, showing to the left as the main motif a couple, a man and a woman, and to the right, a mother and child, both surrounded by ornaments (Peschlow-Bindokat 2007: 163).

Before continuing I want to summarize the arguments for understanding the meaning of these paintings. The most important point seems to be their relation to the mountain and to the water, which is evident from three perspectives: a. The distribution of the sites around the peak; b. The orientation of some sites directly towards the peak; and c. The proximity of water in a generally arid mountain region.

The second point is the subject of the paintings: the human figure in its social context, especially in the form of a couple — man and woman, dancing groups, groups of mother and child — shown in what seem to be family and wedding scenes. The subject is the family and its survival. In a metaphorical sense, the couples of men and women can be understood as symbols for fertility. The sites with the paintings are little sanctuaries; they are places where people perhaps came together to celebrate weddings or births in front of the cult place on the top of the mountain from which they asked for blessings for themselves and their fields.

Within the multitude of family pictures one rock painting stands apart. It was placed in a cave on the northern slope of the deep, romantic valley of Karadere. Other than the peak, this may be the most important prehistoric cult place of the Latmos (Peschlow-Bindokat 2003: 57-65, figs. 50-58b).

The incline of the slope at the site is set off, forming a terrace-like area which, except for a gap at the eastern side, is enclosed by rocks all around. This creates a small courtyard which, similar to Göktepe, brings to mind the setting of a nature sanctuary. The cave with the painting is located in the northwestern corner of this courtyard. The interior of the cave looks like the room of a little chapel or temple. The rock face shows traces of different weathering. The floor was paved with rock slabs. At the foot of the rock cliff sits a small rock-cut bench. As exceptional as the cave room is the painting, which shows an assemblage of several human figures and one animal (fig. 4). Most are line drawings of frontal figures. Only the fourth, seventh, and tenth figures are set apart from the others by means of their physical largeness, their hand positions, and their body volume. They apparently are wearing long robes. The principal one seems to be the fourth figure from the left, whose elevated position underneath an arc-shaped weathering edge in the rock raises him above the crowd.

Quite curious is the T-shaped or antenna-like headdress of several figures, especially noticeable on the fourth figure from the left. Since the head of the animal, too, has such a shape, the headgear may connote horns. Such figures go back as far as the Palaeolithic period and they are called God of the Horns or interpreted as shamans.

The picture at Karadere, which has nothing to do with the family scenes of the other Latmian paintings and must have therefore another meaning, probably represents the gods of the Latmos. This interpretation is suggested by the following observation. A shallow, round hollow in the rock is located at the side of the entrance (Peschlow-

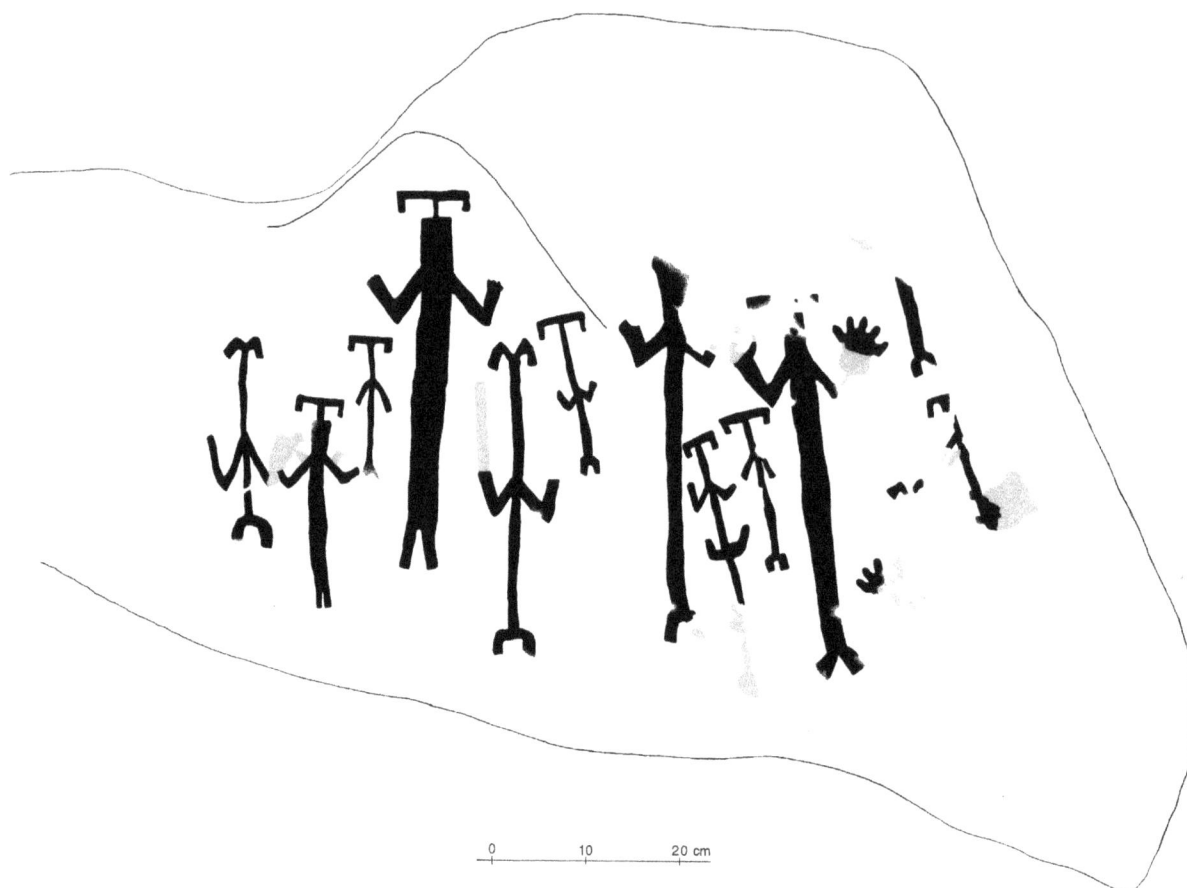

*Figure 4. Karadere Cave, copy of the rock painting with representation of the Latmian (?) gods*

Bindokat 2003: 62, figs. 55 a-b). This cup cut in the rock served probably for certain rites related to the cult practice of this holy place in front of the peak. Perhaps libations were carried out during prayers for rain. Looking from this spot to the main mountain range only the highest peak — which was the sacred stone — becomes visible (Peschlow-Bindokat 2003: 63, fig. 56). The remaining silhouette of jagged mountain peaks is hidden by the rock cliff opposite.

After climbing this cliff one overlooks the entire mountain range (Peschlow-Bindokat 2003: 64, fig. 57). This particular placement raises the question whether the figures on the cave's wall are possibly the personifications of the various mountain peaks. Quite possibly the dominating fourth figure personifies the main peak, the place of the old stone and rain cult. Therefore we consider the Karadere Cave as a sanctuary of the weather and the mountain god. But I don't want to exclude another explanation of the human figures of the cave as shamans, based on the supposition that the idea of shamanism was still alive at this time in western Anatolia. In this case this picture could be understood as a scene of rain magic.

**Conclusions**

What can we say at the moment about cult practices in the

Latmos in prehistoric times? The most important place was the peak as a center of an old stone and rain or fertility cult. We have understood the family scenes of the rock paintings as the expression of a fertility cult related to the peak, but the Karadere Cave, however, as a sanctuary of the weather and mountain god (or perhaps a place where shamans came together for rain magic in front of the peak).

At the Karadere Cave, but also at other sites, we found cup-shaped hollows cut in the rock ground, most of them with a view of the peak, as the example of Basmak Burnu — here fig. 5 — which is located near a rock face with paintings. Perhaps these hollows were used in the Latmos for libations in honor of the weather god. Such cuttings are known from other places in Anatolia (Neve 1996: 41-56) and also elsewhere in the world.

Another example for ritual practices is the miniature vessel from the Cave of Christ, a place that we identified as a sanctuary of the mountain god. In the valley of the Cave of Christ and its neighborhood we found other gifts for the gods which were deposited in rock crevices or under rocks, such as the bear figurine (Peschlow-Bindokat 2006a: 92-93, figs. 91a - 92).

The most exciting find, however, is a fragment of a big

*Figure 5. Basmak Burnu, rock cup in the neighbourhood of a rock painting with view on the peak*

amphora which came to light in 2006 under a rock not far away from the site of the figurine of the bear (Peschlow-Bindokat 2006a: 93, fig. 93). This piece is unique. Above the handle sits a male figure in appliqué with horns on his head. This image immediately reminds one of the main figure of the Karadere Cave (fig. 4). It must represent the same person. If I am right, the main gods of the Latmos were worshipped also in the settlements.

The cult tradition of the weather and mountain gods was taken over by the Greeks and the Byzantines. The weather god was replaced by Zeus Akraios. The Hellenistic temple of this deity on the back side of the main mountain range corresponds to the prehistoric sanctuary of the Karadere on the other side. The peak which lies between these two sanctuaries (fig. 1) was the main cult place of the region. The Byzantines erected here a cross to ban the magic pagan powers of this old place and to adapt the cult site for their own needs. In this context it is interesting to remark that the Byzantines considered also the prehistoric rock paintings as pagan symbols. We know two examples. In one case, the site in the Çinedere (Peschlow-Bindokat 2002: 255), they overpainted the prehistoric painting; in another one at the north shore of Lake Bafa near Sütlü they put a cross above

it (Peschlow-Bindokat 2006b: 269-270, 274, fig. 2); they used the same procedure for the peak.

The Greek successor of the prehistoric mountain god was Endymion, who lived in a cave and can be understood as a personification of the mountain. He had sanctuaries in the old city of Latmos as well as in Herakleia. In Byzantine times his prehistoric sanctuary in the valley of the Cave of Christ became a prayer room and was decorated with frescoes. The same happened with the cave under the "adyton" of Endymion in the city of Latmos, where Christ Pantokrator took his place.

It is a well-known phenomenon that a new people arriving in a country with a different religion takes over the old local cult places to use them for their own convictions (Haas 1982: passim). For this procedure the Latmos is a new and especially convincing example. The local cults of these mountains which emerged from this mysterious rocky landscape in prehistoric times maintained their power into the Middle Ages.

## Note

The manuscript was translated from German into English by W. Rudolph. Photos are by the author.

## References

GERBER, C. 2003. Die Arbeiten des Jahres 2006 in Herakleia und Umgebung (Bafa Gölü/Beşparmak). *Araştırma Sonuçları Toplantısı* 21/2.: 204-210.

HAAS, V. 1982. *Hethitische Berggötter und hurritische Steindämonen*. Mainz: Philipp von Zabern.

LAUMONIER, A. 1958. *Les cultes indigènes en Carie*. Paris: De Boccard.

LOBEL, E. & D. PAGE (ed.). 1955. *Poetarum Lesbiorum Fragmenta*. Oxford: Clarendon Press.

MÜLLENHOFF, M. 2005. *Geoarchäologische, sedimentologische und morphodynamische Untersuchungen im Mündungsgebiet des Büyük Menderes (Mäander), Westtürkei*. Marburg: Marburger Geographische Gesellschaft.

NEVE, P. 1996. Schalensteine und Schalenfelsen in Boğazköy-Hattusa (2. Teil). *Istanbuler Mitteilungen* 46: 41-56.

PESCHLOW, U. 1993. Latmos, in *Reallexikon zur byzantinischen Kunst* V: 651-716. Stuttgart: Hiersemann.

——2005. Die Latmos-Region in byzantinischer Zeit, in A. Peschlow-Bindokat, *Herakleia am Latmos. Stadt und Umgebung*: 161-201. Istanbul: Homer Kitabevi.

PESCHLOW-BINDOKAT, A. 2002. Die Arbeiten des Jahres 2000 in Herakleia am Latmos und dem zugehörigen Territorium (Beşparmak). *Araştırma Sonuçları Toplantısı* 19/1: 255-262.

——2003. *Frühe Menschenbilder. Die prähistorischen Felsmalereien des Latmos-Gebirges (Westtürkei)*. Mainz: Philipp von Zabern.

——2005a. *Feldforschungen in Latmos. Die karische Stadt Latmos*. Milet III 6. Berlin: De Gruyter.

——2005b. *Herakleia am Latmos. Stadt und Umgebung*. Istanbul: Homer Kitabevi.

——2006a. *Tarihöncesi Insan Resimleri. Latmos Dağları'ndaki Prehistorik Kaya Resimleri*. Istanbul: Sadberk Hanım Müzesi.

——2006b. Die Arbeiten des Jahres 2004 im Latmos. *Araştırma Sonuçları Toplantısı* 23/2: 269-278.

——2007. Die prähistorischen Felsbilder des Latmos, in *Vor 12.000 Jahren in Anatolien. Die ältesten Monumente der Menschheit*: 162-165. Karlsruhe: Badisches Landesmuseum.

PHILIPPSON, A. 1936: *Das Südliche Jonien*. Milet III 5. Berlin: De Gruyter.

WIEGAND, T. 1913. *Der Latmos*. Milet III 1. Berlin: De Gruyter.

# From Elyanas to Leto: The Physical Evolution of the Sanctuary of Leto at Xanthos

*Jacques des Courtils*

The marshy character of the Letoon has not failed to strike every modern traveller who has visited the site ever since it was rediscovered in the nineteenth century, even though drainage related to cultivation has attenuated this phenomenon today. Many indications make it possible to think that the situation was the same in antiquity. In this essay my ambition is to attempt to reconstitute the natural environment of the Letoon as well as the archaeological problems which it poses.

The Letoon is located approximately 4 km from the shore of the Mediterranean, at the foot of a completely arid, rocky hill. In antiquity, the shore lay probably somewhat nearer, although the Letoon never was a coastal site. The sanctuary is located in the midst of the estuary of the Xanthos River that, except for the already mentioned hill, forms a 100 km² marshy plain through which the river makes its way towards the sea. Rising from the Taurus range, the Xanthos flows year round; sometimes during the winter or spring it rises above the sand levees built along it by the modern villagers and floods part of the estuary. Water storage done by the farmers of the valley upstream of Xanthos and of the Letoon, although it contributes to a decrease in the amount of water reaching the plain, still allows a considerable quantity to flow through. One can imagine that, in antiquity, the size of the river was greater and floods were even stronger.

A geomorphological survey carried out over two years in the estuary of the Xanthos by a combined French and Turkish team has confirmed observations already made several years ago by French geographers and geomorphologists (Bousquet and Péchoux 1984): the bed of the river itself probably shifted several times in the plain, and could have divided into several arms.

As for the hill that rises 40 m above the Letoon, it constitutes simply a karstic outcrop in the middle of the estuary. It is

thus related to the rock base that rises on either side of the valley, that is the mountains the Ancients called Cragos (to the west) and Massicytos (to the east), whose summits reach an altitude of more than 2000 m.

The site where the Letoon was built is located at the foot of this hill, at the place where the rocky slope meets the alluvial ground of the plain and slips underground. We will describe its general topography in a moment, but it is important to note at this point that the ancient inhabitants built there a terrace cut within the foot of the hill, on which were erected the temples of Leto, Apollo, and Artemis, around 400 BC. This terrace has been on several occasions in modern times the location of a phenomenon which brings information of great importance: at the end of particularly wet winters, the local inhabitants have witnessed the astonishing spectacle of veritable geysers erupting with considerable pressure from the ground through the numerous cracks present in the rock underlying the terrace.

To complete this quick description of the environmental conditions of the region, let us add that the climate of this area is hot, as everyone knows, but also that the presence of the Taurus range ensures a constant water supply throughout the year. In addition, it is notable that 20 km to the north of the Letoon, on the eastern side of the valley, is a place called Saklı Kent where a tributary of the Xanthos gushes out of the rock with such considerable force that the gorge where it emerges has become today a popular location that attracts the inhabitants of the entire region as well as tourists.

These details are essential to understand the reconstruction of the natural environment of the Letoon sanctuary that we will present below. Unfortunately no ancient description of the site is available to us, but only poetic evocations. We will quote only Ovid's impressions from Book VI of the *Metamorphoses*, in which a character arriving at the

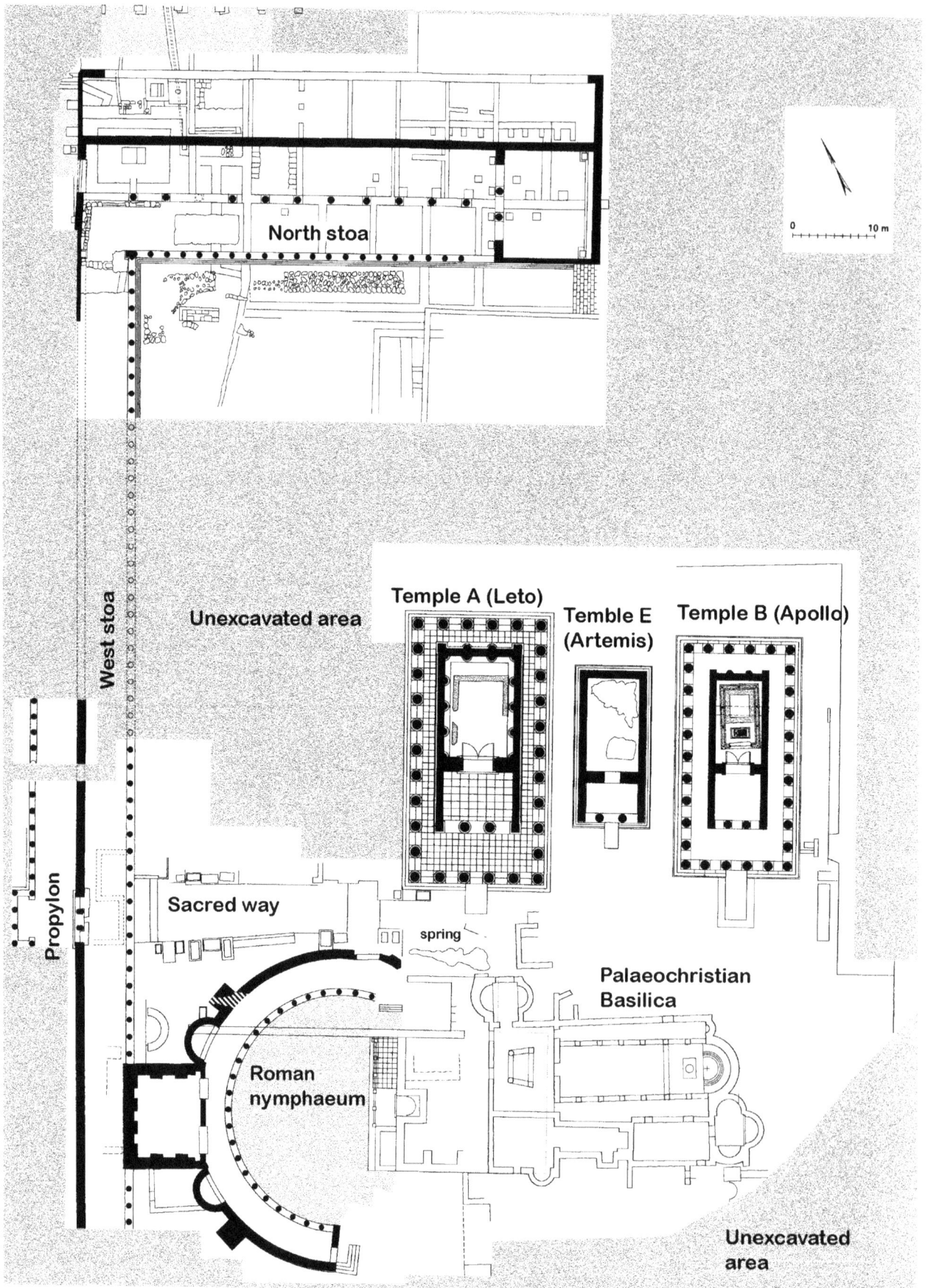

North stoa

West stoa

Propylon

Unexcavated area

Temple A (Leto)

Temble E (Artemis)

Temple B (Apollo)

Sacred way

spring

Palaeochristian Basilica

Roman nymphaeum

Unexcavated area

0    10 m

*Figure 1. Plan of the Letoon.*

Letoon says the following: "I traversed pastures with my companion, when suddenly I saw standing, in the middle of a pond, an ancient altar, blackened by the smoke of sacrifices and surrounded by swaying reeds" (324-326). One should undoubtedly not attribute to this text more historical value than it has; Ovid certainly did not come to the Letoon. However, he may have learned somehow that the sanctuary was built in a wet place, even "in the middle of a pond," which is somewhat exaggerated, because the sanctuary would be at most "at the edge" of a pond, the hill on which it rests preventing its being surrounded by water. Nonetheless, all indications lead one to believe that the surroundings of the Letoon were already marshy in antiquity. Archaeological observations even show that it was a constant problem for those using the sanctuary.

Christian Le Roy (1991), then Alain Davesne (2000), have clearly showed by a topographic and stratigraphic study of the sanctuary that the oldest installations, datable to the seventh century BC, were buried under sandy alluvia and that this phenomenon continued unrelentingly through all periods. When excavations began in 1962, the excavators noted that the remains of Roman and Byzantine times were covered by more than 3 m of alluvia, but that the older vestiges were several meters deeper. Le Roy also showed in detail how the phenomenon of the gradual rise of the water table, caused by aggradation of the whole estuary, had consequences in the way the sanctuary was maintained. Without going over his study in detail, let us recall that the paved "sacred way" that connects the sanctuary's propylon with the foot of the temple terrace must have become submerged. To counter this problem, the ancient inhabitants naively believed that they could prevent the water from penetrating the sanctuary by awkwardly raising the threshold of the door of the propylon by placing within it re-used blocks intended to serve as a barrier.

Whatever one may think of this Sisyphean struggle against the rising waters, we can now try to describe more precisely both the natural characteristics of the Letoon and the man-made installations which made the Letoon a sanctuary so closely related to its surrounding landscape.

We must begin with a natural feature unfortunately no longer visible but which was the subject of an excavation and is of paramount importance. The site of a spring, which had risen in antiquity and whose water was still flowing through a natural crack in the rock and several joints in a pavement of limestone plaques, was discovered twenty years ago during excavations by Christian Le Roy (1990), thus confirming the myth which portrayed Leto coming to bathe her new born twins in a spring. At the same location, the presence of terra cotta figurines ranging from the Archaic period to Roman times attests to the sacred character of the place Le Roy had very convincingly identified as the sacred spring. This is a fundamental discovery since it lends substance to the myth of Leto and her children, and beyond mythology, it accounts for the very

foundation of the sanctuary. Indeed, the Lycians, just as their Anatolian predecessors of the Bronze Age, must have particularly venerated springs, having associated specific divinities with them: the Elyanas, local equivalents of the Nymphs (Laroche 1980; Bousquet 1992: 179). The name of the prehellenic divinity who reigned in this sanctuary before the emergence of the Greek cults is "the mother of this sanctuary", a title behind which one can recognize the presence of a Great Anatolian Mother, here settled by a spring.

The first cult of the "mother of this sanctuary" was probably established above this spring, on a rock outcrop which dominates it, as is quite clearly indicated by the presence of very high quality Attic potsherds discovered in the fill of the later temple, built probably at the end of the fifth century BC by the dynast Arbinas. It was he, as is demonstrated by an inscription, who also had the rocky terrace built, by cutting into the hillside, and had two other temples erected: one for Apollo, one for Artemis. A little further to the south, the terrace was spacious enough to accommodate altars; at any rate this seems the most appropriate location for them, as Le Roy always maintained. The altars no longer exist, but the presence of a church at the place where one can imagine them constitutes almost a proof. The situation here might even confirm the text of Ovid since the altars, on their high terrace, would appear to rise out of the marsh.

These are not the last of Arbinas's installations. When quarrying the rock of the hill to arrange a terrace intended for the temples, the Lycian workmen carved from the hillside two vertical faces laid out at right angles and framing the terrace of the temples to the north and east. We noted that the ground above the eastern face, the tallest because of the greater slope of the ground in which it was cut, was leveled. On the flat area thus created was arranged a terrace whose back wall is exactly parallel with the wall that dominates the temples. Behind this first terrace comes a second one, also parallel, but which retains cross walls either built or directly cut in the rock. All these construction traces lead us to restore a stoa (portico) dominating the sanctuary with, behind it at a slightly higher level, rooms whose function escapes us but that may have been dining rooms rather than any other type of installation (such as a hostel). The portico and the rooms turned at a right angle at their northern end, and continued westwards, following the wall of the terrace of the temples, then turned northwards again. At this point, however, since the rocky surface of the hill lay at a lower level, the buildings needed to be erected on raised foundations; segments of these foundations, in rusticated polygonal masonry, still survive in places.

Two rules thus govern the constructions in the eastern part of the sanctuary, that is, on the hill that dominates the temples: first, strict orthogonality; second, terracing. Information currently available leads us to attribute this construction work to the dynast Arbinas who, in about 400 BC, had three temples built, in purely Lycian building technique, honoring the divinities of the Apollinian triad whose worship he probably imported to the Letoon. We have here an exceptional case for the Graeco-Oriental world: installations on a large scale that follow rigorous geometry. Arbinas put in place here the radically new design of a religious sanctuary placed at the center of a stage based on domesticated nature, or more appropriately, nature carved and modeled with rigor.

The Letoon possessed an *alsos* (sacred grove). Since these sacred groves could be limited to a few trees, it appears useless to speculate where the alsos of the Letoon was located. Common sense, however, leads us to conclude that a sandy, waterlogged soil is not ideal for the growth of trees. One can thus reasonably ask whether the *alsos* could not have crowned the hill that dominates the Letoon. Today the hill presents a rocky and dismal portrait, inhospitable as it is to any vegetation. Nonetheless we might be able to imagine a sacred grove on this hill; its very existence would have prevented solifluction for a few centuries, thus ensuring its own perenniality.

At a date that is not precisely determined but certainly within the Hellenistic period (numerous clues suggest the third century BC), the inside of the sanctuary was refurbished with what one would describe today as "landscape architecture." The natural terrace of the (supposed) altars was lengthened towards the south by a building made up of two massive masonry blocks separated by a vaulted room in which a bench was built, obviously intended to receive small statues or offerings. Everything points to this room being a false grotto and that it was built in honor of the divinities of water, the Lycian Elyanas, or Nymphs in their Greek personification. In front of the entrance of this false grotto stretched a flat area that was certainly filled with water.

In Roman times, undoubtedly following the visit of the emperor Hadrian in Lycia (138), a large half-moon shaped portico was built facing the grotto. The colonnade of this portico was reflected in the water which extended from its base to that of the grotto of the Nymphs. Should we perhaps see here the pond evoked by Ovid?

We finally need to mention a small topographical problem that affects our "reading" of the sanctuary's natural environment. We have known since the excavations of the 1960s that the sanctuary opened to the West via a propylon, already mentioned previously, whose ground plan is rather well preserved. This propylon was inserted in the long north-south boundary wall of the sanctuary that was used also as the back wall of two stoas, one placed inside the sanctuary, the other outside. Close to the northern end of this wall was discovered a door that apparently served as a secondary gate of the sanctuary. Lastly, on the northern side of the sanctuary, the excavations of Davesne revealed the presence of a third gate, located at a higher level since it was placed at the foot of the hill whereas the stoas

mentioned earlier stand at the edge of the marsh of the estuary. This high gate certainly marks the end of an access road to the sanctuary whose existence was revealed during the work of Moretti and Lemaître on the Letoon's theatre (Badie et al. 2004). Indeed, they showed that the theatre was constructed on an ancient road leading from the town of Xanthos. After the theatre was built, the road crossed the diazoma of the theatre. This road possesses a characteristic that is important for us, since it snaked its way along the Letoon hill a few meters above the surface of the marsh; that is, it had been built especially to avoid being made impassable by the floods of the Xanthos.

This arrangement, although it appears perfectly logical and leads us to pay homage to the practical sense of the ancients, nevertheless conceals a problem. If a secure and safe road existed that made access to the Letoon possible, why is it that the propylaia of the sanctuary were not located at the gate to which this road led? A definite answer to this question has recently been found, thanks to an interpretation of Strabo's text that says that the Letoon was accessible from the sea by boat (14. 3. 6). It is, in fact, impossible to imagine that this text alludes to boats sailing up the river Xanthos, since we have already seen that this river has an impressive flow, probably even greater in Antiquity, so that one can exclude that it ever was navigable. Consequently, only one solution remains: that one could reach the Letoon by sailing through the marsh which surrounded it.

Confirmation of this assertion was first reached in the conclusions of the research carried out by French and Turkish geomorphologists in the campaigns of 2006 and 2007. They indeed located near the Letoon traces of an ancient channel, completely filled today, but which could have provided access to the Letoon by water. This discovery explains the construction of propylaia opening onto the marsh. Furthermore, these observations lead us to conclude that the main entrance of the sanctuary was this lake gate that understandably consisted of a built propylon. One could go to the Letoon on foot by walking on the road that ran along the hillside, crossing the theatre and arriving at the northeast corner of the sanctuary, but the beautiful entrance, the grand gate, was what one reached by crossing the watery expanse that separated the Letoon from the Mediterranean shore. The Letoon was thus a sanctuary of water par excellence: surrounded by more or less stagnant water, containing captive water, giving rise to the running waters of a spring, it dealt entirely with the liquid element. Thus the legend that reports the arrival of Leto, the bathing of her children in a spring, and the transformation of the inhospitable peasants into frogs directly derived from the natural features of the place. The Lycians who built this sanctuary there were undoubtedly attracted by the presence of the spring, but they were also able to take extraordinarily ingenious advantage of the omnipresence of water. It was fated then that this same water which gave rise to the sanctuary also caused its death by submerging it slowly but unrelentingly. In the meantime the Lycian architects and "landscape artists" were able to develop one of the most decorated and best ordered sanctuaries of all Anatolia, by toying with a landscape that continued to retain eloquent testimonials of their actions.

**Note**

The manuscript was translated from French into English by Jacques Morin.

**References**

BADIE, A., S. LEMAÎTRE, & J.-C. MORETTI. 2004. Le théâtre du Létôon de Xanthos. Etat des recherches. *Anatolia Antiqua* 12: 145-186.

BOUSQUET, B. & P.Y. PÉCHOUX. 1984. L'évolution de la plaine alluviale du Xanthe (Turquie) depuis le début de l'holocène. *Recherches géographiques à Strasbourg (Hommages à René Raynal)*: 22-33.

BOUSQUET, J. 1992. Les inscriptions du Létôon en l'honneur d'Arbinas et l'épigramme grecque de la stèle de Xanthos. *Fouilles de Xanthos* 9: 155-188.

DAVESNE, A. 2000. La région des portiques du Létôon de Xanthos. *Comptes Rendus de l'Académie des Inscriptions et Belles-Lettres*: 615-631.

LAROCHE, E. 1980. Les dieux de la Lycie classique d'après les textes lyciens, in *Actes du Colloque sur la Lycie antique*: 1-6. Paris: Institut Français d'Etudes Anatoliennes d'Istanbul/Librairie d'Amérique et d'Orient Adrien Maisonneuve.

LE ROY, C. 1984. La lutte d'un sanctuaire contre l'évolution du milieu naturel: le Létôon de Xanthos en Lycie. *Bulletin de l'Association des Géographes Français*: 41-44.

——1990. La source sacrée du Létôon de Xanthos et son dépôt votif. *Bulletin de la Société Nationale des Antiquaires de France* [1988]: 125-131.

——1991. Le développement monumental du Létôon de Xanthos. *Revue Archéologique* 1991: 341-351.

# SACRED LANDSCAPES AND THE COLONIZATION OF THE SINOP PROMONTORY

## Owen Doonan

## Introduction

Sacred landscapes develop over time, across and between cultures. In a colonial situation the landscape is probably the most essential arena for working out relationships between communities who have natural conflicts of interest over land, resources, communications, and authority. Greek colonists seldom, if ever, held the kind of overwhelming military advantage that Roman or modern colonists have had over local groups whose territory they sought to occupy. Greek colonization was less a process of conquest and definition of territory, more an ongoing process of negotiation and relationship-building. Irad Malkin has applied the useful concept of "Middle Ground" to the discussion of cultural formations in the context of west Greek colonization (Malkin 2002). The Middle Ground model emphasizes the mediation of ethnically exclusive frameworks of identity through useful and creative misrepresentations across cultures. The result is a malleable emerging narrative, neither "us" nor "them," that provides a basis for mutually comprehensible social relationships between colonists and local communities. Malkin applies the model to the understanding of western Greek-related mythological traditions; the present paper seeks to offer preliminary thoughts on the colonial landscape as a medium for similar narratives. As in the west Mediterranean, the Middle Ground was expressed through sacred mytho-historical formations. The case of Sinope, however, is examined not through surviving mythological evidence but through monumental elaboration in the landscape.

## A Few Notes of Caution

The direct comparison of the evidence for sacred remains between one archaeological case study and another is highly problematic. Most remains relating to sacred activity outside of town centers are marginal, small-scale, and unevenly distributed, Differences in topography, research design, and interpretation complicate the process of recording sacred

landscapes through archaeological survey. Alcock and Rempel (2005) have recently pointed out the challenges of reconstructing patterns in the distribution of special purpose sites that are the most important archaeological evidence for sacred landscapes. On the whole, the more fine-grained survey designs have much greater success recording the fleeting traces of sacred sites: compare 0.2 sacred sites/ ha for the Laconia survey (Cavanaugh et al. 2002) to 0.001 sacred sites/ ha for the Minnesota Messenia Survey (McDonald and Rapp 1972; see Alcock and Rempel 2005 for a detailed comparison of these examples). Special sacred sites most often were unmarked by formal architectural monuments. More common are the small-scale offerings to the spirits (*daimones*) of a place like a wood, a spring, or a cave (de Polignac 1995: 14). Such places by their nature offer little visibility to survey archaeologists unless they survey off-site areas with closely-spaced (10-20 m) field walkers and carefully examine marginal locations like springs and caves.

De Polignac divided sanctuaries into several types based on their relationships to the urban center (*astu*) and function: urban, suburban or peri-urban, and extra-urban (de Polignac 1995: 21-25). His work established the great importance of the extra-urban sanctuaries for the organization of communities and suggested an important tension between the *astu* and the wilder spaces at or beyond the edge of the formal territory (*chora*) of a polis. He showed that the polis was an integrated sacred space in which urban, rural, and marginal places all played important and complementary roles. His thesis challenged the predominant perception up into the 1980s that the *astu* was the center of sacred life and thus archaeological interest.

## Sacred Landscapes in the *Chora* of Sinope: Methodology

Before discussing the evidence for sacred landscapes in the Sinop hinterland it is necessary to consider how that evidence

*Figure 1. CORONA photograph of the Sinop promontory highlighting the Boztepe, Demirci and Karasu valley sample quadrats. Dark areas are heavily forested offering almost no potential for systematic archaeological survey.*

was created. Since 1996 the Sinop Regional Archaeological Project (SRAP) has investigated the hinterland of one of the most important Greek colonies on the Anatolian Black Sea coast through systematic archaeological survey, geomorphological and palaeoenvironmental studies and limited excavations. The SRAP research program was primarily designed to characterize the patterns of land use, habitation, and organization of the various parts of Sinop promontory and to establish local patterns of exchange and infrastructure in order to reconstruct a history of community. Sinop is one of the most heavily forested provinces in Turkey. Conditions on the ground and the scale of the promontory as a unit for research (ca. 500 km²) require that we sample the survey zone rather than attempt to cover every part equally (Doonan 2004b; fig. 1). Our intent is to create a record in the major topographic and ecological zones of the promontory to assess how the various sub-regions functioned together economically and socially through time. These zones include the territory immediately surrounding Sinop port, the east and west coasts, the Karasu valley, and the highlands. In each of these zones we are identifying several 1-5 km² units called quadrats that we examine intensively in a series of 20-50

field-walking tracts. Field-walkers are closely spaced (for the most part 10 m apart) so that they should notice small, isolated deposits where present. Contextual (topographic, environmental), spatial, and material data are collected from each tract. We map all survey tracts regardless of whether archaeological loci (places where evidence of human use is identified) are identified. We interpret different kinds of archaeological loci based on analysis of the nature of archaeological finds, their distribution, and context. It is important to understand that our record of sites in Sinop is strongly conditioned by factors of preservation and visibility – we have glimpses rather than a census of past times and practices (see discussion of the effects of landscape preservation in Wilkinson 2004).

The survey is supported by programs of geomorphological and palaeoenvironmental research (Doonan et al. 2001), historical analysis and ceramic studies (Bauer 2006) that permit us to analyze production and distribution of goods throughout the promontory. The overall design of SRAP tends to be more oriented towards economy and settlement than specifically to understanding sacred landscapes. Although the closely-spaced intensive fieldwalking

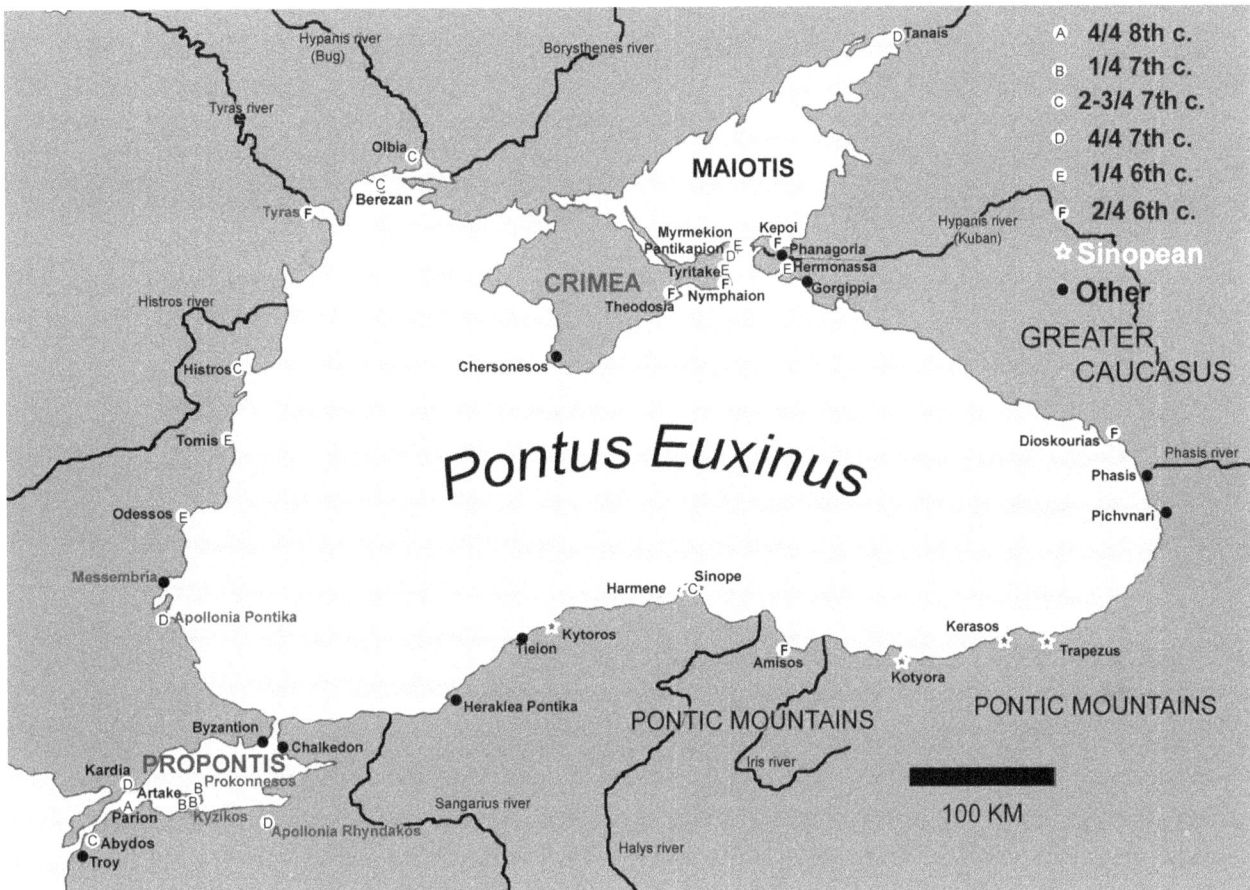

*Figure 2. Map of the Black Sea, showing major Milesian colonial foundations*

conforms to the recommendations of Alcock and Rempel it is still possible that the nature of our survey has resulted in the under-representation of small sacred sites.

**Overview: Settlement and Colonization, Seventh – Second Centuries BC**

The archaeological record shows that the Greeks founded their port town of Sinope at the edge of a territory that was inhabited by other groups. The Greek colony of Sinope appears to have been established in a time of intensifying trans-Pontic or circum-Pontic maritime interaction (fig. 2). In 2000 SRAP excavated a pre-Greek settlement just beneath the later city walls that showed significant parallels in ceramics and architecture to the pre-Greek settlements of the North Pontic region (Doonan 2004a; 2007). This may have been a colony or a fishing camp, and similar coastal settlements have been identified around the promontory (Gerze, Akliman and others) suggesting a new coastal-oriented settlement pattern (Doonan 2007). Because location on the coast decreases a settlement's agricultural catchment by 50% or more we can argue that these communities pursued maritime economic benefits through fishing, trade, or some other means. Non-Greek communities were also present in the hinterland at the time of colonization (Doonan, Casson, and Gantos 2008). The ceramics and architecture typical of these inland

communities were distinct from those found on the coast, suggesting the Greeks may have come into a rather complex social situation.

According to the available archaeological and historical record, Greek colonists from the city of Miletus established the port city of Sinope in the later seventh century BC (Boysal 1959). Shortly after the foundation of Sinope the town established a chain of colonies extending to the metal-rich eastern Pontus. The eastern colonies maintained close economic and political ties with the mother city from the sixth century at least down to around 400 BC, since Sinope was represented as the guarantor of the town of Cotyora when the latter was threatened by Xenophon's army (*An.* 5.5.7-10). In contrast to a rather aggressive approach to controlling the eastern Pontus, there is very little evidence for Greek engagement with the hinterland on the Sinop promontory before the fourth century BC.

Persian influence in the eastern Pontus expanded greatly during the early fourth century, driven in part by the ambitions of the local satrap Datames (Doonan 2003b). At this time Sinope's relationship with its colonies was likely severed and Sinope itself fell under Persian sway. Around this time suburban amphora production was established on the Boztepe coast about 1 km east of the town (Garlan and Tatlıcan 1997; 1998). SRAP has recorded several sites on

Boztepe that are likely to be farmsteads contemporary with the kilns (Doonan 2004a). Amphoras identical to the ones from Boztepe have been documented in several parts of the Sinop hinterland, in particular the coastal site of Keçioğlu in the Demirci valley.

Also dating to the fourth century are several columnar grave monuments with non-Greek names from the Kumkapı cemetery on the mainland just outside the town wall (French 2004: 14-45; 47-54). This had been a primarily Greek cemetery before the fourth century and these finds suggest that Greeks and non-Greeks were mixing in the city and the countryside. A fifth/fourth century miniature column of *Manes elaiopoles*, an oil seller of Paphlagonian origin, is particularly interesting for this discussion (French 2004: no. 28). Manes's monument, coinciding with the expansion of Hellenized settlements on Boztepe and in the hinterland, may point to the emergence of Sinope's olive industry famous in later Hellenistic and Roman times (Doonan 2003a). The products of this industry may be traced through the extensive distribution of Sinop amphoras from the fourth-third centuries BC (Avram 1999; Fedoseev 1999; De Boer 2001).

Contemporary with these changes SRAP has documented a significant increase in settlement density along the coasts of the promontory, the establishment of contacts between inland, coastal, and overseas communities and the establishment of Greek-related sanctuaries in the highlands (Doonan 2004a: ch. 4; Doonan and Bauer 2005). Although the process of colonization began with the Milesian colony in the late seventh century, the effective colonization of the Sinop hinterland took place in the fourth century as part of the reorganization of the city's economy.

**Evidence for Temples and Cults**

Much of the monumental evidence for cultic activity at Sinope is concentrated near the town center, as with other Greek cities. A fourth-third century inscription detailing the rights and responsibilities of the priest of Poseidon Helikonios was seen on the grounds of the Greek school at Sinop in the late nineteenth century (Mordtmann 1884; cited from French 2004: no. 8). Another fourth century inscription recording a dedication by the *prytany* to Hestia Prytaneia (guardian of the *prytany*) was found on Boztepe overlooking the city (French 2004: no 7). One of the best-known religious monuments of Sinope is the suburban temple of Sarapis excavated by Budde and Akurgal just to the east of town within the grounds of the museum (Akurgal and Budde 1956). Decorative architectural terrracottas including the well-known Gorgon antefixes establish the religious use of the site at least as early as the sixth century. A wide variety of terracotta votives in association with the temple were dedicated to Sarapis, Dionysos, Herakles, and Isis (Akurgal and Budde 1956). The terracottas were the basis of Budde's argument that the temple was dedicated to Sarapis and Isis, following a tradition preserved in

Tacitus (*Hist.* 4.83-84) that Sinope had a grand temple to Sarapis from which Ptolemy I brought the cult image to Egypt (Doonan 2003b). Several Roman (first-second c. AD) inscriptions from the town are dedicated to Sarapis and Isis (French 2004: no. 115), Heliosarapis (French 2004: no. 114), and a statue base honoring Reipane, possibly a priestess in the cult of Sarapis (French 2004: no. 172).

A third-second century BC funerary inscription honoring Saitta daughter of Nymphodorus and priestess of Ino Leukothea was also found in the city (French 2004: no. 84). Saitta's non-Greek name is particularly interesting, again raising the possibility that significant intermingling of Greeks and non-Greeks was taken for granted up to the higher social strata of the community.

One of the few sacred inscriptions found outside of the port of Sinope was a dedication to Zeus Dikaiosynos by Pythes son of Dionysios. This inscription was found in the town of Gerze, 40 km southeast of the town of Sinope (French 2004: no. 75). It dates to the second-first centuries BC, making it one of few indications of cultic activity outside of the city before Roman times. A sanctuary site on top of Asar Tepe in the highlands above Gerze was first reported by Işın (1998: 109; pl. 23). Remains from the site included numerous terracotta bull figurines, fine wares including lamp fragments and a spindle bottle, and Mithridatic coins that were purchased by the Sinop Museum. Based on the finds, Işın suggested this was a sanctuary of Zeus. Extensive traces of burning and fine ware deposits were documented by the SRAP team in 2003. At 1040 m above sea level, Asar Tepe is one of the highest points of the coastal mountain chain. Rising more than 600 m above the Sorkum Dere, the mountain has a dramatic peak and distinctive form (fig. 3). The site still has sacred associations as a burial spot for a local saint (dede) and the focus of annual rituals dedicated to Hızır İlyas.

**Tumulus at Kayanın Başı, Sorkum**

The sanctuary at Asar Tepe is intervisible with a small sanctuary complex that may help us to understand a key strategy for the creation of the "Middle Ground" between Greeks and locals. Locus L03-01 was a small prehistoric settlement that caught the attention of the later Hellenistic inhabitants of the valley, who built a tumulus at the site and left a small deposit of bones and fine wares (figs. 4, 5, 6). The prehistoric settlement has also attracted the attention of looters who have dug a large pit into the site. The main ceramic scatter marking the prehistoric site measures approximately 35 x 30 m (0.1 ha). The tumulus measures approximately 15 m across with little pottery present. The deposit of Hellenistic fine wares was small and isolated (about 40 m east of the tumulus), perhaps representing a small shrine, a single sacrificial offering or burial.

Tumuli and tombs have been linked by several authors to the development of "ancestralizing strategies" – narratives that

*Figure 3. Profile of Asar Tepe (Sorkum village, Gerze district – Sinop), site of an extramural sanctuary, possibly of Zeus Dikaiosynos.*

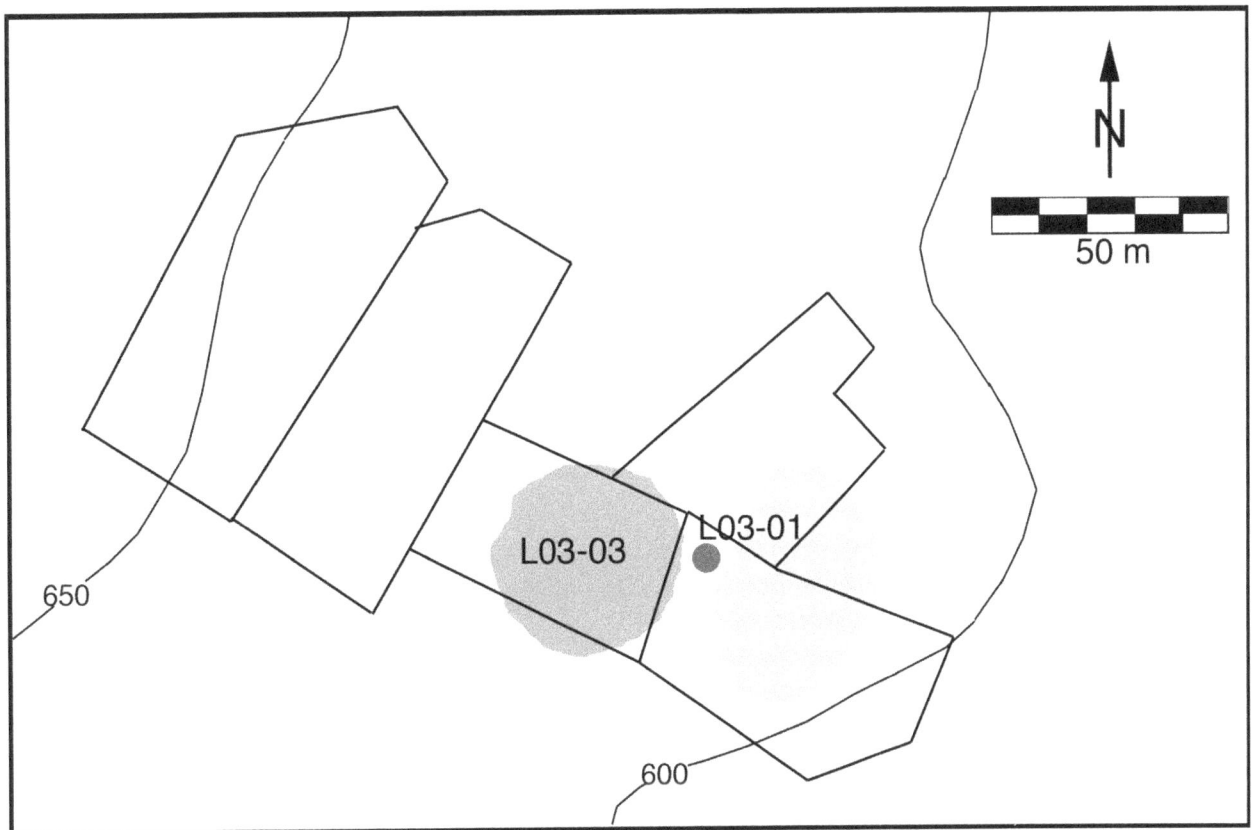

*Figure 4. Plan of the prehistoric site and Hellenistic deposit (L03-01) and tumulus (L03-03) at Kayanın Başı. The darker shading marks the extent of the tumulus while the lighter shading indicates the extent of the prehistoric scatter. The grey dot indicates the position of the votive deposit.*

Figure 5. Site of Kayanın Başı showing the area of ceramic scatter. Note the profile of Asar Tepe on the opposite side of the gorge.

Figure 6. Ceramics from the site of Kayanın Başı including (A) Early Bronze Age ceramics, (B) chipped blades and ground stone tools, and (C) Hellenistic fine wares and an amphora handle.

establish authority over territory (Hall 1997: 138-40; 2002: 23). This phenomenon is mostly connected to the Archaic and even earlier periods in Greece. An interesting exception was cited by Alcock and Rempel (2005: 37-39): the Helots in Messenia established numerous and more monumental tomb cults in the countryside after they were liberated from the Spartans. Tomb cults were part of a process of claiming the lands as ancestral and rightfully belonging to the Helots. In the hinterland of Sinope the process was not one of the liberation of a long-oppressed minority. Colonization of the Sinop promontory was a process of entanglement and integration of Greek and local communities (Doonan 2006). Newcomers were in need of their own ancestralizing strategy to create a shared tradition with locals. The local Bronze Age sites are typically mounded in form and can often be mistaken for tumuli (see fig. 7, the site of Kocagöz Tepe in the village of Demirci). In 1997 SRAP recorded a cluster of tumuli near Kocagöz Tepe (Doonan et al. 1999; Doonan 2004a; Erzen 1956; Burney 1956; Yakar 1985: 244). They look like smaller replicas of the Bronze Age site and are situated on the landward side of a coastal settlement (figs. 8 and 9). Note that these tumuli were not meant to be seen from the sea (where most of the Greek action was), but to be encountered in the Middle Ground

between the Greek-related settlement and the hinterland. A similar pattern can be observed in the Karasu valley east of Sinope where tumulus cemeteries are situated behind settlements at Akliman, Karacakese and Osmaniye (Doonan 2004a: fig. 4-8). The Demirci tumuli appear to be typical of the Hellenistic tumuli in Sinope: located near a prehistoric site and set on the landward side of a coastal settlement.

## Pontic Anatolia: an Emerging Structure

There has been almost no systematic survey conducted in Pontic Anatolia outside of Sinop province, but it is possible to make some tentative observations that should be followed up with additional research. The first point concerns the Asar Tepe – Sorkum pattern of remote highland sanctuaries. A highland temple of Zeus (Bonitenos) has been recorded in the highlands behind the Sinopean colony of Kytoros (Marek 2003: 104-06). The remains include a jumble of limestone blocks set on a high hill overlooking the Devrekanı Çayı near the village of Megre (Marek 2003: fig. 149). Like the site of Asar Tepe, this temple commands a view that encompasses a likely pass through difficult mountains (fig. 10). A similar temple at Kale Tepe overlooking the main highway south

*Figure 7. Kocagöz Tepe, an Early Bronze Age settlement in Demirci village, Sinop.*

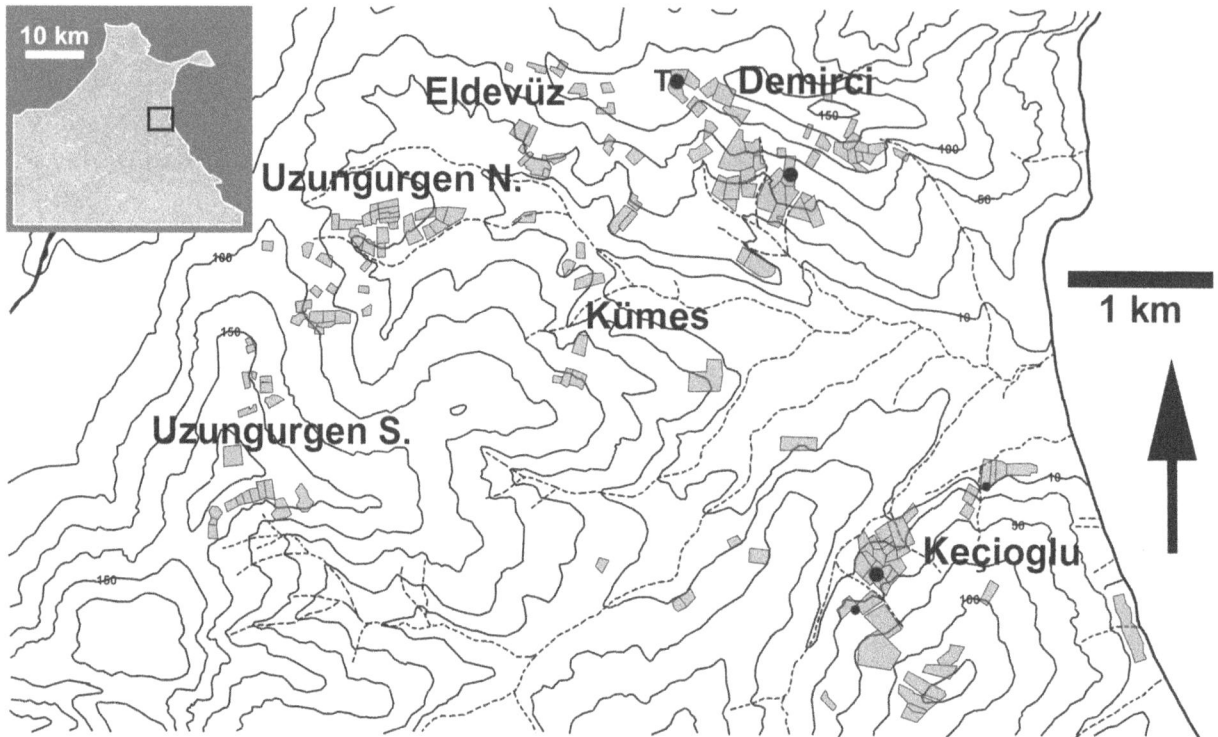

Figure 8. Map of Hellenistic sites identified by the Sinop Regional Archaeological Project in the Demirci valley. Several settlements were recorded in the Keçioğlu and Demirci districts. The distribution of settlements suggests a coastal orientation as in the Roman period when a major industrial site was established along the beach. This important beach site was not surveyed by SRAP as it was under investigation by the team led by Dr. Dominique Kassab of Bilkent University. Note the position of the tumuli marked by the letter "T" along the northern ridge. The tumuli are inland of the settlements along the coast.

Figure 9. Tumulus on the north ridge of Demirci valley.

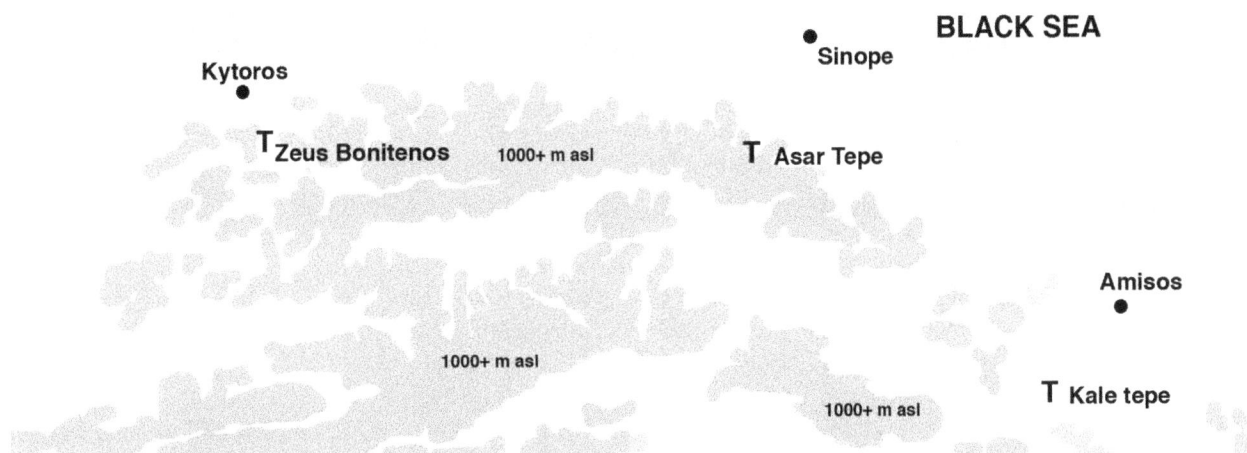

*Figure 10. Map of mountain temples in the central Black Sea region: Zeus Bonitenos (Bartin), Asar Tepe (Sinop), Kale Tepe (Samsun). Shaded areas indicate highlands above 1000 m elevation.*

of Amisos (Samsun) has recently been documented (Bilgi et al. 2004: 133; Atasoy 2003: 1334). Early excavations by Biliotti in the 1880s yielded numerous terracotta figurines of bulls and human (especially female). A first century BC inscription recorded the temple to Apollo Didymeus and the extant architecture is a double set of walls (outer structure 12.8 x 9.7 meters) surrounding a spring. As in the case of Asar Tepe, Kale Tepe is thought to be the burial spot of a local dede and a focus of continuing votive traditions.

Passing through the difficult and under-populated Pontic mountains in the fourteenth century, the famous traveler Ibn Battuta stopped at a "hospice in the mountains where there was no habitation" (Gibb trans. 1962: 465). From that time until the travels of William Hamilton in the 1830s (Hamilton 1842), religious installations offered a safe haven for those passing through this difficult territory (Doonan 2004a: 140). Temples, churches, mosques and saints' tombs are common but powerful reminders of the traditions of making and refashioning the ancestors of place, and of the persistence of such narratives in the sacred landscapes of Anatolia.

## References

AKURGAL, E. & L. BUDDE. 1956. *Vorläufiger Bericht über die Ausgrabungen in Sinope.* Türk Tarihi Kurumu V.14, Ankara: Türk Tarih Kurumu.

ALCOCK, S. & J. REMPEL. 2005. The more unusual dots on the map: "special purpose" sites and the texture of landscape, in P. Guldager Bilde & V. Stolba (ed.) *Surveying the Greek chora: a region in comparative perspective*: 13-26. Aarhus: Aarhus University Press.

ATASOY, S. 2003. Amisos, in D.V. Grammenos & E.K. Petropoulos (ed.) *Ancient Greek colonies of the Black Sea*: 1331-1377. Thessaloniki: Archaeological Institute of Northern Greece.

AVRAM, A. 1999. Matériel amphorique et non amphorique dans deux sites de la Chora d'Istros (Histria Pod et Cogealac), in Y. Garlan (ed.) *Production et commerce des amphores anciennes en Mer Noire*: 215–230. Aix-en-Provence: Publications de l'Université de Provence.

BAUER, A. 2006. *Fluid communities: maritime interaction and cultural identity in the Bronze Age Black Sea.* PhD Dissertation, University of Pennsylvania.

BILGI, Ö, S. ATASOY, Ş. DÖNMEZ & L. SUMMERER. 2004. Samsun (Amisos) Bölgesi'nin Kültürel Gelisimi Projesi. *Belleten* 68: 387-402.

BOYSAL, Y. 1959. Über die Älteren Fünde von Sinope und die Kolonizationsfrage. *Archäologischer Anzeiger*: 8-20.

BURNEY, C. 1956. Northern Anatolia before Classical times. *Anatolian Studies* 6: 179-203.

CAVANAUGH, W.G., J. CROUWEL, R.W.V. CATLING & G. SHIPLEY. 2002. *Continuity and change in a Greek rural landscape: the Laconia survey I: results and interpretation.* London: British School at Athens.

DE BOER, J. 2001. Sinopean amphora stamps on the northern and western Black Sea coasts, in S. Solovyev & G. Tsetskhladze (ed.) *Taman Antiquity 3: Greeks and natives in the Cimmerian Bosphorus*: 132-133. St. Petersburg: The State Hermitage Museum.

DE POLIGNAC, F. 1995. *Cults, territory, and the origins of the Greek city-state.* translated by J. Lloyd. Chicago: University of Chicago Press.

DOONAN, O. 2003a. Production in a Pontic landscape: the hinterland of Greek and Roman Sinope, in M. Faudot et al. (ed.) *Pont-Euxin et commerce: la genèse de la «Route de la soie»* (Actes du IXe Symposium de Vani): 185-198. Besançon: Presses Universitaires de Franche-Comté.

——2003b. Sinope, in D.V. Grammenos & E.K. Petropoulos (ed.) *Ancient Greek colonies of the Black Sea*: 1379-1402. Thessaloniki: Archaeological Institute of Northern Greece.

——2004a. *Sinop landscapes: exploring connection in the hinterland of a Black Sea port.* Philadelphia: University of Pennsylvania Museum of Archaeology and Anthropology.

——2004b. Sampling Sinop: archaeological survey in

a low visibility environment, in L. Wandsnider & E. Athanassopoulou (ed.) *Recent developments in Mediterranean survey archaeology*: 37-54. Philadelphia: University of Pennsylvania Museum of Archaeology and Anthropology.

——2006. Exploring community in the hinterland of a Black Sea port, in P. Guldager Bilde & V. Stolba (ed.) *Surveying the Greek chora: a region in comparative perspective*: 47-58. Aarhus: Aarhus University Press.

——2007. Colony and conjuncture: the early Greek colony at Sinope, in J. Cobet (ed.) *Frühes Ionien: Eine Bestandsaufnahme* (= DAI, *Milesische Forschungen* V): 613-620. Mainz-am-Rhein: Philipp von Zabern.

DOONAN, O. & A. BAUER. 2005. Sinop Province archaeological project: report on the 2003 field season. *Araştırma Sonuçları Toplantısı* 22: 275-284.

DOONAN, O., A. CASSON & A. GANTOS. 2008. Sinop Province archaeological project: report on the 2006 field season. *Araştırma Sonuçları Toplantısı* 25: 133-150.

DOONAN, O., A. GANTOS, F. HIEBERT, M. BESONEN & A. YAYCIOĞLU. 2001. Sinop regional archaeological survey 1998-1999: the Karasu Valley survey. *TÜBA-AR. Turkish Academy of Sciences Journal of Archaeology* 4: 113-135.

DOONAN, O., A. GANTOS, D. SMART & F. HIEBERT. 1999. Sinop Ili Yoğun Alan Araştırması, 1997. *Araştırma Sonuçları Toplantısı* 26: 359-371.

ERZEN, A. 1956. Sinop Kazısı 1953 Yılı Çalışmaları. *Türk Arkeoloji Dergisi* 6: 69-72

FEDOSEEV, N. 1999. Classification des timbres astynomiques de Sinope, in Y. Garlan (ed.) *Production et commerce des amphores anciennes en Mer Noire*: 27-48. Aix-en-Provence: Publications de l'Université de Provence.

FRENCH, D. 2004. *The inscriptions of Sinope* I. Bonn: Rudolf Habelt.

GARLAN, Y. & I. TATLICAN. 1997. Fouilles d'ateliers amphoriques à Zeytinlik (Sinop) en 1994 et 1995. *Anatolia Antiqua* 5: 307-316.

——1998. Fouilles d'ateliers amphoriques à Nisiköy et à Zeytinlik (Sinop) en 1996 et 1997. *Anatolia Antiqua* 6: 407-422.

GIBB, H. (transl.). 1962. *The travels of Ibn Battutah*, vol. 2. Cambridge: Cambridge University Press.

HALL, J, 1997. *Ethnic identity in Greek antiquity.* Cambridge: Cambridge University Press.

——2002. *Hellenicity: between ethnicity and culture.* Chicago: University of Chicago Press.

HAMILTON, W. 1842. *Researches in Asia Minor.* London: John Murray.

IŞIN, M.A. 1998. Sinop region field survey. *Anatolia Antiqua* 6: 95-139.

MALKIN, I. 2002. A colonial middle ground: Greek, Etruscan and local elites in the Bay of Naples, in C. Lyons & J. Papadopoulos (ed.) *The archaeology of colonialism*: 151-181. Los Angeles: Getty Research Institute.

MAREK, C., 2003. *Pontus et Bithynia: die römischen Provinzen im Norden Kleinasiens.* Mainz- am-Rhein: Philipp von Zabern.

MCDONALD, W.A. & G. RAPP, JR. (ed.). 1972. *The Minnesota Messenia expedition: reconstructing a Bronze Age regional environment.* Minneapolis: University of Minnesota Press.

MORDTMANN, J. 1884. Inscriptions of the province of Pontus. *Hellenikos Philologikos Syllogos* 15, appendix: 44-49 (in Greek).

WILKINSON, T. 2004. *Archaeological landscapes of the Near East.* Tucson: University of Arizona Press.

YAKAR, J.1985. *The later prehistory of Anatolia: the late Chalcolithic and early Bronze Age.* British Archaeological Reports International Series 268. Oxford: BAR.

# Sacred Boundaries and Protective Borders: Outlying Chapels of Middle Byzantine Settlements in Cappadocia

## Veronica Kalas

### Introduction

The rock-cut settlement located at the northern opening of the Peristrema Valley, in and around the modern Turkish villages of Selime and Yaprakhisar in western Cappadocia, offers an ideal opportunity to explore how sacred spaces in the form of churches and chapels interrelated with secular spaces identified as residential courtyard units in the Anatolian landscape during the Middle Byzantine period, around the tenth to eleventh centuries AD (fig. 1).[1] At Selime-Yaprakhisar, over a dozen courtyard dwellings consist of churches, halls, kitchens, stables and a variety of other multifunctional rooms arranged around open courtyards. They are situated along a one-kilometer stretch of the river in a nucleated pattern of settlement at an area of the valley that provided ample land for cultivation between the riverbed and the volcanic rock cliffs into which the medieval dwellings were carved. In addition to the courtyard complexes themselves, which usually include a church opening to one side of the courtyard, several chapels are scattered throughout the settlement, located either nearby one of the complexes or outside the settlement core. This paper aims to unravel the nuanced meanings of these chapels found at Selime-Yaprakhisar by examining their spatial relationships to the other architectural features recorded at the site and to the landscape as a whole. Often the chapels are placed close enough to either the settlement or the single dwelling unit, and oriented toward the latter in that case, so they appear to belong either to the settlement or the unit. Because of their location and spatial orientation, they form a type of sacred boundary or protective border that envelopes the medieval dwellers' living spaces. By recording and studying groups of dwellings as a whole and not simply the churches in isolation, it appears that certain chapels found encircling the settlements create a kind of

sanctified boundary in the landscape around the homes of the living.

In Byzantium, churches and chapels could function in a variety of ways depending on their contexts. For example, there are parish churches and cathedral churches; monastic churches and churches of the imperial palace; household churches and cemetery churches. Individual churches can be composed of multiple chapels as well (Babić 1969; Ćurčić 1977; Popović 1995/96). The use and meaning of these various churches and chapels, however, cannot be adequately surmised without understanding their archaeological, architectural, and topographical surroundings. This is especially true if epigraphic or textual sources that could offer more precise information on the churches' function or dedication are lacking. This point cannot be emphasized enough with regard to Capppadocia, where no such written documents record any kind of evidence for the churches that have been studied, moreover, in isolation. Thus far the only information available to interpret their function and meaning has been intrinsic to the physical characteristics of the churches themselves. In particular, most scholarship on Cappadocia has tended to focus on the church paintings (Jerphanion 1925-45; Thierry 1963; Restle 1967; Thierry 1983; Wharton 1988; Kostof 1989; Jolivet-Lévy 1991, 2001). Though Cappadocia's ecclesiastical paintings enrich our understanding of the developments in style and iconography of monumental religious imagery of the medieval period, they often remain isolated examples of religious and ceremonial spaces without their architectural settings and topographical surroundings.

In Cappadocia, a wide variety of carved spaces, including churches that are both painted and unpainted, have been found arranged around open courtyards to form complexes in which the local, landed aristocracy of the tenth to eleventh centuries lived and worked. The courtyard complex known

[1] I am grateful to Charles Gates, Robert Ousterhout, Amy Papalexandrou, Svetlana Popović, and Alicia Walker for reading various versions of this paper and offering their valuable insights and suggestions.

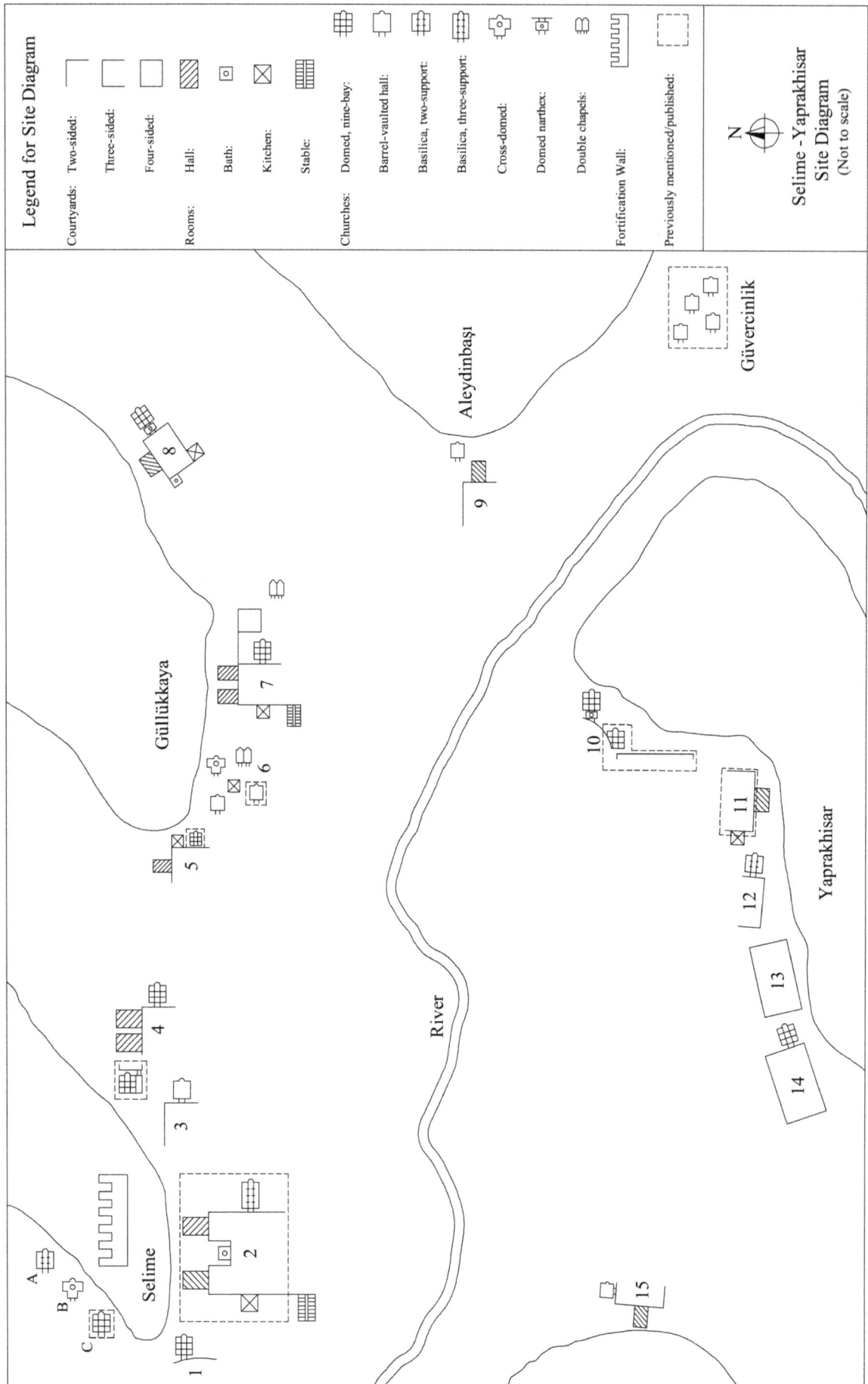

Figure 1. Selime-Yaprakhisar site diagram

as Hallaç Manastır first recorded by Lyn Rodley is often used as the typical example of a domestic Cappadocian courtyard unit (Rodley 1985: 11-26; Ousterhout 1997a; Mathews and Daskalakis-Mathews 1997). Some courtyard units, like Hallaç, are located randomly and in isolation, dispersed throughout the many volcanic valleys of the region. In other cases, several units numbering from half-a-dozen to over two dozen are concentrated in one locale, carved within a single geological outcrop or deposit of volcanic rock. These include the settlements at Selime-Yaprakhisar (Kalas 2000a, 2007a, 2007b), Çanlı Kilise (Ousterhout 2005a), Açık Saray and Göreme (Rodley 1985).

**The Settlement at Selime-Yaprakhisar**

At Selime-Yaprakhisar, fifteen courtyard units are carved into the thick volcanic outcroppings of Selime and Yaprakhisar, tall and imposing cliffs situated across the river from one another. The settlement's complexes are also carved into the outcrops of volcanic cones dispersed in and around these two cliffs. The courtyard complexes form the nucleus of the settlement, and the numerous outlying chapels that stand independently from the centrally located complexes are important for defining the settlement's outer limits. The settlement consists of not only the fifteen courtyard units themselves, but also the innumerable multi-level habitations that cannot be recognized as individual units because of their haphazard state of preservation due to natural erosion, continuous reuse over time, and inaccessibility. They are carved into the thick outcroppings as much as 200m above the valley floor in some examples at both Selime and Yaprakhisar. Most likely many more dwellings are not visible today because they have either been covered by thick layers of landslide or were carved below ground level. In addition, the stylistic features and working methods of the carvers show that most of the architecture at Selime-Yaprakhisar appears to belong to one period of settlement that could have begun in the early tenth century and ended by the late eleventh century, though many spaces that are stylistically indistinct could have been made earlier and used much later. In some areas rooms and façades appear to have remained unfinished which may indicate that the settlement was abandoned at some point shortly after its main period of habitation. The courtyard units themselves, including their monumental sculpted façades, fill a noticeable gap in the available evidence for Byzantine domestic architecture and secular use of space. Yet the types of churches attached to these units as well as the numerous chapels found nearby and beyond the settlement core also reveal significant aspects of medieval Byzantine settlement patterns (Kalas 2000a: 117-125).

One might expect a settlement the size of Selime-Yaprakhisar to require a large, centrally located public church, perhaps built out of masonry in order to distinguish it from the rock-carved examples, which the entire community of the valley and visitors from beyond could

have attended for worship. It appears that the masonry church of Çanlı Kilise, which is larger than the other churches on site and painted with high-quality frescoes, was the parish church of the town consisting of over two dozen courtyard units, each of which has its own private church (Ousterhout 2005a). Perhaps a similar analysis may apply to the large, unusually planned, and elegantly painted Tokalı Kilise for the settlement at Göreme though it is rock-cut (Epstein 1986; Kalas 2000b). At Selime-Yaprakhisar, however, a single, dominant church is absent. Similarly, the settlement of Açık Saray, which consists of seven or more courtyard units, does not have one large public church for the entire community (Rodley 1985). The notable absence of such a church at Selime-Yaprakhisar may simply be due to a lack of preservation, especially if it had been erected somewhere near the valley floor where erosion could have easily swept away a rubble-core masonry building or where the modern villagers could have quarried the cut stone of the building to construct their homes.

Although lacking a central church, Selime-Yaprakhisar does offer a myriad of other churches and chapels that can be divided roughly into two groups. The first group consists of the single, possibly private churches that form an integral part of individual courtyard complexes. The second group consists of two subtypes: outlying chapels serving either the courtyard dwellings (with their own, integrated churches) or the settlement as a whole. The first subtype marks the outer limits of the separate courtyard dwellings (Kalas 2000a). The second subtype includes isolated chapels that lie outside the settlement proper; they have no apparent attachment to any courtyard unit. Such chapels are located to the north of Selime and to the south of Yaprakhisar yet still within the Peristrema Valley. These latter outlying chapels define the outer limits of the settlement, because even though there is abundant rock suitable for dwellings beyond these two groups of chapels, none have been found.

**The Chapels**

As one approaches the Peristrema Valley from the wide Melendiz plain to the north, the imposing outcropping at Selime slowly comes into view. The majority of carved structures appear as one turns the corner of the cliff where it faces toward the south and the river valley. The modern village of Selime begins just before this point, however, where a group of three outlying chapels can also be found carved into the cones facing west (fig. 2). These chapels — labeled A, B, and C — in the cones to the north and west of Selime establish the northern limit of the settlement, about 500 m away from the settlement's first courtyard unit. Their plans are published here for the first time.[2] All three remained unpainted, and none appears to have been attached

---

[2] I discovered these chapels during field research conducted in the summers of 1996-1998 and discussed them in my doctoral dissertation (Kalas 2000a). They were measured and drawn in 2004 with the assistance of Zeynep Kutlu, and subsequently Eda Pekmezi. About a twenty minute walk northeast from here and below the high plateau of Selime is another isolated area of rooms carved into a group of cones surrounding a small,

Chapel C

*Figure 2. View of cones north of Selime with Chapels A, B, and C.*

to a courtyard unit, a fact apparent even in older photographs of the area from the beginning of the twentieth century before local villagers built their houses here (Sterrett 1919: 292).[3] Each one is small in scale, at about 5m x 5m, so that more than a handful of people standing inside would make the space cramped. All three chapels lack a narthex, and one enters the nave by way of a simple, barrel-vaulted porch. Although it is difficult to identify whether there were tombs inside these churches because of the hay and agricultural implements stored within, it is likely that they functioned as funerary chapels. They stand independently from one another and from the settlement at Selime further to the south, thereby resembling spatially the outlying chapels to the south of Yaprakhisar presented below, though they are different in plan. Perhaps the placement of these chapels on the outskirts of the settlement harkens to the common practice of locating cemeteries outside of settlements from the late antique to the medieval and modern periods as well (Nixon 2006: 22). In late antiquity, martyrs' shrines and

cemeteries were often placed outside city walls, and this practice appears to continue through the medieval period.

Chapel A is a basilica with a barrel-vaulted nave separated from barrel-vaulted side-aisles by an arcade, with two supports in each arcade (fig. 3). The two supports are beveled piers, of which only one remains intact. Though the supports have collapsed, the structure remains standing. At the east end of the chapel the two side aisles terminate with truncated sanctuaries containing altars. The central sanctuary contains the main altar but is unusual because of its square plan surmounted by a cupola instead of the traditional semicircular apse with a conch.[4] Chapel B has a domed, inscribed-cross plan (fig. 4). The dome rests on four arches that create the central square space but without supports and corner bays as in the cross-in-square plan, which is the more typical plan for the period. Three barrel-vaulted cross-arms extend from the central dome to the north, south, and west, while the semi-circular apse and

---

barrel-vaulted, single nave church known as the Doğan Yuvası Mevkiindeki Kilisesi, dated to the Middle Byzantine period on account of its frescoes. I consider this church and its loosely associated set of rooms as a separate settlement because it is located far from the main settlement at Selime and is relatively isolated (Jolivet-Lévy 1991: 332-333, pl. 185; Thierry 1975: 185; Giovannini 1972: plan 6, no. 23).

[3]    I thank Robert Ousterhout for bringing this reference to my attention.

[4]    Though rarely seen elsewhere, this innovative interpretation of the east end of a Byzantine church with a square apse surmounted by a cupola is also evident at another small chapel of the settlement associated with Area 6, discovered and recorded during the 2004 field season. This chapel has a barrel-vaulted nave and two barrel-vaulted cross arms immediately west of the sanctuary to create a Latin cross shape in plan; the sanctuary itself is a domed square.

NORTH OF SELİME
CHAPEL A

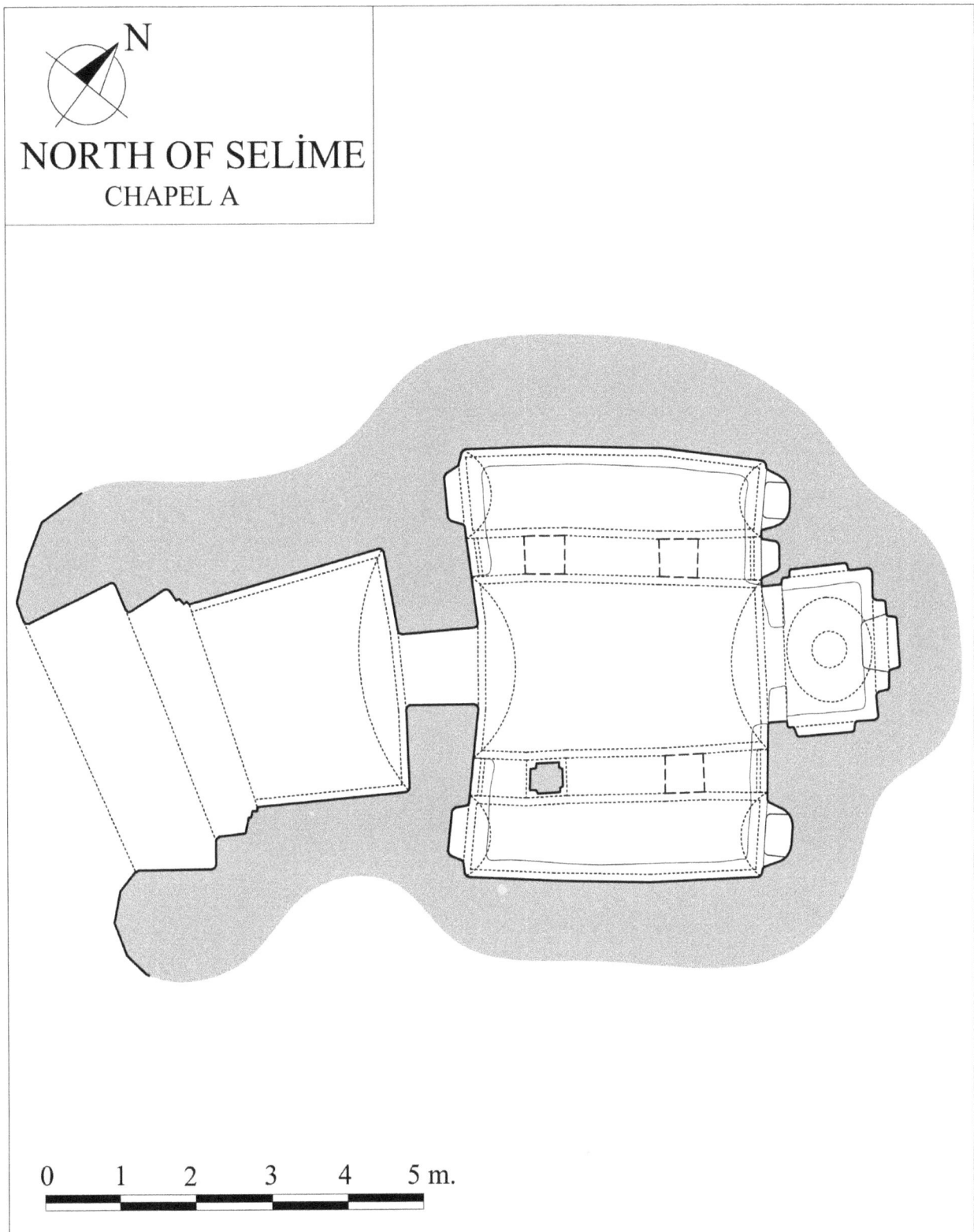

*Figure 3. Plan of Chapel A.*

sanctuary extend to the east of the central square. A low bench runs along the base of the walls of the chapel nave.

Chapel C is also small and unpainted, but precisely carved into a domed, four-column, cross-in-square plan, also known as a domed, four-support, nine-bay plan,

or a quincunx (fig. 5). Chapel C presents one of the more common plans for the Middle Byzantine period in Cappadocia, second only to the frequently found barrel-vaulted, single nave church. In Cappadocia the domed, cross-in-square church usually has piers instead of columns for supports, as in this example. The supports are strictly

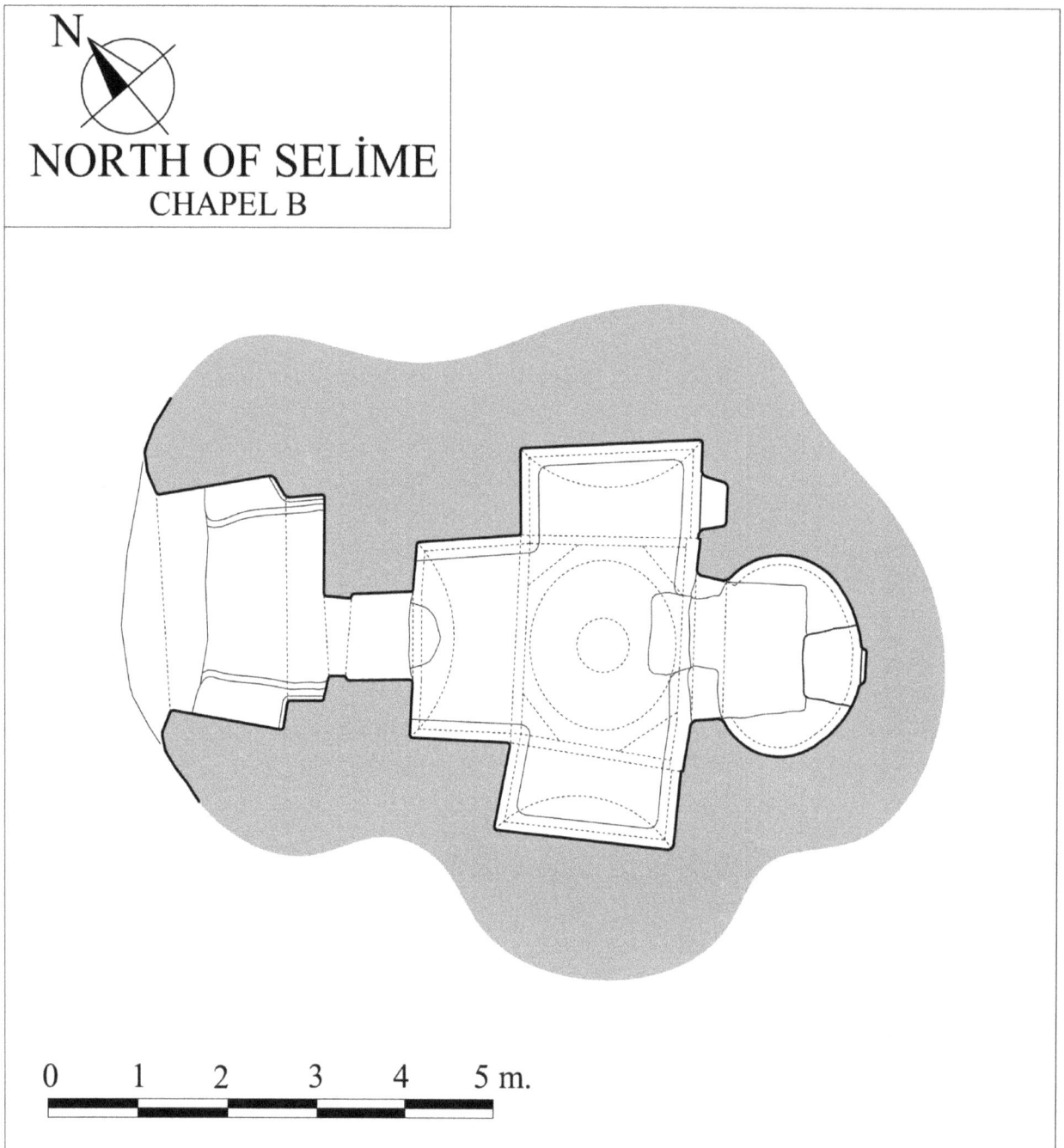

**NORTH OF SELİME**
**CHAPEL B**

0   1   2   3   4   5 m.

*Figure 4. Plan of Chapel B.*

stylistic and symbolic because in the carved environment of Cappadocia they merely imitate built forms and do not serve a structural purpose. Therefore, although the piers have collapsed, as in the basilica of Chapel A, the elevation of the church is fully understandable and can be accurately measured and drawn.[5] For Chapels A and C, a rectangular, stepped façade frames the barrel-vaulted porch, whereas the entrance porch to Chapel B also has a rectangular frame but is much simpler. This chapel is also the smallest of the

group. Although each chapel presents a different plan type, from the more common domed, nine-bay plan to the far less common basilica plan, their location in relationship to the settlement and to the landscape more generally is similar. Perhaps this common feature among the chapels is a better indicator of the manner in which they were intended to function than their architectural typology alone.[6] They also demonstrate the enormous flexibility on the part of

---

[5]   The chapel is filled with agricultural implements and hay so that some walls could not be reached during the survey; they are drawn with dashed lines on the plan.

[6]   In Cappadocia it is difficult to ascertain why one plan type is used over another, and why so many numerous and different types appear simultaneously in similar contexts. Though certain patterns are noticeable, indeed they are not consistent. For example, the domed four-support, nine-

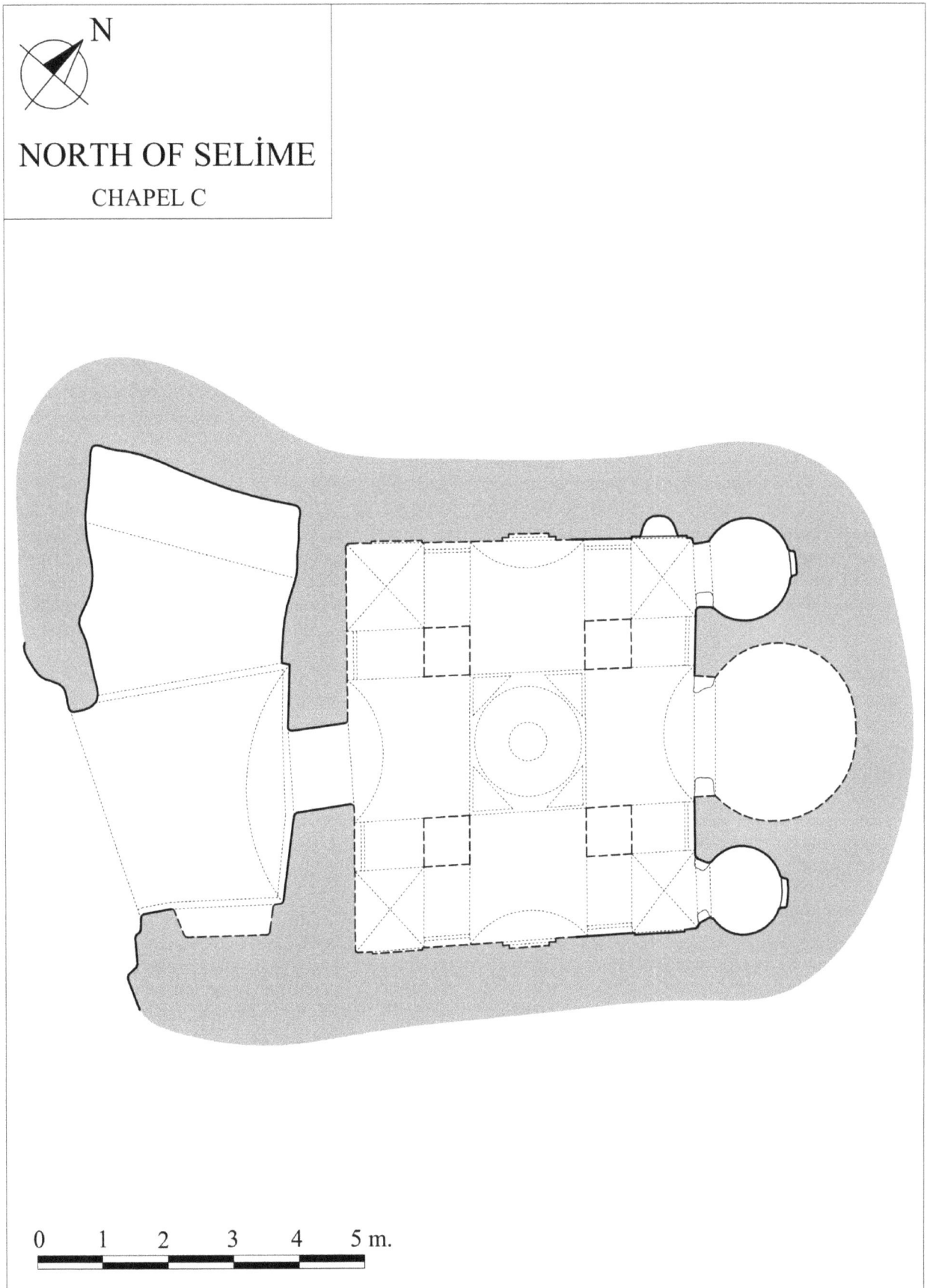

**NORTH OF SELİME**
CHAPEL C

0    1    2    3    4    5 m.

*Figure 5. Plan of Chapel C.*

the Cappadocian carvers. Their familiarity with a range of designs allowed them to manipulate and execute a wide variety of church plans and elevations with ease as they engineered a ceremonial and living environment out of the landscape (Kalas forthcoming; Ousterhout 2005a: 156-169; 2005b).

Like the group of three chapels to the north of Selime, a group of four chapels to the south of Yaprakhisar were carved into the cliff on the east bank of the river in an area known as Güvercinlik, and all are similarly diminutive in scale. These four chapels are known as the Davullu Kilise, Çohum Kilise, Yazılı Kilise and Alaygediği Kilisesi, and they define the southern limit of the settlement. Unlike the group to the north of the settlement, however, all four chapels in this group present the same plan. They are small, single nave, barrel-vaulted chapels with a single apse and altar at the east end, the most common chapel design in Cappadocia. Additional features include a low parapet on either side of the step up into the sanctuary. In the sanctuary itself consists of a rock carved altar underneath the conch of the apse, which is semicircular or horseshoe-shaped in plan. A rectangular molding at the springing of the barrel-vault of the nave continues into the apse at the level separating the wall of the apse from the conch rising above. These chapels south of Yaprakhisar show clearly that they were used primarily for burials, because graves have been carved out of the floor in the naves and into the base of *arcosolia* that appear along the chapel walls. This format is fairly standard for funerary spaces and can be found throughout Cappadocia's chapels and in the *nartheces* of larger churches.[7] The tombs themselves consist of a long, rectangular cavity oriented west to east, and curved at the short ends, with a lip at the surface into which a stone lid could have been inserted. These graves may have contained multiple burials but all have been destroyed and nothing remains of their contents.

In two of the four chapels, the most important details are two funerary inscriptions that further assert a Middle Byzantine date for the settlement. The inscriptions are found at Yazılı Kilise and Alaygediği Kilisesi, dated 1024 and 1023, and both name Theodule as the deceased (Thierry 1975: 189, nos. 7-10, figs. 7-10). They complement a similar inscription found at a tomb in a chapel associated with Area 9 of the settlement further north. This inscription dates to 1035, and the deceased is named Eustathous (Kalas 2007a: 276). The chapels remained devoid of figural imagery, though simple red decoration is painted either immediately

on the rock surface or on an intervening layer of white plaster and is mostly used to accentuate architectural design features. There are no further settlements carved into the cliffs of the valley on either side of the river for several kilometers south of Güvercinlik until one reaches the modern town of Belisırma, even though there is abundant soft rock and farmland surrounding the river to make this part of the valley viable for settlement. This spatial configuration suggests that the Selime-Yaprakhisar settlement constituted an entity separate from the remaining churches and dwellings of the valley, and its outer limits were defined by the groups of chapels north of Selime and south of Yaprakhisar at Güvercinlik.

A multiplication of chapels at the settlement of Selime-Yaprakhisar can also be seen within the core of the settlement itself. Several chapels at the site are not directly attached to any of the courtyard complexes, yet they are relatively close to one of the units and usually oriented toward it as well. They appear to demarcate the outer limit of the individual habitation in the same way the two groups of chapels discussed above define the outer limits of the settlement as a whole. In addition, these chapels may have had a religious function different from the churches integrated within the courtyard complexes. The most striking examples are found at Selime Area 4, Güllükkaya Area 6, and Güllükkaya Area 7 of the Selime-Yaprakhisar settlement.

At Güllükkaya Areas 6 and 7, a distinct set of two funerary chapels found in a pair accompanies each courtyard complex that also includes, within its courtyard, a household church. In both cases the paired chapels are carved side by side at a higher elevation than the courtyard complex and into a single cone about 50-100 m to the east of the complex. In other words they are toward the right as one faces the main approach to each of the complexes with the river behind the viewer (fig. 6; see also Kalas 2009: fig. 6.8). The chapels' apses face east and their doorways face west toward the courtyard. They are almost exact copies of each other. Each has an arched doorway at the center of a rectangular stepped frame and presents a distinctly funerary character with tombs carved into their floors as with the chapels to the south of Yaprakhisar at Güvercinlik described above. Because the paired chapels occupy similar positions in the landscape in relationship to the courtyard units of the settlement, they may have served the same function. Perhaps they signify a double dedication or that one chapel was reserved for female and the other for male burial and therefore could suggest a concern for the separation of genders in a funerary context. In addition to their internal features, their placement at a high elevation on the individual cones may further point to a funerary use. Difficulty of access could signify that the chapels were not used on a daily or weekly basis for prayer or worship; instead the settlers ascended to these chapels once for the interment of a deceased family member and once each subsequent year for his or her commemoration.

---

bay plan is most commonly found in the courtyard units recorded by Ousterhout, Rodley, and myself. Yet occasionally barrel-vaulted, single-nave churches, basilica churches, domed-cross churches and other varieties are included as well. For a general discussion of this issue in the built churches of Byzantium, see Ousterhout 1999.

[7]   At Selime Kalesi (Area 2) and Güllükkaya 7 at the Selime-Yaprakhisar settlement, tombs were carved in the narthex and not the nave of the churches (Kalas 2000a). At Güllükkaya 5 the cross-in-square church, which is part of the courtyard complex, has a small, single nave, barrel-vaulted chapel attached to the south side of the narthex. In this case tombs appear in the attached chapel and not in the main church or its tiny narthex.

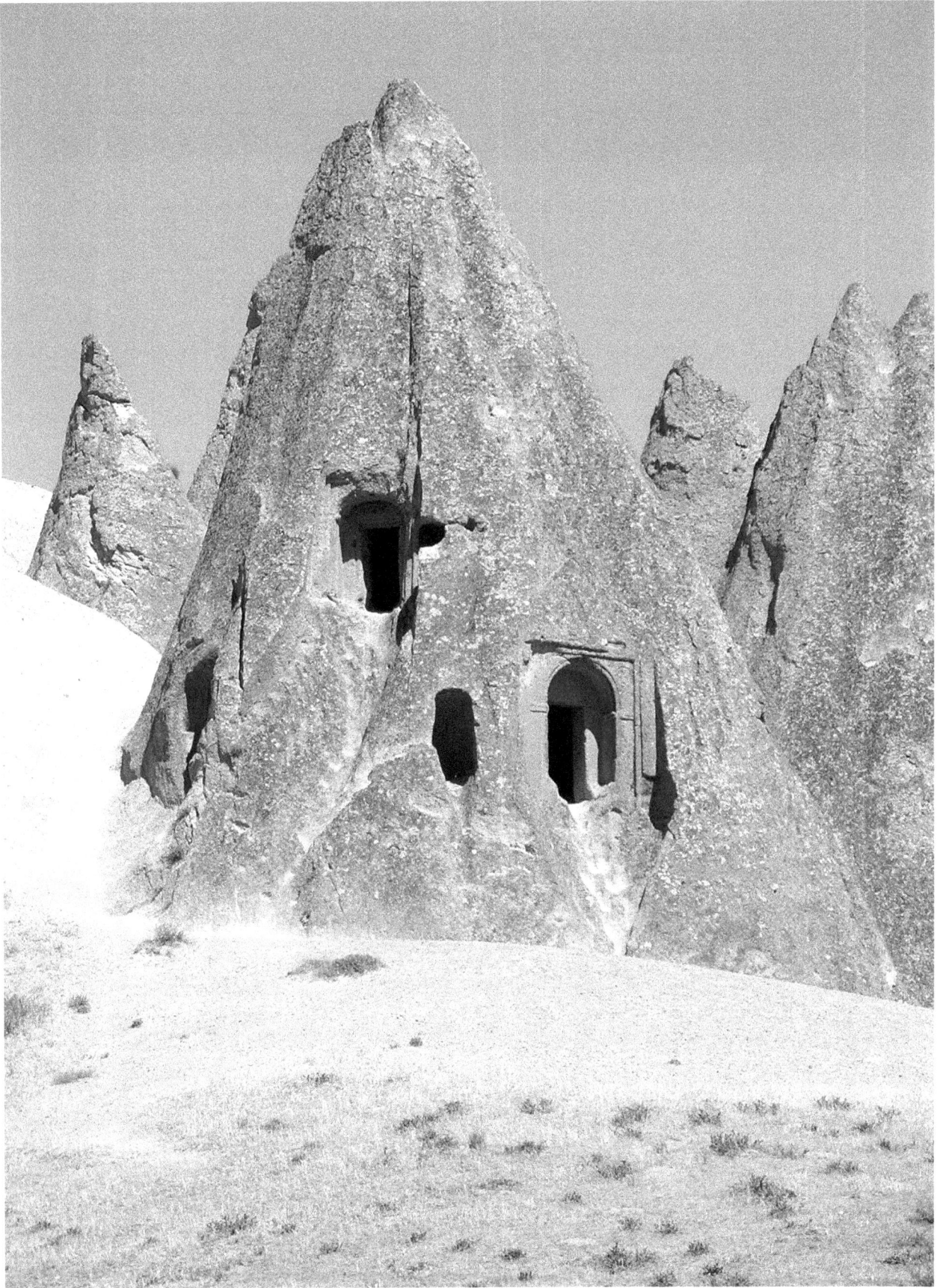

*Figure 6. View of double chapels associated with Area 7*

This proliferation of chapels, and in particular the doubling of funerary chapels found outside a complex yet associated with it, reveals that the funerary aspect was not served by the household church proper but by separate architectural spaces. For the churches that are part of the courtyard complexes, in Area 5 a chapel with tombs is attached to the main household church. In Area 7 a narthex is added to the main church of the courtyard complex and the tombs are inserted there. In Areas 6 and 7, entirely independent chapels included more graves. In addition to these, Area 4 provides a further example of an independent church near a courtyard complex that is also oriented toward it. The independent church is known as the Derviş Akın Kilisesi (fig. 7). Because of its position and orientation, I posit that it belonged to the courtyard unit of Area 4 and likely served both a funerary purpose as well as defining a boundary. The church is elegantly carved into a spacious domed, four-support, nine-bay plan with a large funerary narthex containing several tombs. It includes an elaborate, monumental façade and interior painted frescoes, some with donor images, and a funerary epigram in a provincial form of Greek. Because the plan and funerary epigram of the Derviş Akın Kilisesi have not yet been fully published, and because it is one of the more significant churches at the settlement in terms of its architectural layout and decorative program, it will be fully examined elsewhere. In the context of the present discussion however, it should be noted that it shows the same spatial relationship to the courtyard of Area 4, as do the double chapels of Areas 6 and 7 to their respective courtyard units.

## Conclusions

In Byzantine culture, a church hosted a variety of functions beyond the weekly Sunday liturgy, and different churches were also erected for different purposes. Many could serve multiple functions as well. Moreover, churches and chapels could be clustered to create a multi-apsed, many-domed building complex. What is most striking about Cappadocia is the sheer number of churches that survive. When the unpainted examples are counted, the number rises considerably. It would seem that these numerous churches not only provided ceremonial spaces in which to perform the liturgy, pray, and bury the dead in both congregational and private worship, but also functioned as landscape markers with which to define settlement space. It may be that the centrally located cathedral/village/parish church of the settlement, which I posit to be now lost at Selime-Yaprakhisar, functioned like the church attached to an individual courtyard unit. In other words, both are public in that one serves the entire community while the other the smaller household community and their guests; the latter church type is more often described as private (Mathews and Daskalakis-Mathews 1997; Ousterhout 2005a). In like fashion, the churches outlying the entire settlement may have functioned the same way as the examples that lay outside the individual courtyard units. Perhaps placement within the landscape of the settlement carried a greater

significance than their intrinsic formal characteristics and plan types. As we have seen here, although the various outlying chapels present different floor plans and elevations, they maintain the common characteristic of lying outside the settlement or household unit. A chapel located within a village or courtyard dwelling differed from one located outside of the village or dwelling. Although they are located in the more public areas of the settlement, and conspicuously visible in the landscape, they may have actually hosted a more private or perhaps personal purpose as funerary chapels, especially given their often diminutive scale and inaccessible positioning. It is possible that they were used only once or twice a year, during the commemoration of the deceased individuals buried within or on the feast day of the chapel's dedication.

This kind of settlement pattern is reminiscent of the earliest periods of Christianity when churches were erected around and above Christian cemeteries and martyrs' shrines located outside the walls of late antique cities, and of a type of pattern that can still be detected today in rural chapels and icon stands in the countryside of parts of the Orthodox world. On Crete, for example, chapels and icon stands are placed at the entrances into villages and at the outside of houses to form sacred boundaries and protective borders to the settlements, be it the entire village or the individual house (Nixon 2006). The numerous small chapels and icon stands erected throughout the countryside of medieval and modern Greece are noticeably absent in the rural landscapes of Turkey, apart from the region of Cappadocia. Most likely the landscape of many regions of Anatolia would have appeared today much like the one described by Lucia Nixon in *Making a Landscape Sacred* for the island of Crete were it not for the Seljuk and later Ottoman occupations of the late eleventh century onwards which restricted the development of Byzantine Orthodox communities in its territories (Nixon 2006; Vryonis 1971). As Nixon notes in her study, there is a word in Greek to designate an outlying chapel, *exokklisi*, but no such word exists for a church included as part of a settlement, whose equivalent would be something like an "*esokklisi.*" This interesting observation raises the fundamental question of whether inhabitants of settlements did indeed have the concept of inside and outside spaces, and if so, were these spaces considered to be in opposition to one another. Furthermore, if certain chapels were considered to occupy either the inside or the outside of a settlement, would they also present other formal, stylistic, or functional elements to enable one to further characterize the distinction. According to Nixon, it is generally regarded that the parish or congregational church in Cretan villages is the norm, and the outlying chapels are later additions. These chronological relationships cannot be demonstrated, however (Nixon 2006: 14), which is the case for Cappadocia as well. If sufficient differentiation between the two types exists spatially in their relationship to the landscape and to their associated settlements, then perhaps it would be possible to state that they functioned in different ways as well, a hypothesis that proves especially

*Figure 7. View of Area 4 and the Derviş Akın Kilisesi.*

significant in the interpretation of Cappadocia's settlements where other kinds of information for sacred structures such as these do not exist.

A brief comparison with the situation of other similarly recorded sites in Cappadocia reveals the special characteristics of Selime-Yaprakhisar. For example, because the landscape at Selime-Yaprakhisar is open and there is ample rock into which to carve dwellings, the residences tend to spread out along the landscape with seemingly empty land between the end of one complex and the beginning of a neighboring example. It is interesting to note that this is not the case at Çanlı Kilise, where the courtyard units are set side by side, next to one another within a single horizontal layer of volcanic rock to form a compact settled line. Though there are more recognizable, individual courtyard units at Çanlı Kilise, almost double the number found at Selime-Yaprakhisar, the settlements within the massive outcrops at Selime and Yaprakhisar that extend vertically along the cliffs possibly hosted a larger population. At Çanli Kilise several chapels are noted adjacent to the courtyard groupings as well as at a distance from the settlement (Ousterhout 2005a: 79-126), resembling the pattern at Selime-Yaprakhisar. At Açık Saray, the units

are also carved in a sprawling fashion so that the beginning and end of the individual units are set at a distance from one another, but unlike Selime-Yaprakhisar, no outlying chapels have been recorded thus far; some of the units at Açık Saray do not even include churches (Rodley 1985: 121-150). At Göreme there are many churches, but no clearly recognizable courtyard units, which necessarily would have to be identified first in order be able to understand whether any churches lay outside a particular settlement space (Rodley 1985: 160-183; Giovannini 1972: plan no. 4). At Selime-Yaprakhisar, the outlying chapels appear to have been used for funerary purposes; they could also be interpreted as a means of marking the landscape. They are invaluable for understanding how Middle Byzantine culture made a landscape sacred through the insertion of sacred structures along its rural terrain.[8] They establish the outer limits of either their larger collective, nucleated settlement

---

[8]    Several other regional surveys throughout the coastal and inland territories of Anatolia have recently brought to light the presence of rural chapels dated to the late antique and Byzantine periods and located in the countryside surrounding larger cities or settlements, as at Aphrodisias, Pisidian Antioch, Anavarza, and Silifke; see the website for the 2008 conference "Archaeology and the Cities in Asia Minor in Late Antiquity" held at the University of Michigan in Ann Arbor: http://sitemaker.umich.edu/late-antiquity/home.

or the individual courtyard settlement unit. Furthermore they serve not only to demarcate the border of that space or its outer edge, but to also protect it and provide a sacred barrier between the outside and the inside worlds of the inhabitants. The first man-made feature encountered along the landscape as one approaches the settlement are the chapels, and the last one encountered leaving the settlement are the chapels once again. By marking the landscape surrounding the settlement as sacred, chapels such as these also served to protect its inhabitants while also establishing where the space of an outsider ended and the space of an insider began. Perhaps this boundary also helped in defining the social status and identity of the region's inhabitants of the tenth to eleventh centuries. At least at Selime-Yaprakhisar, settlement space consisted not only of the physical features carved into the landscape designated for occupation and use, but also the spaces in between and beyond the houses. By applying this contextual and sociological focus as a new tool for understanding the significance of the components of such settlements as Selime-Yaprakhisar, fresh questions can be asked of the religious architecture of Byzantine Cappadocia.

**References**

Babić, G. 1969. *Les chapelles annexes des églises byzantines*. Paris: C. Klincksieck.

Ćurčić, S. 1977. Architectural significance of subsidiary chapels in middle Byzantine churches. *Journal of the Society of Architectural Historians* 36.2: 94-110.

Epstein, A.W. 1986. *Tokalı Kilise: tenth–century metropolitan art in Byzantine Cappadocia*. Washington, DC: Dumbarton Oaks.

Giovannini, L. (ed.). 1972. *Arts of Cappadocia*. Geneva: Nagel Publishers.

Hild, F. & M. Restle,.1981. *Kappadokien: Kappadokia, Charsianon, Sebasteia und Lykandos*. Vienna: Österreichische Akademie der Wissenschaften.

de Jerphanion, G. 1925-45. *Une nouvelle province de l'art Byzantin: les églises rupestre de Cappadoce*. 4 vols. Paris: Paul Geuthner.

Jolivet-Lévy, C. 1991. *Les églises byzantines de Cappadoce: le programme iconographique de l'apside et de ses abords*. Paris: Éditions du CNRS.

——2001. *La Cappadoce médiévale: images et spiritualité*. Saint-Léger-Vauban: Zodiaque.

Kalas, V. 2000a. *Rock-cut architecture from the Peristrema Valley: society and settlement in Byzantine Cappadocia*. PhD Dissertation, New York University.

——2000b. Cappadocia, in W. M. Johnston (ed.) *Encyclopedia of monasticism*: 238-239. Chicago: Fitzroy Dearborn.

——2004. Early explorations of Cappadocia and the monastic myth. *Byzantine and Modern Greek Studies* 28: 101-119.

——2007a. Survey of the Byzantine Settlement at Selime-Yaprakhisar in the Peristrema Valley, Cappadocia. *Dumbarton Oaks Papers* 60: 271-293.

——2007b. Cappadocia's rock-cut courtyard complexes: a case study for domestic architecture in Byzantium, in L. Lavan, L. Özgenel & A. Sarantis (ed.) *Housing in late antiquity: from palaces to shops*: 393-414. Leiden: Brill.

——2009. Challenging the sacred landscape of Byzantine Cappadocia, in A. Luyster & A. Walker (ed.) *Negotiating secular and sacred in medieval art: Christianity, Islam, and Buddhism*: 147-173. Aldershot: Ashgate.

——forthcoming. Middle Byzantine art and architecture in Cappadocia: the Ala Kilise in the Peristrema Valley, in J. Alchermes, H. Evans & T. Thomas (ed.) *Anathemata Eortika: studies in honor of Thomas F. Mathews*. Mainz: Philipp von Zabern.

Kostof, S. 1989. *Caves of God: Cappadocia and its churches*. Cambridge, MA: MIT Press.

Mathews, T. & A.-C. Daskalakis-Mathews. 1997. Islamic-style mansions in Byzantine Cappadocia and the development of the inverted T-plan. *Journal of the Society of Architectural Historians* 56.3: 294-315.

Nixon, L. 2006. *Making a landscape sacred: outlying churches and icon stands in Sphakia, southwestern Crete*. Oxford: Oxbow.

Ötüken, Y. 1984. Selime'de Derviş Akin Kilisesi ve Mezar Odası, in G. Renda et al.(ed.) *Suut Kemal Yetkin'e Armağan*: 293-316. Ankara: Hacettepe Üniversitesi.

Ousterhout, R. 1997a. Secular architecture, in H. Evans & W. Wixom (ed.) *The glory of Byzantium: art and culture of the Byzantine era, A.D. 843-1261*: 193-199. New York: Metropolitan Museum of Art.

——1997b. Questioning the architectural evidence: Cappadocian monasticism, in M. Mullett & A. Kirby (ed.) *Work and worship at the Theotokos Evergetis 1050-1200*: 420-431. Belfast: The Queen's University of Belfast.

——1999. *Master builders of Byzantium*. Princeton: Princeton University Press.

——2005a. *A Byzantine settlement in Cappadocia*. Washington, DC: Dumbarton Oaks.

——2005b. The ecumenical character of Byzantine architecture: the view from Cappadocia, in E. Chrysos (ed.) *Byzantium as oecoumene*: 211-232. Athens: National Research Foundation.

Popović, S. 1995/96. Disposition of chapels in Byzantine monasteries. *Saopštenja* 27-28: 23-37.

Restle, M. 1967. *Byzantine wall painting in Asia Minor*. 3 vols. transl. by R. Gibbons. Greenwich, CT: New York Graphic Society.

Rodley, L. 1985. *Cave monasteries of Byzantine Cappadocia*. Cambridge: Cambridge University Press.

Sterrett, J. R. S. 1919. The cone dwellers of Asia Minor. *National Geographic Magazine*. 25.4: 281-330.

Thierry, N. 1963. *Nouvelles églises rupestres de Cappadoce: région du Hasan Dağı*. Paris: C. Klincksieck.

——1975. Études Cappadociennes: région du Hasan Dağı: compléments pour 1974. *Cahiers Archéologiques* 24: 183-190.

——1983. *Haut Moyen-Age en Cappadoce: les églises de la région de Çavuşin* vol. 1. Paris: Paul Geuthner.

——1994. *Haut Moyen-Age en Cappadoce: les églises de la région de Çavuşin* vol. 2. Paris: Paul Geuthner.

VRYONIS, S. 1971. *Decline of medieval Hellenism in Asia Minor and the process of Islamization from the eleventh through the fifteenth century.* Berkeley: University of California Press.

WHARTON, A. J. 1988. *Art of empire: painting and architecture of the Byzantine periphery: a comparative study of four provinces.* University Park, PA: Pennsylvania State University Press.

# The Church of Mren and the Architecture of Intersection[1]

## Christina Maranci

The church of Mren, constructed sometime between 638 and 641, has long been discussed in terms of its imperial associations. Erected during the reign of emperor Heraclius (610-641), the church offers key evidence for relations between the Byzantines and Armenians during the height of the Persian wars. While Timothy Greenwood (2004: 37) believes that the church was intended as a show of local support to the empire, Jean-Michel and Nicole Thierry argue that Mren commemorated Heraclius's recovery of the True Cross (J.-M. Thierry and N. Thierry 1971; N. Thierry 1997). These assertions are valid—indeed, I offer elsewhere further testimony toward the latter argument.[1] Yet if a broad historical perspective situates Mren at the edge of empire, and as a provincial bid of allegiance to Byzantium, a closer look suggests a very different, if not contrary, set of claims. I will argue here that Mren's text inscription and sculptural reliefs place emphasis on messages of centrality and universality, locating the monument as the focus of authority in the landscape. I will ultimately assert that the evidence invites a reinterpretation of the relationship between the built form of the church and its physical setting.

Mren stands on the Ayrarat plain, a high tableland located in modern eastern Turkey, about a 90 km drive southeast of the city of Kars, and just 1 km from the border of the Republic of Armenia (fig. 1). Now largely uninhabited, the site is bounded by two rivers which have gouged deep canyons into the earth: the Arax river to the south and its tributary,

the Akhurean (Arpachay), to the east. The cathedral rises some 25 m into the sky, its tall drum and dome punctuating the horizon line. Facing stones have fallen from the walls, in some cases replaced later by sculpted slabs known as *khachk'ars* (cross-stones).[1] Much of the uppermost roofing lies at the foot of the building, and several large seams have now rent the fabric of its walls. What remains, nevertheless, is imposing: upon first viewing, the length of the building is deflected by its height. Four cross arms mark out the strong upright of the elevation, which is surmounted by a faceted drum. This simple, almost severe massing is enlivened by the portals of the façades, a series of tall arched windows, and many passages of architectural sculpture.

Those who enter the church find little to affirm Richard Krautheimer's description of the "cramped" and "hemmed" character of Armenian architecture (Krautheimer 1986: 327, 340) (fig. 2). Space stretches upward: the cross arms rise high into the narrow curves of the barrel vaults, while the drum and dome, supported on piers, extend six meters farther over the central bay. Fan-shaped squinches, thrown across the corners of this space, are echoed in a smaller set of eight higher up at the base of the dome. At its summit, eight thin ribs meet at a central boss.[2]

In his study of the architecture of Mren, Jean-Michel Thierry sought to locate the monument within the development of Armenian architecture (J.-M. Thierry and N. Thierry 1971: 51-53). He grouped Mren with two other inscribed-cross plans of the seventh century: the churches of Gayanē and

[1] I would like to thank Charles Gates for his very useful comments and questions regarding an earlier version of this essay. This essay seeks to use evidence from the epigraphy and sculptural reliefs at Mren to propose a mode of interpreting Mren and its physical setting. In this sense, it offers only a preliminary consideration of questions of landscape in early Medieval Armenia. Further examination of the subject, particularly related to questions of memory, is offered by the author in a forthcoming book, *Powerful geometries: building churches in early medieval Armenia*.

[2] A study by this author confirming the identification of the north portal lintel as a scene of Heraclius returning the True Cross to Jerusalem is forthcoming: "The humble Heraclius: Revisiting the north portal at Mren," to appear in the *Revue des Études Arméniennes*.

[3] Traditionally regarded as objects of veneration, these rectangular slabs may have also performed apotropaic and devotional functions.

[4] The monument may have already suffered damage during Arab and Seljuk raids in the early Middle Ages. Its later fate is known only through sporadic sources. An inscription on the church attests to its restoration during the Georgian domination of Armenia in the thirteenth century. The addition of a structure to the west of the church probably dates to the fourteenth century or later (see J.-M. Thierry and N. Thierry 1971: 44). Now, much of the roofing has fallen, and large cracks threaten the walls. Most alarming is the collapse of the southwest corner, exposing the interior space to the sun and wind, and rendering the entire structure vulnerable.

*Figure 1. The Church of Mren, northeast Turkey, ca. 638, from the southwest. (photo: courtesy of Richard and Anne Elbrecht)*

Bagavan. Both were constructed by the catholikos Ēzr between 630 and 641. Acknowledging the significance of the local family of domed basilicas to which Mren belongs, this essay seeks to explore the broader meanings the form may have carried for its contemporary audiences. Often connected by scholars to the rise of centralized planning in sixth-century Constantinople, the monument may alternately be read as an expression of intersecting authorities at a crucial moment on the Transcaucasian frontier.

**The West Portal Inscription**

High on the west façade of Mren is an inscription of three lines, spanning nine of the facing stones on the wall. In large, carefully-incised, upper-case (*erkatgir*) letters, the text relates the date of construction of the church and its intercessionary purpose. It names four individuals: the emperor Heraclius, a Prince of Armenia and Syria, the bishop T'eovp'ighos, and Nerseh Kamsarakan, the local lord:

> *[In the 29]th year of the victorious king Heraclius, in the office of Prince [Dawit'] the all-praiseworthy patrik, kourapalate, and sparapet [of Armenia] and Syria and in the office of bishop [T'e]ovp'ighos and in the office of tanutēr Nerseh lord of [Shira]k*

*and Asharunik', this holy church was built [for the intercession] of the Kamsarakank' and Mren and all [---] (after Greenwood 2004: 83).*

The surviving text thus describes the synchronism within which Mren was built, beginning with the imperial level and extending to the local, and suggesting a date of 638 or shortly after. This period saw a rapid reversal of Byzantine fortune in the Near East. Although Heraclean campaigns had enjoyed great success in the previous decade, the late 630s saw the faltering of imperial power, in the wake of a multiple defeats to the Arabs in Syria, Palestine, and Egypt.

The seventh-century chronicle of Sebeos provides a close context for the inscription, describing the relationship between the first two named figures, Heraclius and the "Prince of Armenia and Syria." The second, who can be identified as Dawit' Saharuni, was involved in a court plot to replace Heraclius with the emperor's illegitimate son (Sebeos 1990: 92-94; Kaegi 2003: 260-261). As soldiers were escorting Dawit' to court for his punishment, he escaped his bonds and returned to Armenia. There, he united local forces under his command, used them to attack and defeat the Byzantine commander, and took control of the forces stationed in Armenia. Heraclius, in no position to contest Dawit''s actions, acknowledged his power and named him "prince over all the territories [of Armenia],"

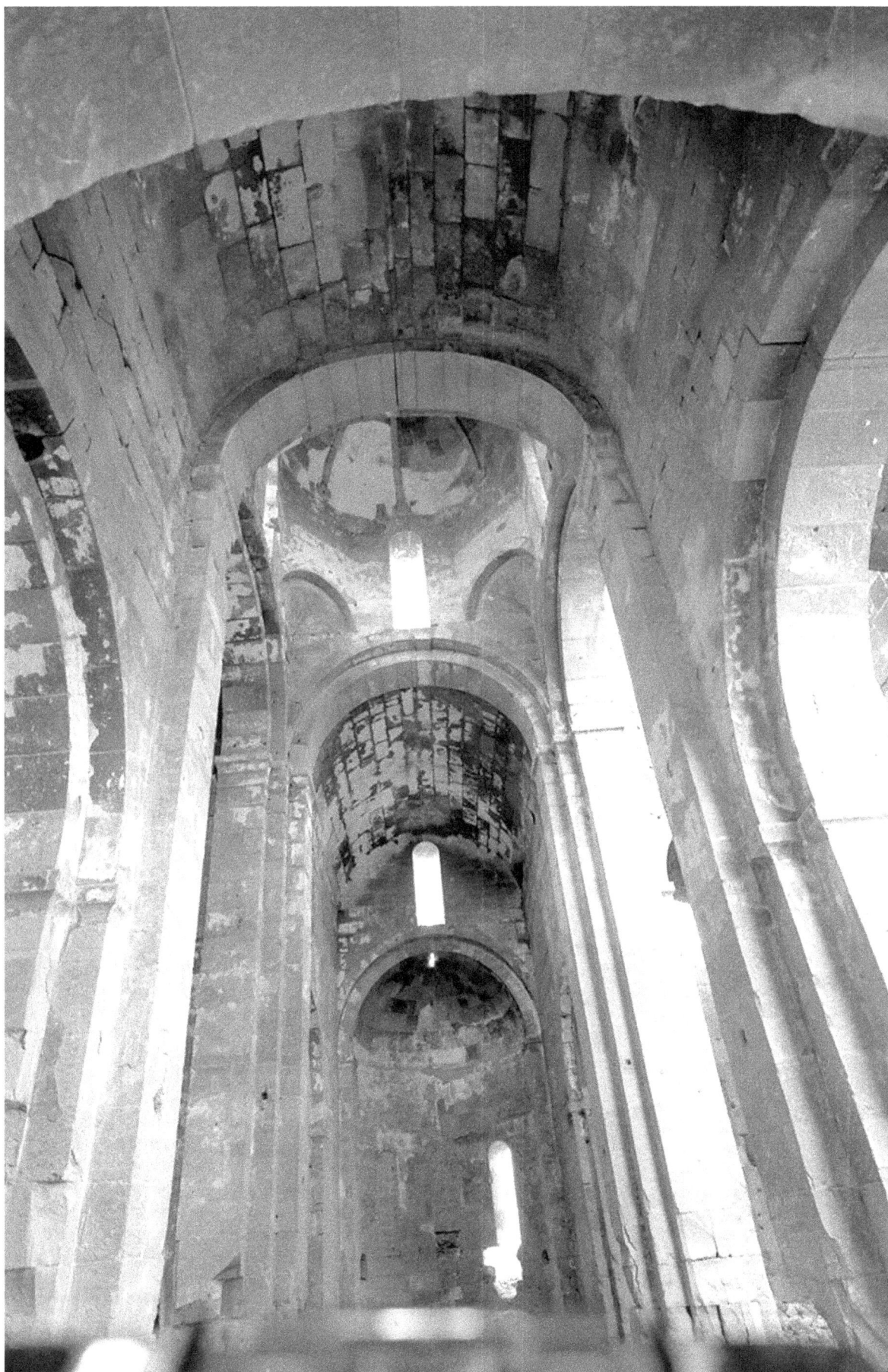

*Figure 2. The Church of Mren, interior from west (photo: Richard and Anne Elbrecht)*

*Figure 3. The Church of Mren, west façade portal (photo: Richard and Anne Elbrecht).*

a position of unprecedented authority in the Caucasus (Sebeos 1990: 94).

Of the third and fourth figures in the inscription, bishop T'eovp'ighos and Nerseh Kamsarakan, no mention is made in Sebeos's *History*. Yet Nerseh, who the epigraph names as "lord (ter) of Shirak and Arsharunik" and "tanutēr," or "head of the household," belonged to one of the most important Armenian clans of the early Middle Ages. Related to the Arsacid line, the Kamsarakans and their cadet branches inherited a substantial portion of the old royal domains: the northern part of Ayrarat, a large and central block of territory in the south Caucasus. As was traditional of aristocracy in early Medieval Armenia, each clan elected its own bishop, hence the presence of T'eovp'ighos in the inscription (Garsoïan 1999).

The Kamsarakan lands were also of strategic importance to the Byzantine military, as the broad plateau formed the easiest point of access across eastern Anatolia into Persarmenia: both Heraclius's campaigns of 628 and 631 passed through the plains of Ayrarat and Shirak. Based on their geopolitical importance, and the wealth and political sway of the Kamsarakans in Armenia, it is tempting to imagine that Nerseh himself was sought after as an ally of the empire. A specific relationship between Nerseh and Heraclius is further suggested by the title "tanutēr." As

Greenwood has argued, evidence from Sebeos suggest that this term was used only when authority was conferred and recognized by external powers (2004: 67).

When collated with the testimony of contemporary chronicles, therefore, the individuals named in the synchronism at Mren suggest a set of interdependent relationships. By the 630s, Heraclius was in need of a strong ally in the Caucasus, particularly in the wake of the court conspiracy and the first of the Arab conquests. Dawit''s election to prince by Heraclius was probably also enabled by Nerseh, lord of one of the most prominent families of early medieval Armenia. In this case, one may take slight issue with the contention that the synchronisms "[reflected] the political hierarchy that existed within Armenia in the 630s as perceived by a contemporary" (Greenwood 2004: 64-5). To judge from the immediate contexts of the named figures, the articulation of ramified power would seem less important than an expression of coalition, attested particularly at the level of emperor and prince.

**The West Portal**

The theme of accord also informs the sculpted portal just a few feet below the inscription (fig. 3). The portal consists of a heavy arch which shelters a sculpted tympanum depicting the archangels Michael and Gabriel. They are dressed

*Figure 4. Detail of left hand noble, west portal lintel, Mren.*

*Figure 5. Detail of right hand noble, west portal lintel, Mren.*

identically in long, trimmed cloaks, which are pinned at the shoulder and fall to the ground in heavy pleats. In their hands are scepters and orbs, positioned gently by the fingers. Below them is a large rectangular lintel. Christ appears in full length, slightly left of center, holding a book in his right hand. Flanking him are Saints Peter and Paul, who make the gesture of benediction. Paul, with beard and tonsure, stands to the left holding a book while Peter carries his keys. Accompanying the central group of the lintel are three additional individuals. To the right of Peter is a large

figure standing frontally, bisected by a gash in the masonry. The undisturbed passages nevertheless suggest a man with a short beard in a garment of elaborate folds, holding a book similar to Paul's. He appears to be blessing with his right hand, suggesting his identity as a member of the clergy, and most probably the bishop T'eovp'ighos mentioned in the inscription. Two figures, finally, frame the group (figs. 4, 5). Unlike the others, they look towards the viewer but stand in three-quarters position, each gesturing towards the center. Their forearms extend from magnificent cloaks, which, although fastened at the shoulders, are only partially worn. Their extraordinarily long sleeves hang empty, almost sweeping the groundline of the image. These two figures are invariably identified in the literature as the Armenian nobles named in the inscription, Dawit' and Nerseh.

The central iconography of the portal, Christ between Peter and Paul, might seem self-explanatory in the context of early Christian art. I would like to suggest, however, that it served a particular function within the immediate context of the seventh-century frontier, as an affirmation of alliance between Byzantine and local powers. While Nicole Thierry describes the central imagery as a scene of the "adoration of Christ," it may be linked to more specific pictorial themes of late Antiquity (J.-M. Thierry and N. Thierry 1971: 57). As seen in apse mosaics, the scene of Christ standing between Peter and Paul is commonly known as the *traditio legis*, or "transfer of the law". Based on imperial imagery, this formula appeared at Old Saint Peter's and Santa Costanza, both ca. 370, and on fourth-century sarcophagi in Rome and Ravenna.[3] Variations on the theme include the depiction of Christ enthroned or shown handing a closed scroll to Paul. Consideration of the iconographical evolution of the *traditio legis* and its context, however, is less important here than inquiring into its initial Armenian appearance at the church of Mren. Previous studies have explained its use as a reflection of the widespread popularity of the subject at that time (Thierry 1971: 67 and Der Nersessian 1977: 57). Its placement in a semi-circular field has been regarded as further evidence for a link with Roman apsidal spaces (Der Nersessian 1977: 58).

From a local perspective, however, it is difficult to ignore how the theme would have resonated at the time of Dawit''s election. Just as Heraclius transmitted imperial authority to the municipal level, so Christ transferred his power to the saints, a power, if we are to read the lintel as a whole, which ultimately extended outwards to the Kamsarakan bishop T'eovp'ighos, Dawit', and Nerseh. Presiding over this transaction are the archangels, keeping watch as divine sovereignty is channeled from the heavens down to the plain of Mren. In light of the immediate political context, there could have hardly been a more felicitous subject for public display.

The theme of accord is furthered by the two figures of Dawit' and Nerseh. With their placement on either side of the composition and offertory gestures, these individuals are frequently discussed in terms of donor portraiture. Yet neither the image nor the inscription above offers a clear sense of the donor's identity, and a range of theories have been offered. Iosef Orbeli, the first scholar to undertake an epigraphic study of Mren, believed it was Dawit', noting that Armenian sources beginning in the ninth century attribute to him the construction of the church (1963: 395-401). Jean-Michel and Nicole Thierry argue

that the building was founded by either Ēzr, patriarch of Armenia, or the Armenian general Mzhezh Gnuni, and subsequently completed by Dawit' (1971: 48). Timothy Greenwood has considered the possibility that the founder was Nerseh Kamsarakan, reminding us of the last line of the inscription, which declares the purpose of the church: "built [for the intercession] of the Kamsarakank'…" (2004: 66). For my part, I have argued that the evidence suggests a collaborative effort, in which the construction of Mren was enabled by imperial funds, perhaps in the form of gifts (Maranci 2006).

While discussion has thus revolved around the circumstances of the donation, I would suggest that the church's silence on the subject is itself interesting, particularly in light of the sartorial detail of the parenthetical portraits and the rich onomastic data provided by the inscription. The latter is particularly telling in this regard. Its synchronistic structure is well attested in seventh-century Armenian foundation inscriptions. However, the other surviving examples of this type feature an additional textual component in which the donor is mentioned by name (Greenwood 2004). In these cases, the synchronism acts as a dating mechanism, within or after which appears the record of donation. The now-destroyed church of Alaman, for example, featured a large exterior inscription reading:

*In the 27th year of Heraclius pious king in the time of Nerseh lord of Shirak and Arsharunik' and of T'eop'ighos bishop of Arsharunik' I Grigor eghustr and Mariam my wife we built this holy church for the sake of our souls (after Greenwood 2004: 81-2).*

The churches of Bagaran, completed in 629, and Bagavan, begun ca. 631, also preserve this structure (Greenwood 2004: 80-82). At Mren, however, the lengthy text offers no such first-person declaration, employing instead the passive "this holy church was built" (shinets'aw surb ekeghets'[is…]). The absence of an agent in the donation thus lends more emphasis to the synchronism itself, and on the simultaneity of reigns in which the church was constructed.

If the text describes the "sameness" of time in its synchronism, the noble figures in the relief below may be seen to offer a visual analogy, as sculpted messages of equivalence and unity. Although the gesture of the right hand individual is more open, and he wears a close-fitting cap, the figures are otherwise dressed almost identically, appear of equal stature, and motion toward the center of the image. Also notable is the tightly-knit composition of the lintel. In contemporary donor portraits of the Transcaucasus, as at the church of Ateni, individuals are distributed across a series of architectural surfaces. The composition at Mren, by contrast, forms a single group, creating a strong relationship between sacred and secular figures. Thus the

---

[5]  Buddensieg 1959, Schumacher 1959, Davis-Weyer 1961, and Carr 1991.

individuation of the noble pair seems less important than stressing their parity and unity.[4]

The practice of wearing the same costumes may be intended formally to convey an alliance between the two nobles. In an episode recorded in the fifth-century *Epic Histories* (*Buzandaran Patmutiwnk'*), the Persian King Shapur attempts to win the loyalty of the Armenian king Arshak. The Armenian is received with great honor and gifts, and invited to participate in an elaborate ceremony. Together, the kings recline on "one and the same banqueting throne in the hour of festivity, [wearing] the same garments of the same color with the same insignia and ornaments" (*Epic Histories*, transl. Garsoïan 1989: 146). Although the lintel at Mren depicts nobles rather than royals, the survival of Persian court traditions in seventh-century Armenia invites one to regard the symmetrical portraits as a visual testimony of solidarity.

Evidence from tenth-century Armenia would seem to support this point. The royal portraiture of the Bagratid dynasty offers rich comparanda with Mren, as this tradition also features closely-paired figures. One of the earliest such representations appears at the main church of the monastery of Sanahin, in the north of the present Republic of Armenia. At the summit of the east façade of the church, founded in 967, is a scene of the brothers Gurgen and Smbat, sons of Ashot III (Jones 2001: 370). They are posed identically, with equal stature, the same divided beards, draped garments, headdresses, and *prependoulia*.

In an analysis of such scenes, it is worth recalling that the formation of political alliance, like its visual representation, does not necessarily denote equality, loyalty, or understanding between parties (Walt 1987). Rather, the gesture only creates an appearance of accord and the coordination of policy for both constituents and the public. Regarding the relief of Sanahin, Lynn Jones has observed that the twin portraits of Gurgen and Smbat seem at odds with the political reality of the 960s and 70s (Jones 2001: 376-377). She notes the image includes only the eldest and youngest of Ashot's three sons. The middle son, Gagik, was expelled for treachery and perhaps suspected as a potential usurper. Six years before the Sanahin image was sculpted, moreover, Ashot's right to the throne was contested by his brother, Mushegh. Although Mushegh was offered a compensatory title, he continued to refuse his brother's status as king. Jones has thus argued that the mirror-image figures at Sanahin may be understood as a claim for dynastic unity in the midst of crisis.

At Mren, too, the visual parallel between the two donors is in fact illusory, for it suppresses a great disparity in rank. Nerseh was the lord of a powerful and wealthy clan in Armenia, but Dawit''s authority was unprecedented in scope. Named in the inscription as "the all-praiseworthy *patrik*, *kourapalate*, and *sparapet* [of Armenia] and Syria," and in Sebeos as "Prince over all the territories [of Armenia]," Dawit' most likely united both the Byzantine and Persian sectors of Armenia under his command (Howard-Johnston 1990: 230). Yet his dramatic rise to power was followed by an equally abrupt fall: only three years after his election, Dawit' was discredited by the army and demoted. Such swift hiring and firing recurs throughout Sebeos's account of the mid seventh century, and I suggest that the very ephemerality of allegiances drove a new documentary culture on the frontier, as particularly attested by inscribed churches. The pairing of Dawit' and Nerseh, I would argue, may have served as a visual response to a climate of political turnabout, generating a sense of solidarity which could reassure a broad spectrum of visitors to the church, including the Armenian nobility, military troops, and delegates from Constantinople. Thus the elements of the west façade – the synchronism, the *traditio legis* scene, and the symmetrical nobles – are not a reflection of existing political reality as much as claim of coalition at a time when diplomatic relationships were anything but secure.

**Frontier or Center?**

Mren has recently been described as evidence of the "short high tide" of Byzantine hegemony in the Caucasus (Whittow 1996: 208). Yet a closer look at the evidence suggests an alternate explanation of the monument. The universalizing messages of the inscription locate Mren at the center of a series of political relationships. Opening with the date of the reign of Heraclius, the text starts expansively, and then proceeds to increasingly smaller spheres of authority, from the prince, to bishop, to the local lord. In the closing of the inscription, the circles grow larger again, as the text pleads intercession for the Kamsarakan family, the town of Mren, and "all…" Carved into the west façade of the building, the inscription seems to assert the centrality of the church in the landscape, as the nucleus of a series of concentric realms of authority. Coordination is also expressed visually in pictorial themes of loyalty and alliance on the west façade reliefs. Within its immediate context, Mren thus offers a material assertion against the social and political crises of the late 630s: when relationships between emperor and frontier nobility had become fragile, and when Byzantium was no longer triumphant.

The textual and visual evidence invites a rethinking of the architecture of the church and its setting in the landscape. When viewed through the traditional lens of typology, Mren offers few surprises: its cross-domed form can be grouped within a category of plans in seventh-century Armenia, generally referred to as "post-Justinianic building" in

---

[6] The depiction of identically-dressed figures appears also at the Georgian church of Mtskheta, where the nobles Stephanos I, Demetre, and Adrnerse I appear together as donors of the church. Commenting on this ensemble, of which two individuals are of the Guaramid family and one of the Chosroid (Adrnerse I), Wachtang Djobadze writes that "whatever antagonism might have existed [between the two families] it did not prevent members of both families from being depicted together" (1960: 123). Yet as in the case of Sanahin and Mren, one wonders whether it was for just this reason that the three were pictured together: as an illusion of accord in the midst of dispute.

the Christian East (Krautheimer 1986: 327). Yet the lofty height of the building in comparison to its breadth creates an emphatic vertical punctuating the flat stretches of surrounding plain. The elevated cross arms, intersecting at the tall drum and dome, also underscore the centeredness of the monument. Like the bulls-eye of geopolitical realms described in the text, and the radiating ribs of the dome, the tall superstructure of the exterior locates Mren not on a distant shore of Constantinople, but at a vortex of earthly and sacred power.

## References

BUDDENSIEG, T. 1959. Le coffret d'ivoire de Pola. *Cahiers Archéologiques* 10: 157-195.

CARR, A. W. 1991. Traditio Legis, in A.P. Kazhdan (ed.) *Oxford Dictionary of Byzantium*: 2102. New York: Oxford University Press.

DAVIS-WEYER, C. 1961. Das Traditio Legisbildt und das Nachfolge. *Munchner Jahrbuch der bildenden Kunst*, series 3, 12: 7-45.

DER NERSESSIAN, S. 1977. *L'art arménien*. Paris: Arts et Métiers Graphiques.

DJOBADZE, W. 1960. The sculptures on the eastern façade of the Church of the Holy Cross of Mtzkhet'a. *Oriens Christianus* 44: 112-135.

EPIC HISTORIES. 1989. *The epic histories [Buzandaran Patmut'iwnk']*. translation and commentary by N.G. Garsoïan. Cambridge, MA: Harvard University Press.

GARSOÏAN, N.G. 1999. *L'église arménienne et le grand schisme d'Orient*. Leuven: Peeters.

GREENWOOD, T. 2004. A corpus of early medieval Armenian inscriptions. *Dumbarton Oaks Papers* 55: 2-91.

HOWARD-JOHNSTON, J. 1990. *The Armenian History attributed to Sebeos. Part Two: Historical Commentary.* Liverpool: Liverpool University Press.

JONES, L. 2001. The visual expression of Bagratuni rulership. *Revue des Études Arméniennes* 28: 341-398.

KAEGI, W. 2003. *Heraclius. Emperor of Byzantium*. Cambridge and New York: Cambridge University Press.

KRAUTHEIMER, R. 1986. *Early Christian and Byzantine architecture*. 4th edition, revised by R. Krautheimer and S. Ćurčić. New Haven and London: Yale University Press.

MARANCI, C. 2006. Building churches in Armenia: medieval art at the borders of empire and the edge of the canon. *Art Bulletin* 88: 656-675.

—— forthcoming. The humble Heraclius. Revisiting the north portal at Mren. *Revue des Études Arméniennes*.

ORBELI, I.A. 1963. The inscription of 639 at Bagavan and other Armenian inscriptions of the seventh century, in *Selected Works*: 395-401. Erevan: Academy of Sciences. (in Russian).

SCHUMACHER, W.N. 1959. Eine römische Apsiskomposition. *Römische Quartalschrift* 64: 137-202.

SEBEOS. 1990. *The Armenian History attributed to Sebeos. Part One*. translation and notes by R.W. Thomson. Liverpool: Liverpool University Press.

THIERRY, J.-M. & N. THIERRY. 1971. La cathédrale de Mren et sa décoration. *Cahiers archéologiques* 21: 43-77.

THIERRY, N. 1997. Héraclius et la vraie croix en Arménie, in J.-P. Mahé & R.W. Thomson (ed.) *From Byzantium to Iran. Armenian studies in honour of Nina G. Garsoïan*: 165-186. Atlanta: Scholars Press.

WALT, S. 1987. *The origins of alliances*. Ithaca: Cornell University Press.

WHITTOW, M. 1996. *The making of Byzantium (600-1025)*. Berkeley: University of California Press.

# Sacred Spaces in the Yezidi Religion

## Birgül Açıkyıldız

The thrust of this paper is to examine the relationship between the material culture and the contexts in which Yezidi sacred monuments take their form, by focusing on three principal Yezidi settlements: Sheykhan, Sinjar, and Behzanê/Ba'shiqe in northern Iraq (fig. 1). It aims to discuss how form, content, and function sanctify a place in the Yezidi world. Among the questions to be asked: What do Yezidi monuments do to the places in which they were built? What makes a building "Yezidi," its form, its function, or its meaning for the Yezidi faithful? In other words, how is the "spirit" of Yezidism reproduced visually? Is there a correlation between Islamic art and Yezidi funerary art? What is the innovation in Yezidi material culture?[1]

In the Yezidis' world there is no tradition of communal prayer, or a temple to carry out their devotions. Thus, buildings were not purposely planned for religious practices and teaching. However, any such structures that do exist are, for the most part, all mausolea, shrines for saints, and the houses of the men of religion (Sheikhs and Pîrs) which, to a large extent, take the place of absent temples, though sometimes a stone, or a spring next to a plant will also fulfil the function of a place of worship. Despite their modest and rural appearance Yezidi mausolea and shrines are an important part of the cultural environment of the Yezidi areas and constitute material signs of the general Yezidi belief system. In particular, the mausoleum denotes the presence of Yezidism and its unity, which are the most important hallmarks of the Yezidi settlements.

Yezidis are a heterodox religious community who live in northern Iraq, western Iran, northern Syria, and southeastern Turkey, as well as in the Armenian Republic and Georgia (fig. 1). Their estimated number is 600,000 throughout the world. Yezidis are ethnically Kurdish, speak the northern, Kurmanji, dialect of Kurdish, and comprise 2% of the total Kurdish population.

Yezidis are the inheritors of several cultural and religious beliefs, such as Zoroastrianism, Magism, and Mithraism, and these became mixed with the Sufi teaching of Sheikh 'Adī[2] in the twelfth century. The form of each influence remained visible with every new addition. Thus, a syncretic belief system was established, and a unique religious tradition developed. Although contemporary religious practices and hymns, transmitted from generation to generation by oral tradition, hint at various layers in the religion, there is no liturgical or historical writing before the twelfth century that can facilitate an examination of the periods for evidence of the cults that influenced and formed Yezidism. On the other hand, it is obvious that the Sufism practised by Sheikh 'Adī's order, 'Adawīyya, had a predominant influence on its development. Arabic sources and the observances and practices of modern Yezidism confirm this strong Sufi influence. The earliest historical source, the Kitāb al-Ansāb written by 'Abd al-Karīm al-Sam'ānī (d. 563/1167), mentions the presence of the Yezidis for the first time (Frayha 1946: 20-21). According to al-Sam'ānī, at the beginning of the twelfth century Yezidis were living in the mountains of Ḥulwān, in the vicinity of al-Yazīd and Sinjar. This region continues to be the homeland of the Yezidi community in modern times. Other Arabic sources (Al-Hafiz al-Dhahabī 1983: 20: 344; 23: 223; Ibn Kathīr 1932: 12: 243; Ibn Khalikān 1978: 3: 254-55; 4: 163; Ibn Taymiya 1906: I: 262-317; Yāqūt

---

[1] This article originated in a somewhat different form as part of my doctoral dissertation (Açıkyıldız 2006).

[2] For the Yezidis, Sheikh 'Adī is both a historical personage and a religious and mystical person from whom the spirit crossed the centuries, following the example of founders of other religions such as Moses, Jesus Christ, and Muhammad. An Arab from the Kuraysh tribe of Umayyad origin, he was born in 1073 in Beit-Far in the province of Baalbek, Lebanon. He spent the first half of his life in Baghdad where he met famous Sufi mystics of his epoch and with whom he studied – men such as the founder of the Kadiriyya order Abd al-Qādir al-Djīlānī, the two Ghazalī brothers, and Abū'l-Nadjīb 'Abd al-Kāhir al-Shuhrawardī. His good practices won him the respect of others. He later received a Sufi education from Abū'l-Khayr Hammād al-Dabbās, 'Oqely al-Manbidjī, and Abū'l Wafā' al-Ḥulwanī, and went twice to Mecca for the pilgrimage. On becoming an appreciated and sought after spiritual master, he brought together a number of disciples and retired with them to the Kurdish mountains at the beginning of the twelfth century.

*Figure 1. Map of the expansion of Yezidism in the Middle East (B. Açıkyıldız)*

1814: 5: 28) from the thirteenth and fourteenth centuries also talk about Sheikh 'Adī and his early successors, such as Ḥasan ibn 'Abī'l-Barakāt who played a crucial role in the formation of the dogmas and doctrines of Yezidism. According to the same sources, Sheikh 'Adī, who was an Arab Sufi, came from Baghdad and withdrew with his disciples to Lalish in order to spread his own orthodox Islamic teachings and to live a contemplative life in this remote and peaceful place. However, particularly following his death in 557/1162, his successors changed the direction of the religion from orthodox Islam towards the Yezidism that we know today. Thus, his teachings developed under the influence of local Iranian beliefs and practices, and took a different path to syncretism.

The Yezidis believe in one eternal God, named Xwedê. However, there are also divine and semi-divine creatures that are intermediaries between God and the Yezidi people. It is believed that God manifests himself in three different forms: the Holy Trinity in the shape of a bird, Tawûsê Melek, the Peacock Angel; as an old man, Sheikh 'Adī, a historical personality and considered to be the reformer of the Yezidi religion; and in the form of a young man, Sultan Êzî (Joseph 1919: 147). In Yezidism, God has a transcendental character and is perceived only through the activities of this Trinity. The Yezidis' God is interested only in heavenly affairs. He delegated his power to the seven angels (Heptad of seven Holy Beings) and appointed the Peacock Angel, Tawûsê Melek, responsible for worldly affairs and human fortune. It is also believed that the Seven Holy Beings (Heptad) have successive manifestations in human form, called khas/mêr, and Yezidis approach God through these khas/mêr (Kreyenbroek 1995: 83). The most recent manifestations of this Divine Essence were the members of Sheikh 'Adī's family who were his early successors. Moreover, Tawûsê Melek ('Azazil) and six individuals with high spiritual rank are believed to be incarnations of the Seven Holy Beings, namely: Sheikh Ḥasan (Darda'il), Shams al-Dīn (Israfil), Sheikh Abu Bekir (Jibra'il), Sajadin ('Azra'il), Sheikh Nasr al-Dīn (Shemna'il) and Sheikh Fakhr al-Dīn (Nura'il) (Guest 1993: 210). Four of these figures, Shams al-Dīn, Fakhr al-Dīn, Sajadin, and Nasr al-Dīn also comprise the "four Mysteries" who are believed to be sons of Ezdina Mīr, eponyms of the lineage of Shamsani sheikhs (Kreyenbroek 1995: 102). Thus, these figures are objects of devotion for Yezidis and are manifested in the mausolea and shrines, called khas/ mêr, that constitute the main Yezidi sacred buildings and are regarded as symbols of the religion. It is principally in

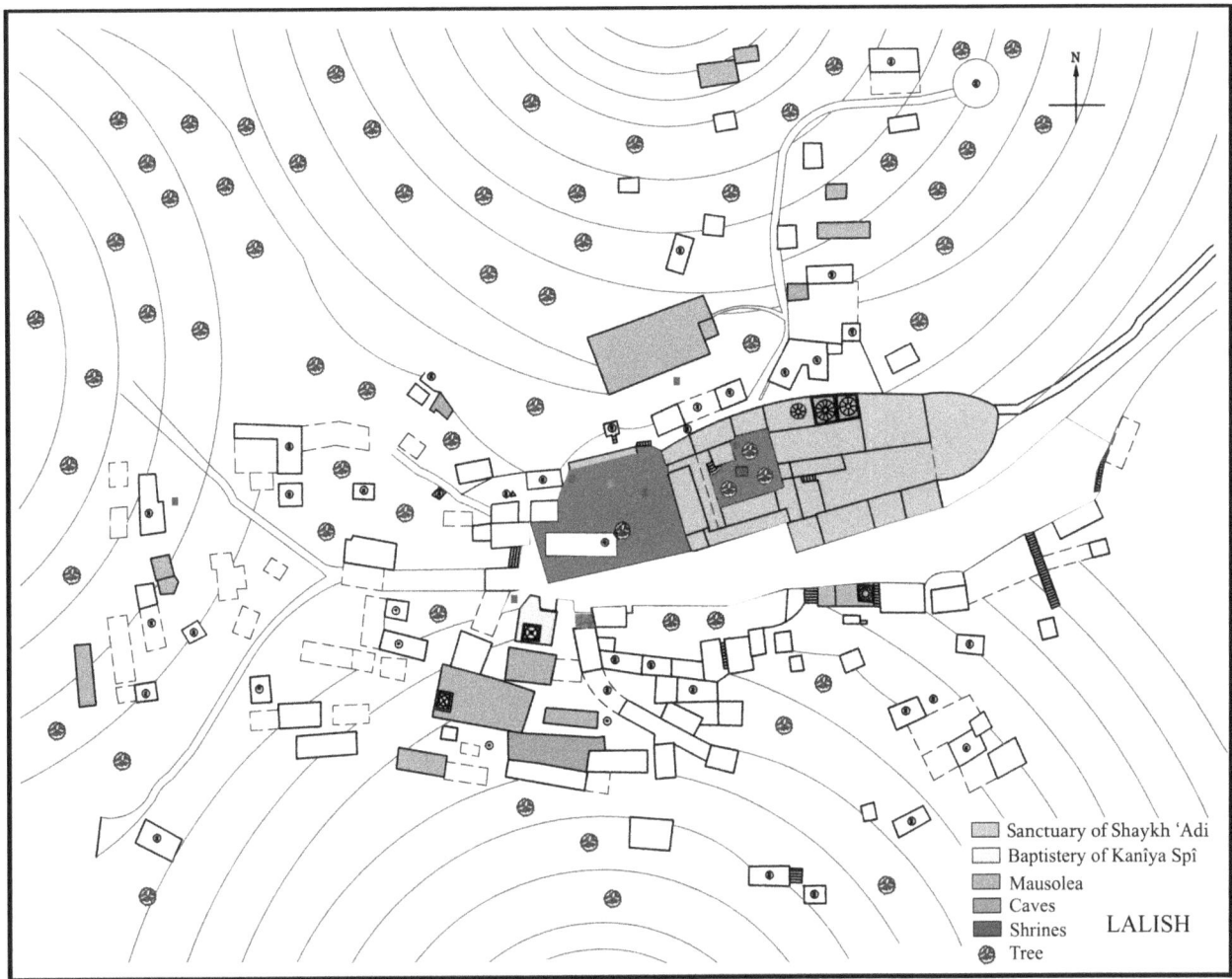

*Figure 2. Map of Lalish (B. Açıkyıldız, based on the map of Suleiman Havend).*

the Kurdish region of northern Iraq that natural phenomena are emphasised by Yezidi sacred buildings.

The Yezidi heartland lies, more precisely, in a triangle between Jazira, Amadiyya, and Mosul. This was a heterogeneous area where various religious, ethnic, and linguistic communities lived side by side, and it maintains its particularity today. Two distinctive Yezidi regions are well-known, namely Sheykhan and Sinjar, with the twin town of Behzanê/Ba'shiqe between them. Although the Yezidi communities in these locations have a strong relationship between them, they have developed differently over the centuries and it is worth glancing briefly at each settlement to see the significance of each location for the Yezidi community and to examine the relationship between faith and buildings in each area.

Sheykhan, the administrative and spiritual centre, is probably the most ancient homeland for the Yezidi community. Most of the important Yezidi villages such as Lalish, 'Eyn Sifni, Ba'adrê, and Bozan are located here. Lalish, which stands in a small valley, is regarded as holy in its entirety. Enclosed by mountains on three sides it has springs and streams running in every corner. These irrigate

many kinds of trees including those sacred to the Yezidis: the olive, the mulberry, and the grape vine. Maintained as a rural area, it is untouched by the modern world. Time seems to stand still here. As both countryside and architecture are together, considered to constitute an integral part of a sacred environment, each stone, plant, and building in this valley has a sacred meaning for Yezidi pilgrims. Thus, it is forbidden to cut down trees in Lalish, or to step with shod feet on its stones. Out of respect for nature, Yezidis remove their shoes on arrival in the valley. Even the Mounts of Hezret, 'Erefat, and Meshet, which encircle the valley, are regarded as sacred and have roles to play during the rituals and ceremonies. In Yezidi popular belief the mountain, the neighbour of the sky where God resides, is the meeting point of earth and sky, while Lalish, which houses the Sanctuary of Sheikh 'Adī, is the focal point of Yezidism. Moreover, with their modest appearance many mausolea, shrines, caves, the baptistery of Kanîya Spî and the bridge of Silat are in harmony with the wild nature of the village (fig. 2). The bridge of Silat, located on a small stream that runs through the valley, is viewed as the bridge between this world and the hereafter, and has symbolic meaning for the faithful. Several ceremonies are performed on it at times of pilgrimage as well as during simple visits on Wednesdays,

*Figure 3. General view of the Sanctuary of Sheikh 'Adī, Lalish (photo: B. Açıkyıldız)*

the holy day for Yezidis, when animals are sacrificed for the souls of the dead and the meat distributed. In addition, more modern, small-scale dwellings for the needs of pilgrims are scattered on the lower slopes of the mountains. In fact, apart from a group of religious people responsible for the upkeep of the sacred buildings, and who greet devotees, there is no permanent habitation in this valley as pilgrims reside here only during religious festivals. According to the Yezidis, God alone lives in this idyllic place.

The existence of springs, which are believed to have mystical properties, caves, which have become constructed edifices, and rocks, around which most of the mausolea are built, and the placement of the sacred buildings in relation to the Sanctuary of Sheikh 'Adī allow us to think that in this valley sacred spaces have been dominated for most of the time by a religious monument. Lalish, however, became an entirely holy place only after the construction of Yezidi buildings from the twelfth century onwards. In the course of time as rituals took place there, Lalish became the qibla of the Yezidi faithful for their devotions. The principal pilgrimage centre, the sanctuary of Sheikh 'Adī, occupies the centre of the valley and is surrounded on three sides by other buildings (Fig. 3). The mausoleum of Sheikh

Mushelleh, located on the western side of the sanctuary, is considered to guard the sanctuary of Sheikh 'Adī. A narrow road separates these two buildings. The baptistry of Kanîya Spî is situated in the southwest of the sanctuary, and to its west are the mausolea of Êzdîna Mîr and Sheikh Shams. The latter is attributed to Sheikh Shams, the divinity of the sun. The Yezidis believe that the first rays of the sun fall on the conical fluted dome of the mausoleum of Sheikh Shams. In order to ensure this solar peculiarity the mausoleum in question, which is considered to be particularly sacred, was built in this place. Several celebrations are performed in honour of the divinity of the sun, and a bull sacrifice takes place once a year in autumn during the ceremony of Cejna Jema'iyyê. The Yezidi faithful turn towards the sun when they pray. In addition to these buildings, there are many others in Lalish. These edifices give the impression of belonging to a single complex, developed around the sanctuary and spreading into a hilly area. Each building in Lalish has a religious meaning for Yezidi pilgrims and has its part to play during the seasonal Yezidi ceremonies and rituals.

It was probably not accidental that the sanctuary of Sheikh 'Adī, originally just a zāwiya building composed of eight rectangular cells for the contemplation of the 'Adawis, was constructed next to a grotto which may have been used in the religious practices of other communities prior to the arrival of Sheikh 'Adī. In the course of time this simple structure developed into the big complex that we know, and became a place of pilgrimage for Yezidi and non-Yezidi visitors of the region, especially following the construction of the tomb of Sheikh 'Adī after 557/1162. In the Yezidi world this monument is also known as the Perisgaha Lalish, Lalish Temple.

The complex which is irregular in shape and oriented east-west, houses the tombs of Sheikh 'Adī and Sheikh Ḥasan, the assembly hall, several chambers, visitors rooms, and a kitchen, as well as a forecourt and inner and lateral courtyards. Although the sanctuary has an abundance of springs that run underneath the complex, the Yezidis do not use the water for ablutions. However, water is collected into the basins in the assembly hall and the inner courtyard, to be used during religious ceremonies when it is sprinkled over the congregation. Yezidi ceremonies, which are usually held in the fore and inner courtyards, provide a valuable picture of the dramatic and sensually charged religious environment of Yezidi culture, in which procession and music play important parts. Each season is marked by a major celebration: the New Year (Serê Sal) in April, the Forty Days of Summer (Chîlê Havînê), the Festival of Assembly (Cejna Jema'iyye), and the Forty Days of Winter (Serê Chil Zivistanê). In this way, the entire year is imbued with sanctity. Branches from mulberry trees and grape vines provide some shade in the courtyards which are also used as venues for discussions about community affairs. Thus, the sanctuary is used both as a place of worship and for social and political purposes.

The water of Kanîya Spî where Yezidis perform the baptismal rite "mor kirin" is also sacred, a fact which reveals similarities to Christian baptism. The baptistry building is located in Lalish near the Sanctuary of Sheikh 'Adī (fig. 2). Although we do not have any historical source or an inscription to date this edifice, a comparative study with Mosulian architecture, especially the décor applied to the frieze of the door of Kaniya Kurke, and which is similar to the décor used on the portal of the Mār Behnam Monastery, makes us think of a date sometime in the thirteenth century (Gierlichs 1996: 59.4). The baptistry is composed of three rooms: the Kanîya Keçka designated for girls, the Kanîya Kurke for boys, and the Kanîya Spî – from which the name of the building derives – for people who are baptised at a later age. In the middle of each room a square-shaped stone basin is located where the water from the spring that gushes up from the beneath the building, is collected. This is where either a Sheikh or a Pîr who is officiating at Lalish as a Mijêwir "guardian" performs the ceremony, alone but for the presence of the child's parents. The Mijêwir takes water from the pool and sprinkles it three times on the head of the child while reciting incantations in Kurdish "Ho, hola, Prince Ezî. You became the lamb of

Êzî, the chief of the faith Êzî (Ho, hola, Êziyê Siltan. Tu buyî berxê Êzî, serekê riya Êzî). He then declares the child to be a servant of Êzî.

Apart from the mausolea of Sheikh 'Adī and Sheikh Ḥasan, I catalogued twelve well-preserved mausolea in the Lalish valley attributed to Yezidi saints, most of whom were Sheikh 'Adī's immediate successors or his early disciples, and from whom current Sheikh and Pîr families are descended (Açıkyıldız 2006: 116-129). More than one of the mausolea are attributed to the same saint. Thus, it is quite usual to find a mausoleum with the same name in another Yezidi village or region. As most Yezidi mausolea are commemorative it is almost impossible to know in which of them the body of the saint lies. Yezidi saints and their mausolea are worshipped for several reasons. For instance, it is believed that these buildings serve to cure illnesses; the mausoleum of Sheikh Ḥasan is effective against liver problems and rheumatism, that of Sheikh Sharaf al-Dīn is effective against jaundice and skin problems, while the mausoleum of Hajali helps to cure madness and the possession of the soul by djins, and so on. Some of the Yezidi saints are also considered to have a direct relationship with nature. Memê Resh is the lord of rain and protector of the harvest; Pîr-Afat is associated with floods and storms. Some Yezidi saints have power over animals. For example, Sheikh Mand is believed to have influence over serpents, and his mausolea and shrines are effective against snakebites. Thus, a vertical black snake is frequently depicted on the façades of his mausolea and shrines (fig. 4). Lastly, Pîr Cerwan protects people from scorpion stings because he is associated with the scorpion (Kreyenbroek 1995: 103, 105-6, 109-11).

Shrines, where oil wicks are lit and wishes made, are particularly numerous and serve several functions. No inscriptions or historical sources date these shrines which appear, with the exception of two examples in Sinjar, only in the region of Sheykhan. Frequently used as memorials for dead saints, they are believed to possess the spirit of the deceased. These shrines, which differ in shape, are small constructions around which pilgrims, individually or as a group, perform their devotions, kissing them, burning oil wicks, and making wishes. Visitors may also donate money at these shrines, each of which has a square or circular niche where the oil wicks are burnt, and which are usually located as freestanding edifices in the courtyard of mausolea, or in the cemeteries. It is possible to suppose that the Yezidis inherited these shrines from their Zoroastrian ancestors who practised fire rituals. Fire has a symbolic importance in the Yezidi culture which considers it to be a manifestation of the Sun, the source of life on earth, and one of the four elements of creation in Yezidism, i.e. Earth, Fire, Air, and Water. Yezidis observe the dualism in fire: fire as light, and fire that burns and harms, as the symbol of creation, destruction, and renewal, and small oil wicks are always lit by the faithful in the niches of shrines and mausolea during their visits. Furthermore, fire is used during the seasonal ceremonies, notably as the central feature of the New Year

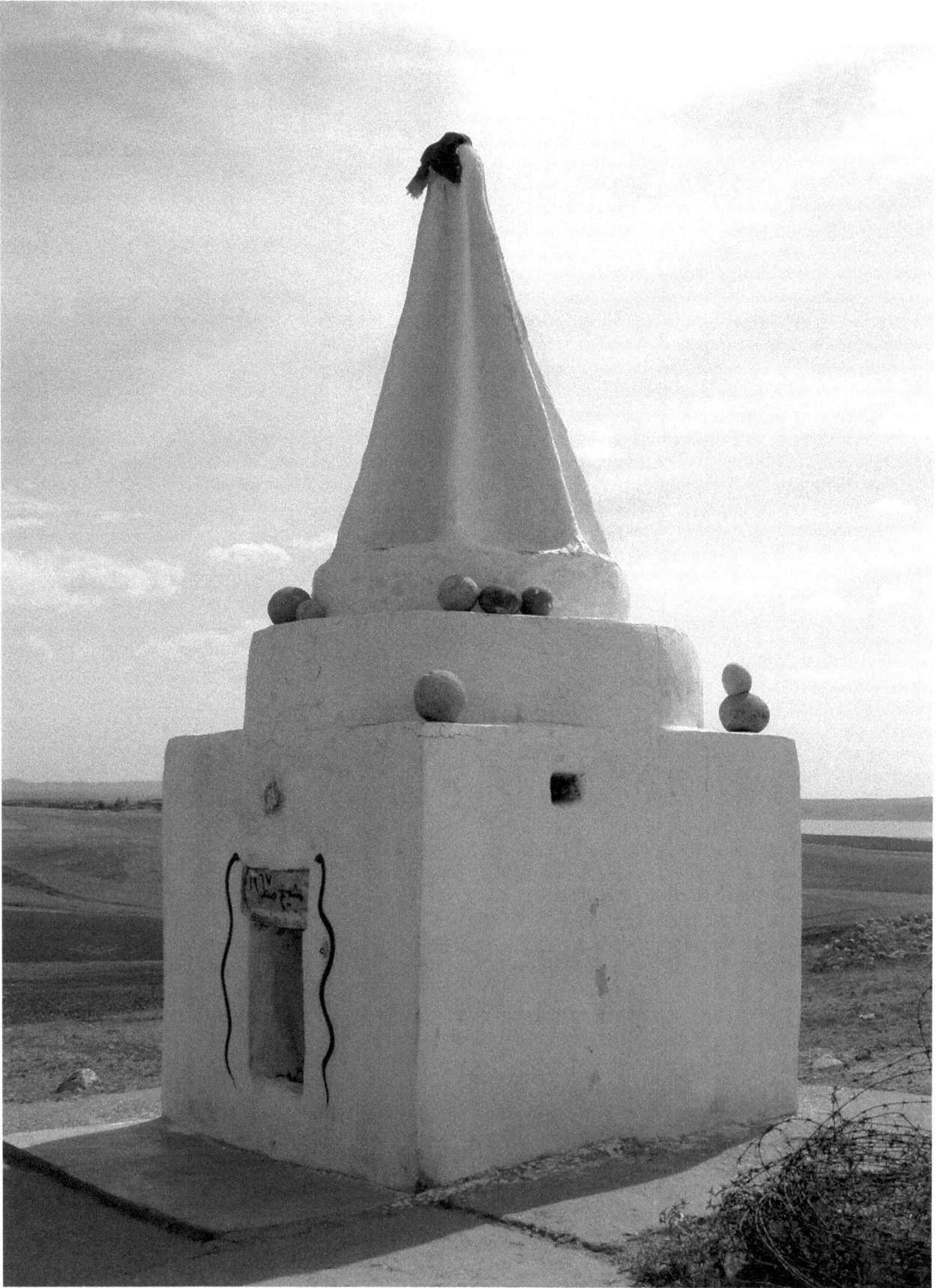

Figure 4. Mausoleum of Sheikh Mand Pasha, Kabartu (photo: B. Açıkyıldız)

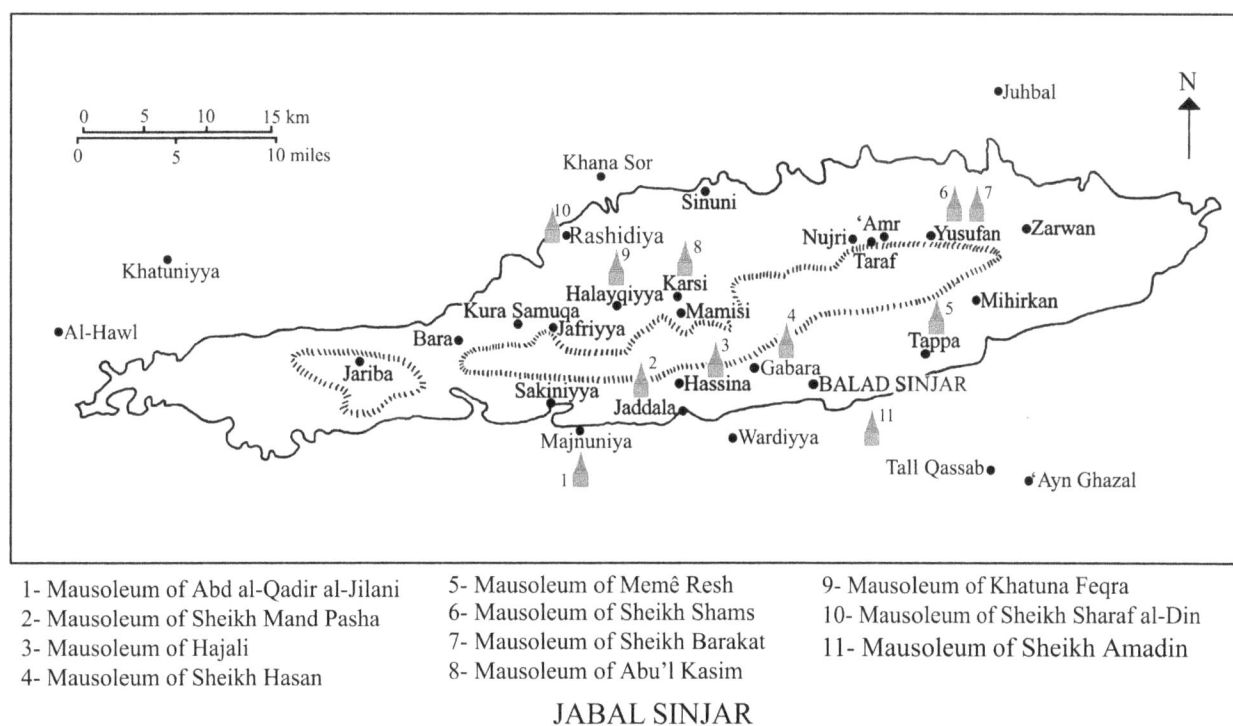

1- Mausoleum of Abd al-Qadir al-Jilani
2- Mausoleum of Sheikh Mand Pasha
3- Mausoleum of Hajali
4- Mausoleum of Sheikh Hasan

5- Mausoleum of Memê Resh
6- Mausoleum of Sheikh Shams
7- Mausoleum of Sheikh Barakat
8- Mausoleum of Abu'l Kasim

9- Mausoleum of Khatuna Feqra
10- Mausoleum of Sheikh Sharaf al-Din
11- Mausoleum of Sheikh Amadin

JABAL SINJAR

*Figure 5. Map of Jabal Sinjar (B. Açıkyıldız, based on the map in Fuccaro 1999: xiv)*

ritual performed in April in Lalish. This ritual is enacted only in the forecourt of the sanctuary of Sheikh 'Adī. Together with Baba Sheikh, the clerics, and laypersons – a mix of men, women, and children, light oil wicks on the paving stones of the courtyard and recite litanies in the Kurdish language. The ceremony lasts for just a few minutes. Yezidis also light fires in the front gardens of houses during the feasts and on Wednesdays.

Another important Yezidi region is Sinjar, located on the Iraqi-Syrian border. It is a mountainous area and the settled plains are limited to the north and east where the majority of Yezidi villages are located (fig. 5). Its mountainous features offered ideal shelter for the Yezidi community, which fled from Sheykhan due to persecution by Muslim sovereigns from the thirteenth century (Patton 1991b: 65). Almost all Yezidi funerary buildings are located in rather isolated areas and remote countryside, mostly on the summit of a mountain, totally cut off from the modern world. The location of Yezidi buildings can be explained by two factors: the need for security, and the ascetic life style of early Yezidi saints. Unfortunately, most Yezidi villages were destroyed by the Ba'ath regime in the 1970s, and their inhabitants now live in collective villages in the plain of Beled Sinjar, with only their saints' mausolea remaining in the mountain villages. Following visits to ten ruined Yezidi villages in the mountains,[3] I studied eleven mausolea, most of which have been restored recently by local people

(Açıkyıldız 2006: 166-76). Yezidi pilgrims return to these buildings regularly during each festival and take care of them.

The most popular building in the Sinjar region is the mausoleum of Sheikh Sharaf al-Dīn, located in the village of Rashidiya. It is situated in a courtyard where two shrines for fire rituals are also found. Sheikh Sharaf al-Dīn is a historical figure; one of Sheikh Ḥasan's sons, he was killed in 1256. According to Yezidi tradition, it was he who converted the local people of Jabal Sinjar to the Yezidi faith. Thus, in this region, his position is comparable to that of Sheikh 'Adī. According to an Arabic inscription on the façade of the building, the mausoleum in question was built in 1274. It presents a square-plan tomb chamber with an antechamber. The tomb chamber has two entrances. The main one leads from the antechamber, while the second, auxiliary entrance, is in the east wall. In the Sinjar region this arrangement is typical of mausolea that have an antechamber. The tomb chamber is roofed by a polyhedral dome. The drum of the dome rises on three levels with forty fluted sections around the cone. Some small windows let daylight into the tomb chamber, while the windows in the walls of the antechamber are of normal size. Most mausolea in this region also have a wish column called "stuna mirza." Located in the middle of the room, it rises to one meter in height and, as oil wicks are burnt on it, serves as a kind of fire altar.

Behzanê/Ba'shiqe, the third settlement of the Yezidi community examined here, lies in the foothills of the

---

[3] The villages visited in Sinjar were: Gabara, Halayqiyya, Hassina, Jaddala, Karsi, Majnuniya, Mihirkan, Rashidiya, Tappa, and Yusufan.

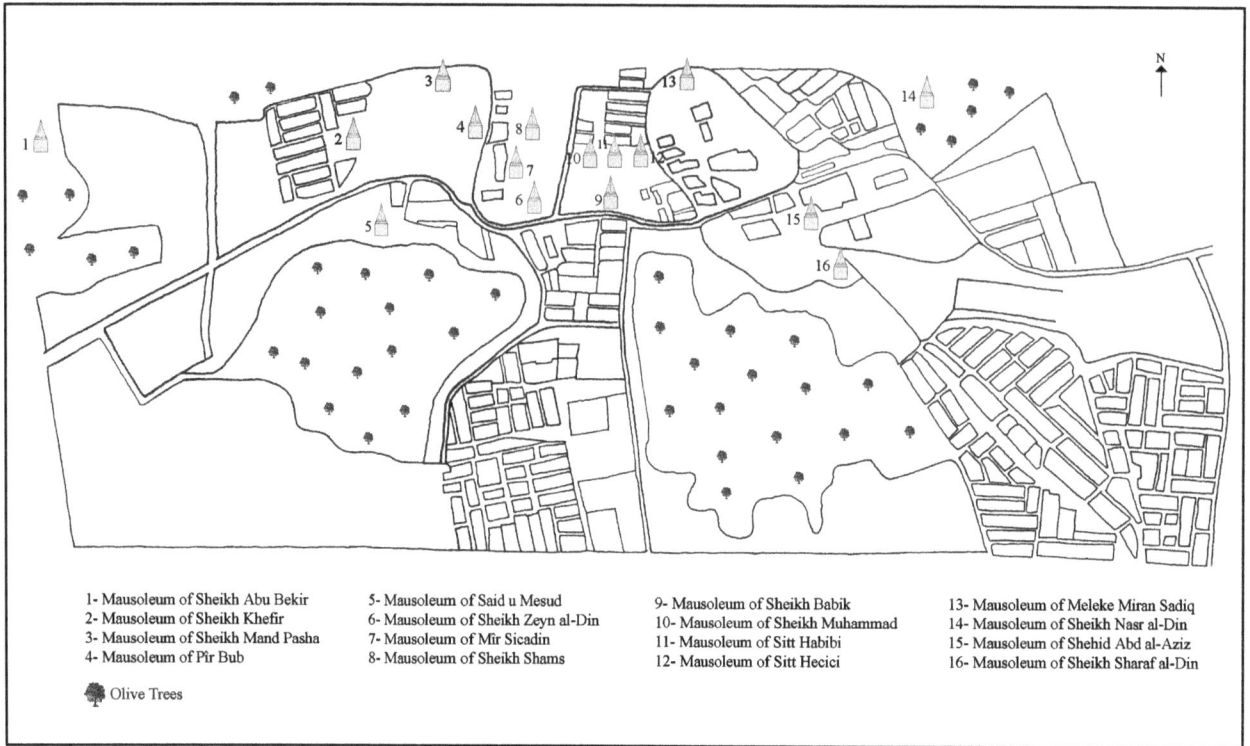

1- Mausoleum of Sheikh Abu Bekir
2- Mausoleum of Sheikh Khefir
3- Mausoleum of Sheikh Mand Pasha
4- Mausoleum of Pîr Bub

5- Mausoleum of Said u Mesud
6- Mausoleum of Sheikh Zeyn al-Din
7- Mausoleum of Mîr Sicadin
8- Mausoleum of Sheikh Shams

9- Mausoleum of Sheikh Babik
10- Mausoleum of Sheikh Muhammad
11- Mausoleum of Sitt Habibi
12- Mausoleum of Sitt Hecici

13- Mausoleum of Meleke Miran Sadiq
14- Mausoleum of Sheikh Nasr al-Din
15- Mausoleum of Shehid Abd al-Aziz
16- Mausoleum of Sheikh Sharaf al-Din

Olive Trees

BEHZANÊ/BA'SHIQE

*Figure 6. Map of Behzanê/Ba'shiqe (B. Açıkyıldız, based on the map found in Ba'shiqa Town Council)*

Maqlub Mountain in northern Mosul province. It probably became a new homeland for the Yezidi population when Badr al-Dīn Lu'lu', the Atabeg of Mosul, began to massacre the Yezidis in the middle of the thirteenth century. His hostile attitude towards the Yezidis is very well documented (Patton 1991b: 65). Fearing a Kurdish rebellion against him, in 1254 Badr al-Dīn Lu'lu' assassinated Sheikh Ḥasan (Lescot 1938: 102; Patton 1991b: 65) who was both the administrative and religious leader of the Yezidis in that epoch. The geographical features of Behzanê/Ba'shiqe differ from the Sheykhan and Sinjar regions, which are mainly mountainous or hilly. A twin town, it lies on a plain between Mosul and the Sheykhan region and is the major gateway between the mountainous Kurdish heartland and the flat desert of the Arab world. One of its particularities is that all members of Qewwals, the Yezidi religious musicians and narrators, reside only in these villages.

In Yezidi architecture, the concept of space has expressed itself in isolated, individual buildings. Although constructed for public use, they are set apart from habitation. Even in Behzanê/Ba'shiqe where the majority of Yezidi sacred buildings are located in the centre of the village, they are generally built on the top of a hill to isolate and separate them from public spaces. Furthermore, each, without exception, is encircled by a high-walled courtyard. In this village Yezidi sacred buildings manifest themselves entirely in mausolea (fig. 6). I worked on sixteen mausolea from various periods, but as all follow the same ground plan and

façade particularities, they give the impression of coming from the same mould (Açıkyıldız 2006: 147-65). A tomb chamber with a square plan covered by a dome raised on a square or octagonal drum is the characteristic type found in this town as well as in Yezidi architecture in general. As the principal architectural element of the mausoleum is the dome, it is made higher by increasing the height and number of the drums as well as the height of the conical fluted dome itself, so making it more visible and giving the impression that it is rising upwards in the sky towards God. The floor of the tomb chamber usually remains unpaved and the door is small in order that the heads of the faithful are bowed before a sacred place. Shoes are removed at the entrance so as not to defile the inner space, and the threshold and lintel of the door are kissed by pilgrims as a sign of respect.

In the light of a comparative study with the Shi'ite architecture of Mosul from the same period, I would like to suggest that Yezidi funerary architecture was influenced by Mosul, which was the artistic centre of Badr al-Dīn Lu'lu' (1211-59), the Atabeg of Mosul. The square plan and fluted, conical-domed mausoleum, which is the principal design of Yezidi funerary architecture, shows similarities with the Shi'ite mausolea of Mosul and Sinjar (Reitlinger 1938: 150, 153; Uluçam 1989: 132-43). On the other hand, the meaning and function that the Yezidis attribute to these buildings differ. For the Yezidis, these mausolea are not simple burial places, but also a kind of place of worship, variously sized, where Yezidis come to perform their devotions and pious duties. These are the main places of worship for the Yezidi faithful since they do not possess any temple in which to carry out their prayers. They are venerated as the tombs of saints and have become centres of pilgrimage, where the faithful expect their prayers to be answered, and which are, in addition, considered to be the houses of the deceased. On every important occasion, such as marriage, festivities, illness, and death, visits are made to these buildings. Commemorative meals are eaten and prayers are offered for the souls of the dead. Moreover, animals are sacrificed, mourning is carried out, and oil wicks are lit in the niches of the mausolea, accompanied by wish-filled prayers.

In addition, the Yezidis revere sacred places where human and divine spaces meet. These are mainly rocks next to a spring where the rituals of animal sacrifice take place and offerings are made. These sacred places are spread across all the Yezidi villages of northern Iraq, Syria, and Armenia. Most holy springs and streams are coupled with sacred trees or plants, generally olive, fig, or mulberry trees where votive rags are hung. The mulberry tree is particularly venerated as it is thought to have sacred qualities, and is believed to hold the power to cure disease. In addition, stones called kevir, located in the cemeteries and around shrines, are also considered to be sacred and believed to contain the essence of God. These stones are not, in themselves, objects of devotion but are used as instruments for spiritual action. A votive wick saturated in olive oil is lit and placed on them in order to obtain something. Yezidis also consider caves to be sacred, and several are visited regularly by pilgrims in Lalish, Bozan, Dere Būn, and so on. The best known of these is located beneath the sanctuary of Sheikh 'Adī where the spring of Zemzem emerges and runs. Zemzem itself is considered to be the holiest place for Yezidis. It is located in an area difficult to penetrate, and access is forbidden to non-Yezidis. Zemzem water has magical and medicinal properties par excellence. It cures, restores, and assures eternal life. Thus, Yezidis make berats, small balls formed from the earth of the sanctuary and mixed with the water of Zemzem. Considered to be sacred they are distributed to pilgrims during ceremonies and feasts and are believed to bring good fortune to the possessor and to protect him from the evil eye.

In the light of the above documentation one can see that the Yezidi community is embodied in its unassuming buildings which are numerous, visible, and vivid in the daily life of every Yezidi individual. Each Yezidi village is recognisable by its fluted, conical-domed structures which are regarded as the symbolic manifestation of Yezidi saints who continue to illuminate their followers after death. The Yezidis were influenced by their surrounding cultures, notably by Shi'ite Muslims of Mosul, and Christians, in their choice of architectural type for their sacred places. On the other hand, they gave a new meaning to these buildings, which unify the followers of the Yezidi faith and differentiate them from their neighbours. The most striking features of Yezidi sacred monuments are the depiction of the serpent and the peacock on the façades.

Yezidi sacred spaces vary. They are sometimes natural rocks and springs and sometimes specifically built places of worship, such as mausolea and shrines. They are considered to be holy because they fulfil certain functions as places of communication with the Divinity where several ceremonies and rituals are performed, but they are also places in which believers make their addresses and expect a response to their demands.

Although small Yezidi communities reside in Iraqi cities such as Dohuk, Mosul, and Baghdad, the majority of the Yezidi population lives in rural areas. It is important to underline here that apart from in Behzanê/Ba'shiqe, no Yezidi religious buildings are located inside cities. Even Beled Sinjar, which supports the largest part of the Yezidi population, possesses no Yezidi building in its centre. One has to go far away into the remote areas to meet Yezidi sacred buildings. Thus, Yezidi architecture is not urban but completely rural.

## References

Açıkyıldız, B. 2006. *Patrimoine des Yézidis: architecture et 'sculptures funéraires' en Irak, en Turquie et en Arménie.* PhD Dissertation, University of Paris I/Panthéon-Sorbonne.

Al-Hafiz al-Dhahabî. 1983. *Siyar al-Alam al-Nubala*, 25 vols. Beirut: Mu'assasat al-Risala.

Al-Hadithi, A. & H.A. Khaliq. 1974. *Conical domes.* Baghdad: Ministry of Information, Directorate General of Antiquities.

Al-Janabi, T.J. 1982. *Studies in medieval Iraqi architecture.* Baghdad: Ministry of Culture and Information, State Organization of Antiquities and Heritage.

Bachmann, W. 1913. *Kirchen und Moscheen in Armenien und Kurdistan.* Leipzig: J.C. Hinrichs.

Blair, S.S. 1990. Sufi saints and shrine architecture in the early fourteenth century. *Muqarnas* 7: 35-49.

Bois, T. 1967. Monastères chrétiens et temples yézidis dans le Kurdistan irakien. *Al-Machriq* 61: 75-103.

Donabedian, P. & J.M. Thierry. 1987. *Civilisation et arts arméniens.* Paris: Editions Mazenod.

Drower, E.S. 1941. *Peacock Angel being some account of votaries of a secret cult and their sanctuaries.* London: John Murray.

Fiey, J.M. 1960. Le temple Yezidi de Cheikh Adi. *Proche-Orient Chrétien* 10: 205-210.

—— 1965. *Assyrie chrétienne: contribution à l'étude de l'histoire et de la géographie ecclésiastiques et monastiques du nord de l'Iraq.* Beirut: Imprimerie catholique.

Frayha, A. 1946. New Yezīdī texts from Beled Sinjār 'Iraq. *Journal of the American Oriental Society* 66: 18-43.

FUCCARO, N. 1999. *The other Kurds: Yazidis in colonial Iraq*. London: I.B. Tauris.

GABRIEL, A. 1940. *Voyages archéologiques dans la Turquie orientale*. Paris: E. de Boccard.

GIERLICHS, J. 1996. *Mittelalterliche Tierreliefs in Anatolien und Mesopotamien: Untersuchungen zur figürlichen Baudekoration der Seldschuken, Artuqiden und ihrer Nachfolger bis ins 15. Jahrhundert*. Tübingen: E. Wasmuth.

GUEST, J.S. 1993. *Survival among the Kurds: a history of Yezidis*. London and New York: Kegan Paul International.

HILLENBRAND, R. 1994. *Islamic architecture: form, function and meaning*. Edinburgh: Edinburgh University Press.

IBN AL-ATHIR. 1965. *Al-Kamil fi'l-Tar'ikh*, 13 vols. Beirut: Tornberg.

IBN KATHĪR. 1932. *Al-Bidaya wa al-Nihaya*, vol. 12. Beirut: Maktabat al-Ma'arif.

IBN KHALIKĀN. 1978. *Wafiyāt al-A'yān wa-Anba' Abna' al-Zamān*, 8 vols. Beirut: Daru's-Sadr.

IBN TAYMIYA. 1906. Al-Risāla al-'Adawīyya, in *Majmu al-Fatwa al-Kubra*, vol. I: 262-317. Cairo: Dar al-Fikr.

JOSEPH, I. 1919. *Devil worship: the sacred books and traditions of the Yezidis*. Boston: Gorham Press.

KREYENBROEK, P.G. 1995. *Yezidism - its background, observances and textual tradition*. Lewiston, NY: Edwin Mellen Press.

KHALID, S. 1988. *Les monuments islamiques de Mossoul aux XIIe et XIIIe siècles*. PhD Dissertation, University of Paris 4.

LESCOT, R. 1938. *Enquête sur les Yézidis de Syrie et du Djebel Sindjār*. Beirut: Institut Français de Damas.

PATTON, D. 1991a. Badr al-Din Lu'lu' and the establishment of a Mamluk government in Mosul. *Studia Islamica* 74: 79-103.

—— 1991b. *Badr al-Din Lu'lu': Atabeg of Mosul, 1211-1259*. Seattle: University of Washington Press.

REITLINGER, G. 1938. Mediaeval antiquities west of Mosul. *Iraq* 5: 143-56.

RICE, D.S. 1950. The brasses of Badr al-Dīn Lu'lu'. *Bulletin of the School of Oriental and African Studies, University of London* 13: 627-34.

SARRE, F. & E. HERZFELD. 1911. *Archäologische Reise im Euphrat -und Tigris-Gebiet*. Berlin: D. Reimer.

ULUÇAM, A. 1989. *Irak'taki Türk Mimari Eserleri*. Ankara: Kültür Bakanlığı Yayınları.

YĀQŪT AL-ḤAMAWĪ. 1814. *Mu'jam al-Buldān*, vol. 5. Beirut: Dar al-Fikr.

www.ingramcontent.com/pod-product-compliance
Lightning Source LLC
Chambersburg PA
CBHW061005030426

42334CB00033B/3371